WALKING A TIGHTROPE

PROFIT FROM THE SALE OF THIS MEMOIR
WILL BE DONATED TO CHARITY

For Liliang who helped me to understand the difficult times her people endured and who was sympathetic to their immense sacrifices, and for Jason who supported the project by joining me in China in his school holidays.

MEMORIES OF WU JIEPING,
PERSONAL PHYSICIAN TO CHINA'S LEADERS

WALKING A TIGHTROPE

OLIVIA COX-FILL

M☉HEDIAN
PUBLISHING

Walking a Tightrope
Published by Mohedian Publishing
P.O. Box No. 80403,
London SW1P 9WQ, UK
www.oliviacoxfill.com

First published in Great Britain by
Skyscraper Publications Ltd. 2019

Second edition published 2025 by
Mohedian Publishing

Copyright © Olivia Cox-Fill 2019, 2025

Olivia Cox-Fill asserts the moral right to be identified
as the Author of this Work, in accordance with the
Copyright Designs and Patents Act 1988.

A CIP catalogue record for this book is available
from the British Library.

All rights reserved. This book is sold subject to the condition
that it shall not, by way of trade or otherwise, be lent, re-sold,
hired out or otherwise circulated, without the express prior
consent of the Publisher.

No part of this book may be reproduced or transmitted in any form
or by any means, electronic or mechanical including photocopying,
recording or by any information storage and retrieval system,
without permission from the Publisher in writing.

Every effort has been made to trace copyright holders and to obtain
their permission for the use of copyright material.

ISBN: 978-1-7385173-2-9
Paperback ISBN: 978-1-7385173-0-5
e-book ISBN: 978-1-7385173-1-2

Maps and Illustrations as accredited

Cover design by Blue Whippet Studio

Typesetting by chandlerbookdesign.com

Printed and bound in Great Britain by
TJ Books Limited, Padstow, Cornwall

CONTENTS

Acknowledgments — vii
List of Photographs and Maps — viii
Author's biographical note — xi
How the book came to be written — xiii
Relationship between China and the USA: then and now — xvii
Prologue — xx
Introduction — xxv

PART ONE

1. 'When Chairman Commands, We Don't Question' — 1
2. Transporting Silver in 1914 — 8
3. China Ungoverned — 24
4. Family Life — 35
5. Submitting to an Arranged Marriage — 46
6. Political Awakening — 58
7. 'Opportunity Favours A Prepared Mind' — 68
8. Questions of Loyalty — 75
9. First Contact with the USA — 82
10. China has stood up — 87

PART TWO

11.	Home into Hospital	93
12.	Had I Embraced Socialism and Communism Completely?	108
13.	"My Genitals Are Smaller"	121
14.	Confucian Solidarity	129
15.	Heroes and History	135
16.	"Don't Let Victory Intoxicate You"	140
17.	"Who Will Save the Cubs?"	154
18.	"China Needs Zhou Enlai, He is the Housekeeper"	169
19.	Return to the USA	179
20.	"Revolution is not a Dinner Party"	188
21.	Friends Reunited	207

Epilogue	227
Appendices	233
Chronology of Chinese History 1911 – 1976	233
Key Dates in the Life and Times of Dr. Wu Jieping 1917 – 2011	235
Key Achievements in the Life and Times of Dr. Wu Jieping	236
Key Places Mentioned in the Text	238
Key Personalities: Short Biographies	245
Bibliography	251
Index	252

ACKNOWLEDGMENTS

I owe an enormous debt of gratitude to the many colleagues and friends of Wu Jieping, who supported the enterprise and helped with their insight, among whom are:

Dr. Yan Ren Ying and Dr. Deng Jiadong, Wu Bing, Wu Xing, Gao Chi Chien, Liu Teh Hua, Chen I-Wan and Simon Campbell-Smith.

I had research help, early on, from Kim Dorman Schroeder, Dominique Dorman and later from Jane Brown.

At different stages in the genesis of this book it has been read and commented on by Dennis Fill, Annemarie Andreae-Jones, Paola Hewins, Renee Landegger, He Liliang, Lena Wei and Glenn Young.

I am especially grateful to Tadeu Soares for his advice and criticisms.

I owe special thanks to Nina Vickery; to Karl Sabbagh; to Blue Whippet Studio for the cover design; to Pink Moon Designs for the logo; and to John Chandler, who helped prepare the manuscript for the press.

LIST OF PHOTOGRAPHS AND MAPS

All from the Author's personal collection, unless otherwise stated.

PHOTOGRAPHS

Biography
Olivia Cox-Fill with Dr. Wu Jieping. London, circa. 1995.

Chapter 1 When Chairman Commands, We Don't Question
Mao Zedong ('Mao Tse-Tung') with Earl Leaf, Zhu De and Wu Lili (Wu Guangwei), Yanan 1946. Copyright Bettman via Getty Images.

Chapter 2 Transporting Silver in 1914
Parents of Wu Jieping.

The four brothers of the Wu family, all Doctors and graduates of Peking Union Medical College.

Chapter 4 Family Life
Wu Jieping (back row, centre) surrounded by his family.

Chapter 5 Submitting to an Arranged Marriage
Dr. and Mrs. Wu Ruiping.

Chapter 20 Revolution is Not a Dinner Party

The Astor Hotel next to Jieping's family home.

Dr. Wu Jieping and Dr. Yang Yuhua following their marriage, 1981.

Four generations of the Wu family following the marriage.

The Chinese Medical Delegation visiting the Squibb Corporation in the United States of America, in 1979.

Train to Chengde for the medical inspection tour. Security Detail convoy alongside with the private railway carriage awaiting the embarkation of Dr. Wu Jieping.

Railway carriage internal scene with Security Detail, Gao Rui, Olivia Cox-Fill, his Secretary and Dr. Wu Jieping.

The Government Official Guest House, Chengde, Hebei Province: street scene with Security Detail.

The Government (official) Guest House at Chengde, Hebei Province: Gao Rui on the terrace.

Gao Rui and Dr. Wu Jieping on their visit to Chengde.

Dennis Fill; Dr. Wu Jieping; Huang Dongsheng; Olivia Cox-Fill; and Haematologist Dr. Teng.

L – R: (back row) Dr. Teng; Dr. Wu Jieping; (front row) distinguished Obstetrician and Gynaecologist Ran Yen Ying; and Olivia Cox-Fill. Circa 1981.

The Chinese Academy of Medical Sciences, Peking Union Medical College Hospital (old building).

The Friends of the Peking Medical College: leaflet illustration.

The Friends of the Peking Medical College, Committee members.

Chapter 21 Friends Reunited

Gao Rui and Wu Jieping with Olivia Cox-Fill at their favourite Beijing restaurant, c. 1995.

Jason Fill; Olivia Cox-Fill; Dr. Wu Jieping; Gao Rui; and Dennis Fill. London UK visit c. 1995.

Dedication to Olivia Cox-Fill by Wu Jieping's step-daughter Marina (Yang Xiaomeng), 'An Extraordinary Journey and a Colourful Life: the Album of Wu Jieping'.

Wu Jieping speaks at the Opening of the Library of the Chinese Academy of Medical Sciences (CAMS) and the Peking Union Medical College (PUMC), 6 June 2001.

Cover photograph from 'An Extraordinary Journey and a Colourful Life: the Album of Wu Jieping' (ISBN No. 9 787 1170809-4-1).

He Liliang and Olivia Cox-Fill

Olivia Cox-Fill visiting Huang Hua at home

The Forbidden City
By kind permission of Dennis Fill

The Forbidden City with golden roof tiles
By kind permission of Dennis Fill

MAPS

Map 1 East Asia	222
Map 2 China	223
Map 3 Illustration of North East China	224
Map 4 Illustration of South East China	225
Map 5 Route of The Long March	226

AUTHOR'S BIOGRAPHICAL NOTE

Olivia Cox-Fill studied Medicine at University College Dublin and subsequently studied Chinese Literature and Journalism at Columbia University. She later took a two-year course in Mandarin at SOAS, University of London.

Olivia Cox-Fill and Dr. Wu Jieping

Previous Publications:

For Our Daughters: How Outstanding Women Worldwide Have Balanced Home and Career, Praeger 1996. ISBN: 9780275951993 (hardback)

Chinese Edition, *Nan Ren Neng Zuo de, Nu Ren Neng Zuo de Geng Hao* Tsinghua University Press, 2012.

Consultancy:

Olivia Cox-Fill was the Cultural Advisor for *Zhuang Zi Tests His Wife* by Su Liqun. [Experimental Theatre, Yadu Enterprise Group, 20 – 25 April 1995.]

HOW THE BOOK CAME TO BE WRITTEN

I was the middle child born into a Catholic family in the West of Ireland, where my mother was a farmer and my father a mechanical engineer. My convent school education finished at the Dominican Convent, Eccles Street, Dublin. At the same time, I was recovering from a car accident following a horrendous sexual assault. My application to Trinity College Dublin was returned, as my stated religion was Roman Catholic. Worried that I would not pass the entrance exams for the Royal College of Surgeons or University College Dublin, my French teacher proposed that I go to France as an *au pair*. It was a wonderful opportunity that I immediately grabbed to escape from my problems.

That summer, I read *Moment in Peking* by Lin Yutang. It would be several years before I recognised the importance of that summer to my life.

I enrolled at and attended UCD, where two of my Professors were priests: one a complete misogynist and the other a clammy-handed pervert. Their treatment obliged me to find another place to study and I applied to University College London in 1966. I secured a summer job in a Harley St. practice and became a temporary researcher for the British Medical Journal. I joined the fledgling Anglo Chinese Society and, as the so-called Feminist movement got traction, I read up and subscribed with moral support.

I was responsible for my University fees and therefore worked evenings and weekends, in the most exciting city in the world in 1960's London. I was a part-time DJ, model, dental nurse etc.; and my homework suffered. After some course failures at both UCD and UCL, I was floundering. Through one of my weekend jobs, I met Scott, an American businessman who offered to assist my application to Columbia University.

Columbia University, 1970-74, was heaven after my earlier experiences and I also volunteered with the World Health Organisation at the United Nations. While studying Creative Writing as my major and Chinese Literature and History as minors, the first Communist Chinese Ambassador was appointed to the UN. Scott was invited to a private function in honour of Huang Hua and asked if he could bring me along because of my interest in Chinese history and culture. By then, I also had a smattering of Mandarin. I was fortunate to become friends with the Ambassador's wife, Mme. He Liliang (who was at the time participating at the UN in writing the Laws of the Sea), her husband Huang Hua, later Foreign Minister of China and his chief Counsel, Zhou Nan, later PRC-designated Governor of Hong Kong and subsequently, Foreign Minister of the People's Republic of China.

I moved with our baby to Hong Kong to join Scott, pet name for Dennis, in late 1974 and, unable to find a job that would pay me a salary equal to male employees, I decided to start a clothing business as the most likely route to gain an entrée to China. I persuaded my youngest sister, then studying in Italy, to move to New York City to become the agent for my childrenswear range. It was the time when Mayor Koch named New York City 'The Big Apple'. We secured our first order from Bloomingdale's parent company, Federated Department Stores, for our design of an apple on a white background. I paired these with solid colour dungarees to match the apples. The buyer at Bloomingdale's was a Miss Birkin, (sister of the famous Jane Birkin) and she asked the parent company to order 200,000 of one style of Tee shirt in a variety of colours. Thanks to her brilliant marketing strategy, the 'little apples' sold like hot cakes.

About a year later, I was scouring the Canton Trade Fair for a textile company that could produce stylish knitwear. I met the head of the Department of Textiles from Shanghai, who was very keen to oblige. This was before Most Favoured Nation (MFN) status was granted to China. When that order eventually went on sale at Bloomingdales, we were approached by major American manufacturers who recognised the quality of our goods at incredibly competitive prices; and we also became their agents.

By this time, my husband had also got the buzz and excitement of doing business in China. He added two male "executives" to our company and secured advances from twelve American companies to be their agents in China. On one of our trips to China, he got an infection and we were exposed to the quality of healthcare. Picture this: my husband had been President of the pharmaceutical company, E. R. Squibb & Sons, accustomed to the best healthcare in the US and was seen running from an Outpatients' Clinic in Guangzhou, pulling his trousers up, hotly-pursued by a lady doctor wielding a hypodermic needle, of a size one could use on a rhinoceros. At that moment, we both determined to do something to improve healthcare in China.

A couple of years later, our private HK company was purchased by Lazard Freres, as China had by then been assigned Most Favoured Nation status by the U.S.A. The granting of MFN status changed the trading relationship overnight and I sensed we could lose our appeal when professional Dragon Ladies could out-manoeuvre us. It had been fun to be in at the beginning, but I really didn't fancy tangling with the professionals. My husband had been invited back to his old company as Chief Operating Officer and so we returned to the US with our 2 children and my husband's son. There Dennis set to compiling a delegation of the best medical brains available and we set up a foundation to implement our ambition: to promote better healthcare in China.

In due course we were invited to meet the leading medical lights of CAMS, the Chinese Academy of Medical Science, of which Dr. Wu Jieping was President. We were hosted to a banquet at the Great Hall of the People by the Minister of Health, and the project was allocated land for a hospital site. Medical delegations from the US were matched by delegations of Chinese doctors to the US, some returning after more than 30 years behind China's Bamboo curtain, the equivalent of the Soviet Union's 'Iron Curtain.' In the end, the hospital site was allocated as a housing site and the funds raised were used instead to upgrade the former Rockefeller-funded hospital, Peking Union Medical College Hospital (PUMCH), which had existed since the 1920's.

I was at that time working on the book, *For Our Daughters* and Dr. Wu Jieping kindly introduced me to some of his colleagues in the Chinese People's Consultative Congress. He was particularly keen to have me meet one of the most senior women, Chen Muhua, Minister of Trade and Minister of Finance. He chaperoned me to meet these extremely accomplished women and became a good friend in the process.

One evening, with our friend Chen I-wan present, he told us stories of the difficult times he had trying to minister to the health needs of Zhou Enlai and being thwarted by Madame Mao, Jiang Qing. When we spoke next morning, I said, "I think I should write *your* biography!" To my astonishment, he replied, "When would you like to start?" I concluded that he had observed enough of my interview prowess by then to feel he could trust me, which was an extraordinary compliment.

Over the next few years, when I was in the city I accompanied Dr. Wu on his Beijing hospital visits. I travelled with him when he was head of Family Planning China, when he visited hospitals: Hunan province one year, Jiangxu province another time, Shanghai and Tianjin. On another occasion, visiting hospitals in Chengde, we travelled in his private railway carriage. He, in turn came to stay in New York, Princeton and various parts of the UK. On most of our trips he was accompanied by his lovely, affectionate wife, Gao Rui.

In 1997, at the time of the handover of Hong Kong to mainland China, his status had become so elevated that Dr. Wu was one of the dignitaries sent to Hong Kong to participate in and witness the return of Hong Kong to the motherland.

It was then that I presented him with this manuscript, but he was horrified by what he read. "Did I really tell you all of this?" He questioned me in surprise. I responded, assuring him that it would be wonderfully helpful and informative to future generations. Nonetheless, it did not suit him to have the book published at that time.

"If you publish this now, you will probably never see me again…"

"But Jieping, you are the most senior doctor in China….."

"And as such, I naturally have enemies who could use this to destroy me. Would you mind waiting until I die?"

Of course, I was extremely disappointed and I sensed that Jieping was sorry to let me down. But I admired him so much, how could I possibly take any other course?

Dr. Wu Jieping died in 2011 and my dear friend He Liliang consoled me, "At least now you will be able to publish his story."

Historical biographies rarely get to the heart of their subject. It was due to the trust in this author that the subject was candid and open in his reflections. This account shows that at the pinnacle of his career, when his status was at its greatest, Dr. Wu Jieping was nonetheless mindful of how his account would be received and the spectre of criticism and consequent punishment.

The Appendices contain several useful annotated lists of people and places which feature in Dr Wu's life.

RELATIONSHIP BETWEEN CHINA AND THE USA: THEN AND NOW

Scholars of US-China history ask the question, "Who Lost China?" The usual scapegoat is Joe McCarthy, but the American Presidents at that time definitely played their part: Eisenhower and Truman. They failed to understand the support, both internal and external, for Mao. Bedazzled by the charm of Chiang Kai-shek's wife, the beautiful Soong Meiling, the US government declared Taiwan to be the true government of China, allocating resources destined for the mainland to the bandits who plundered the art and antiquities of China and moved them, on more than 100 train loads, to Taiwan.

While the USA went to war against Vietnam under J. F. Kennedy, and Lyndon B. Johnson inherited the mess, the USA was desperate to recover its reputation; and so when Chairman Mao reached out a hand to the USA, it was firmly grasped by Richard Nixon who sent Secretary of State, Henry Kissinger, on that first secret mission in 1971. So began the American overture to China, with Nixon's visit following in 1972. Both countries have benefitted commercially and both populations have paid a price.

This book is not an attempt to discredit China. In the case of Dr. Wu Jieping, he co-operated publicly and rebelled privately. Dr. Wu agreed with the need to change China between 1949 and 1999, but was shocked by some of the methods used to accomplish this. Jieping succeeded in implementing changes by burying his head in his research while dealing with new love and the pain of profound loss.

How to maintain one's goodness in a dictatorship? Using medicine for political purposes was a useful tool of control from the 1950's to the 1970's; and because of his profession, Jieping faced challenges on a daily basis but tried, to the best of his ability, to honour his Hippocratic Oath.

President Xi Jinping is selling the notion that improving prosperity is aligned with devotion to the motherland and institutes security measures in the process that ensure a loss of liberty. Soon, he could face critics who challenge this. Today's corollary could tag the whole population, so that not only do the Security Services know the location of the entire population, they could soon also know their very DNA. Given China's phenomenal economic growth in the last fifty years, the American concern is that China will steal a march and threaten its supremacy as the leading economic power in the world. It may be somewhat galling that the USA helped facilitiate the current economic landscape by the need for cheaper products.

China continues to be the most important interest in my life and I only hope the leaders can steer it back to a state that is more trusting and trustworthy.

Notes on Communist Terminology

Russian communism used French versions of the texts of Karl Marx (1818 – 1883) and Friedrich Engels (1820 – 1895) and when China adopted the Russian model, it did not coin a new language. Many Chinese scholars, not to mention the masses, were confused by the language and Mao strove to explain, but was himself confused by some communist terms.

This brings to mind a similar question: the Question of Rites resulting from the disputes over the translation by the Jesuits of Catholic terminology in the Sixteenth Century.

Bourgeoisie vs. Proletariat

Mao used these Marxist terms to criticise the powerful capital class vs. the wage-earners or peasants.

'Cadre' and 'Comrade' replaced 'Official' and 'Peasant'.

Egalitarianism, the very essence of socialism, could not have been further from the Chinese tradition of hierarchical structures.

Revisionism came to represent betrayal.

The bureaucratic class, like *'capitalist roaders'*[1], had to attend work-study sessions in order to learn from the masses. They then had to make self-criticisms.

---

[1] Someone who attempts to move the Communist Revolution in a capitalist direction.

Reactionary authorities were blacklisted because they were *deviating from the party line* and *on the road to revisionism*.

Mao wrote about the Essence of Dialectics, but could not define it. From his various attempts, the intellectuals could only understand that everything in life, the materialist and the metaphysical, had inherent contradictions.

PROLOGUE

Failure is the mother of success

When Dr. Wu Jieping was selected by Chinese Premier Zhou Enlai as his personal physician, little did he know the trouble it would cause him. With that kind of visibility, he soon came to the attention of Chairman Mao, and his wife Jiang Qing who demanded that he also assume responsibility for her medical team. He refused this honour, on the basis that he considered himself a man's doctor. But these protests were ignored. He soon realised that it was not a request, but a command.

Nothing in Jieping's background prepared him for the disappointments of the egalitarian society he supported so selflessly. But in the end, he wanted personal recognition for his sacrifices and for his gifts of medical insight and dedication.

The memoir reveals the appalling conditions in China as experienced by one of its most famous doctors. Dr. Wu Jieping was committed to secrecy by some of his patients, yet had to seek permission from the top to prescribe medicines to help his other patients. Jieping carried out his research in primitive conditions and, in addition to caring for China's leaders, he managed to make valuable discoveries related to tuberculosis and cancer of the kidney. The memoir shows what exceptional talent it took to survive and provides rare insight into life in communist China at a time when most leading intellectuals were expelled to the countryside, imprisoned, or beaten to death.

I got to know Jieping following the death of Zhou Enlai and while the late Chairman Mao's wife was still in prison. I had been in China many times by 1980.

By then, Jieping had been consulted over many years about the health of some of China's leaders, including Premier Zhou Enlai, Chairman Mao, President Liu Shaoqi and Jiang Qing, also known as Madame Mao. Over the following years, our friendship developed.

Before my second husband, Michael, died in 2001, I had travelled annually to China. Following his death, I left the UK and decided to spend more time in the US and China. China's development was such that whole areas of Beijing would be completely transformed in six to twelve months: and with it, the lifestyles of the highest-ranking members of society. Observing this, I decided to move to Beijing to experience personally the march from Communism to Capitalism. And in so doing, I would be close to my old friends.

Over a period of three years, I had interviewed Jieping and gathered vivid and unique recollections of his contacts with the Chinese leadership. But he had insisted that none of these memories should be published until after his death. He had become aware that he could be accused of revealing what the Chinese government had come to regard as "state secrets".

Why have I decided to publish this memoir?

I have done this because it was entrusted to me by someone whose life is a definition of integrity, but who wanted to reveal the skulduggery that went on behind the scenes. Some Chinese friends who had read an early draft commented among themselves that he should never have revealed such personal stories to a foreigner. Regardless of whether, or how, it will be regarded in China, I am doing this as a debt I owe a man whom I greatly admired for many years and in sympathy with his latent captivity by the system he embraced.

It is clear from his life that Jieping acknowledged in the end that he was part of an intellectual elite who, with the best will in the world, could not survive among the multitude of pushing, indifferent masses, who were the recipients of Mao's superficially egalitarian society. Mao reigned for less than thirty years and has been dead for almost five decades. Yet the principles he extolled and inculcated into Chinese society continue to plague it. China's emperors were known as the Sons of Heaven and Mao was, therefore, able to identify with cosmic forces – the sycophants admired him as the "Reddest of all Suns". People worshipped his picture like an icon, asking for guidance as the sun rose and confessing their mistakes as it set. Mao's reaction to criticism of his own failures reflected the patriarchal tradition that sons do not criticize their fathers.

By ignoring the errors of Chairman Mao's administration, the road will be open for a comparably hedonistic "emperor" to thrive in future, at the expense of the Communist Party and of the Chinese people.

The quote at the beginning of this memoir is an idiom, dating to before the Great Wall of China was completed:

> *For one general to achieve fame, ten thousand skeletons must lie exposed.*

I ask myself, what kind of fame – or infamy – should be attributed to one who has been responsible for thirty million skeletons?

He who controls others may be powerful,
But he who masters himself is mightier still.

* * *

The Sage keeps himself behind and he is in the front;
He forgets himself and he is preserved.
Is it not that he is not self-interested
That his self-interest is established?

Laozi
(c. 600 BC),
Legendary sage and author
of Tao Te Ching.

INTRODUCTION

Wu Jieping was born in Jiangsu province in 1917, following the end of the Qing dynasty's three hundred-year rule over the Middle Kingdom, and a few years before China declared itself a Republic under the leadership of Sun Yat-sen.

Less than half a century later, Jieping's telephone number was on the bedside table of the leaders of communist China, the most populous and isolated country in the world. To be known as the best doctor in China during the Cultural Revolution carried certain risks: to subscribe, even inadvertently, to the "Cult of Individualism" meant walking a very fine line. Mao Zedong preached collectivism over individualism but reigned as the final authority, exemplifying the inherent contradictions he touted in his admonitions.

By this time, Chinese values had been turned upside down; the status of the once-revered intellectual class was now on the rubbish dump. It had been consigned there by the very people whose health care was being managed by the intellectual superiority of Dr. Wu Jieping, his brothers and their comrades. But unlike Chairman Mao and his wife Jiang Qing, Jieping made no pretence of being a peasant. He was very proud of his family's inter-generational success and their cultivated tastes. Jieping never shied away from extolling the virtues of the American academic system, which were valued by his father and under which he too had studied.

When he returned to Beijing from the University of Chicago, he became aware of the warning to the Chinese masses that "all dissident scholars, protected by those in power, following the capitalist road, must be eliminated". Jieping had left China believing he was a member of an academic elite and returned to find academia demonized.

When Jieping assumed responsibility for the healthcare of Premier Zhou Enlai, Chairman Mao's wife insisted that Jieping should also assume responsibility for her health care. Jieping demurred, telling her, "I am a *man's* doctor", but to no avail. Over the next decade he was obliged to be at the beck and call of the autocratic Madame Mao, Jiang Qing, whose name means Limpid Stream, responsible for her physical and psychological well-being and frequently expected to compensate for the insecurities caused by her philandering husband.

Jieping was an individual who, unlike his medical colleagues, still sported remnants of values he had acquired in America. He wore polished leather shoes, a dark striped suit with lapels and carried a brown leather medical bag. When his Paul Stuart suits wore out, they were copied by his wife using locally-produced fabric.

Jieping was born into a wealthy family whose senior members were minor officials of the far-flung Chinese empire. His father's mansion was set in the heart of a thriving commercial port, its skyline dotted with colourful junks, sampans, yachts, warships and the myriad characters who tended them.

When I had already known Jieping for some time, after interviewing some of his female colleagues in the Chinese Congress for a book I was editing, we had dinner one evening with a mutual friend, Chen I-wan, known as Chenny[2]. Jieping had earlier told me a number of personal stories about his relationship with Chairman Mao's wife, Jiang Qing, and on this occasion, I asked if I might use my tape recorder to capture the essence of his story. When I saw Chenny the following morning, I asked him why he thought Jieping confided his story to me. Chenny replied, "He wanted someone to know the truth of his experiences."

I presented Jieping with a draft of this book, some years and many interviews later. After reading it, he asked me to wait until he died before publishing it.

It was not easy to give up on a good life story, so I suggested removing the most incriminating parts regarding his patients Zhou Enlai and Jiang Qing.

"That would help; but it is not only the government, but also members of my family who might be offended to read what I have shared with you."

So, seventeen years after meeting him, he had rejected the biography we had both been working on for years. Over the following year I tried

---

[2] Chenny is the Grandson of Eugene Chen, Foreign Minister under Sun Yat-sen. [WJP and Chenny first interview, 1994.]

to revisit the manuscript, omitting the stories that could cause problems. The result was so anodyne, it was not worth publishing.

When Wu Jieping died in 2011, I was living in Beijing and presented the manuscript to the Editor at the Tsinghua University Press.

Tsinghua University Press had already published a book of mine and expressed interest in this memoir, but when I submitted a sampling of chapters, I was informed a year later that the contents had been deleted from their computers as it would "not serve the interests of the Chinese people".

This disappointed me, because what is not visible in any record or archive of those difficult times in China is the kindness, innocence and incorruptibility of anyone who survived those times. Jieping would be appalled at present day practices in China where relatives have to pay sturdy financial bribes to get medical attention. This brilliant man was an exception; he always questioned whether he was making the right decisions and, despite being used by the state and by his in-laws, he retained his innocence and humility to the end of his days. When I last saw him, he confided – like Zhou Enlai – that he had done all that he could. His time was almost up.

Jieping believed in the power of good to change things and wanted to treat people who developed serious illnesses so they could live productive lives, regardless of the corruption and evil that surrounded them. He often quoted a saying of his mother's: "When you yourself are right, nobody and nothing can hurt you." Like many Chinese sayings, it expressed a wish rather than a fact.

While Jieping walked the straight and narrow, he could never have guessed that those he left in his wake would not have the same ethics and would, in fact, become leeches who would bleed him for every last drop.

He believed that his patient, Zhou Enlai, was saving China from the excesses of Mao Zedong and Jiang Qing; and tried to protect Zhou and others from hidden enemies and "minders". His original motivation was to enhance the integrity of health care and the human spirit. His ambition was motivated by goodness. But during the 1950s and '60s, in order to survive, he balanced himself on a tightrope of contradictions and lived into his nineties because he was able to lose himself in the truths of science.

It is ironic that his hard-earned reputation would one day be exploited and marketed, by non-scientists, to promote his name and, in so doing, benefit hugely from the Wu Jieping brand.

Unlike most Chinese, he pulled no strings on behalf of his three children. Jieping believed in meritocracy, and as China entered the world economy under the leadership of Deng Xiaoping, following the deaths of Zhou and Mao in 1976, Wu and other members of the old guard were acclaimed for their contributions to Chinese society. At this time, the handsome widower re-married and his stepdaughter became the chief beneficiary of his esteemed reputation, through the administration of the Wu Jieping Medical Foundation.

Jieping was so uncommercial, and naïve, that perhaps it was predictable that only those who could never understand his motivations were the ones who would capitalize on them.

PART ONE

CHAPTER ONE

'WHEN CHAIRMAN COMMANDS, WE DON'T QUESTION'

Dr. Wu:

"I am a *man's* Doctor. I decided to treat only male patients. There are gynaecologists who are much better qualified than I am."

"But don't you remember me?" Jiang Qing said gently, "You treated me successfully for a stomach problem I had one summer, and I now choose you."

Looking away from me for a moment, she addressed Wang Dongxing, chief administrator of the Communist Party who resided at Zhongnanhai, the central Government compound where Chairman Mao lived, and concluded, "The other doctors were a waste of time."

Premier Zhou Enlai had asked me to treat Jiang Qing when I treated him at Diaoyutai. I felt genuine trepidation at the prospect of tending to the woman who was the biggest firebrand of the Cultural Revolution and at the height of her power. Her raised voice screeched through loudspeakers day and night. Everyone knew her voice better than that of their own mothers or sweethearts. It was familiar, but today it felt as though I was hearing it for the first time. Quoting her husband, Mao Zedong, Jiang Qing reminded me that our primary obligation was "to serve the people wholeheartedly and never for a moment divorce ourselves from the masses, to proceed in all cases from the interests of the people and not from one's self-interest".

I replied mildly, "I am already overloaded with commitments and cannot possibly give you the care you deserve."

She turned to Wang Dongxing once more and in a quiet, lady-like manner said, "Dr. Wu made me feel so much better in such a short time, I believe he knows more than others. He reminds me of Dr. Norman Bethune[3] – and remember what the Chairman felt about him."

Jiang Qing was a brilliant actress and I weakened as I heard her plaintive tone and recalled her pain and unnecessary misery that summer of 1959 at Beidaihe, the coastal resort closest to the capital where government officials stayed at the height of the summer heat.

The British and other foreigners had created the resort in the late nineteenth century, and some of the earlier villas remained. But there were also newer ones, some of them replicas of what had been torn down. One of the most interesting designs was allocated to Chairman Mao's close ally Lin Biao, complete with air raid shelter and underground tunnel leading to the Official Residence and that of Chairman Mao.

I had not been allowed to take my wife, Junkai, that summer and she was very unhappy in the sweltering heat of Beijing where she queued for two hours for a head of celery, while the official medical teams dined well. Now, I was obliged to admit to Junkai that I had agreed to be the personal physician of the actress who captivated our Chairman and that I was to move into the compound of Diaoyutai where she resided.

I told my wife that each leader was allocated their own doctor, but as I was the only one who would also have to practise surgery at several hospitals, I would not have much time left over for Madame Mao. When I explained my schedule to Premier Zhou Enlai, he was encouraging: "Comrade Madame Mao is unlikely to ever trouble you before noon, so you will be able to keep up your surgical practice."

Of course, Junkai did not believe that I had tried to refuse the honour. "You are a urologist who treats men, what does she need *you* for?" she said.

"Look, Junkai, when Chairman Mao commands, you don't question it. It's the same when his wife is giving the order. You know how powerful she is."

"Is there anything you won't do?" my wife asked in fury, looking pitiful as she spun away in her wheelchair. How well I recognized this reaction, as so often in the past she had turned on her heel at the height

---

[3] Norman Bethune was a Canadian doctor who effectively brought modern medicine to rural China. He made a profound impression on Mao Zedong, who wrote a eulogy to him which was memorised by generations of Chinese.

of a furious argument. I sighed, collected some clothes and papers and placed them in my bag.

Later that day the Premier told me, "You should be ready to move in by Monday and, as you have such an important new patient, you may choose whichever medical assistant you deem best."

I suggested a Dr. Wu (who was not related to me), a general medicine specialist who used to be the Chief of Medical Service at Beijing Hospital. Dr. Wu had been severely criticized by the Red Guards and was now doing hard labour. I thought that by requesting this man as my assistant, I could perhaps help him. Dr. Wu turned out to be very helpful and we both survived the Jiang Qing experience. In fact, if it had not been for my hiring him, Dr. Wu would almost certainly have died in prison.

As an intellectual, someone from a bourgeois background, and a man who had studied in America, I had not appreciated that serving that notorious woman would be like walking through a minefield every day. Leaving my ailing wife in our family apartment was heart-breaking, as our children all had their own work commitments and lived far away. To make matters worse, our eldest grandchildren were made to join the hundreds of thousands of urban youths dispersed to the countryside to be re-educated by poor and lower-middle class peasants. They were to become part of the "sent-down" youth generation.

> When Mao married Jiang Qing in Yan'an, those closest to him were appalled that he had divorced – for an actress – the wife who had accompanied him on the Long March. They stipulated that he could only do so if she promised never to become involved in politics. Jiang Qing felt side-lined as other women were highly regarded in their own right.
>
> For fourteen years she complied, albeit unhappily, but maintained a critical interest in the theatre and opera. Many government departments and especially the armed forces had excellent entertainment services.

Mao Zedong with Earl Leaf, Zhu De and Wu Lili
(Wu Guangwei), Yan'an 1946
Bettman via Getty Images

As Minister of Defence, Lin Biao invited her to use her expertise in shaping the "ideology of the armed forces supporting literature and art". Her "expertise" was used to bolster her husband's flagging reputation and to elevate her own position as his right hand. She was finally admitted as a member of the Politburo of the Ninth Central Committee in 1969, whereas Premier Zhou's wife, Deng Yingchao, was admitted four years earlier at the Eighth Central Committee.

Jiang Qing claimed to be exhausted as the Cultural Revolution wound down, but she and the Shanghai Group (later known as the Gang of Four) were at the height of their powers. Her model revolutionary opera productions dominated every category of entertainment within the armed services. But the workers and farmers had had enough of the stalemate that resulted from the anarchy of the Cultural Revolution, and rumours of disaffection were rife. Following years of hardship from famine as a result of

Mao's economic policies, unrest swelled in several provinces, but people were too scared to demonstrate. Jiang Qing and her team believed the revolutionary operas would brighten their moods and infuse them once again with the spirit of the communist revolution.

Jiang Qing, and her devoted Shanghai recruits, Zhang Chunqiao and Yao Wenyuan, (young writers who wrote sycophantic articles lauding Mao) were never members of the Central Committee, but in April 1969 they were made members of the Political Bureau, alarming Zhou Enlai and his circle. Chen Boda, Mao's one-time Secretary and favourite, thought his position was sacrosanct and obstructed the re-establishment of Party and civilian authority. He, too, was honoured in 1962 and made alternate member of the Politburo at the Eighth Central Committee and again at the ninth, when he became a member of the Standing Committee. He was imprisoned in August 1970. Vying for power, the Shanghai clique was supported by Lin Biao (promoted to succeed Mao) against Zhou Enlai and the intellectuals.

Lin Biao's plan to bomb the train on which Chairman Mao was travelling was discovered and, fearing the consequences, Lin and his family made a bid to escape to the Soviet Union; but the plane they had commandeered crash-landed on a plain in Mongolia, apparently having run out of fuel.

In the aftermath, Jiang Qing claimed to be ill. But in an effort to reclaim the initiative from their bureaucratic rivals, the Gang of Four launched several campaigns to bring Zhou and his circle down.

Dr. Wu:

I was to live with other doctors in the Diaoyutai compound in House No. 7, (a splendid mansion by any standards and by the standards of the Cultural Revolution, it was palatial). We avoided taking the best rooms and took those allocated to secretaries. There were six or seven doctors sharing the same living space, but no room for my wife to stay. This infuriated Junkai.

Zhou Enlai and the Shanghai Group, or Gang of Four, also lived at Diaoyutai. This compound was largely the brainchild of Premier Zhou. Its approximately ten acres of landscaped gardens and ponds were interspersed with some twenty mansions designed with the latest creature comforts, ostensibly to house visiting foreign dignitaries.

Everyone travelled by bicycle as there were almost no cars in use at the time, but my situation was very special. Because I had so many surgical roles, I was allocated a car and driver (the Red Flag cars indicated to the masses that a VIP or leader was approaching). My work at Diaoyutai would commence in the late afternoon, whenever Madame Mao deigned to get up, and would usually last until after midnight.

In the mornings, while the others slept, I would go out to the hospitals to start to operate by 8.00 a.m. and I was free to practise surgery until noon at the hospitals. I felt uncomfortable because, in spite of the late nights and trivial demands, my life had become very comfortable and I was probably the only doctor in the country who had a car to take me to work during the Cultural Revolution.

Early on, I was warned by Jiang Qing, "You cannot discuss my treatment with anyone but me; and if you need to consult another doctor, it must be in my presence." If I mentioned anything outside, she could say, "You told my secret." So I revealed no details to Zhou Enlai of my care of Madame Mao, in order to protect both of us.

At this time many of my old Peking Union Medical College classmates were working as porters and orderlies in the hospitals where they'd formerly been department heads. I had no desire to join those accused of spying or being Kuomintang sympathizers who, if they were fortunate to have survived, now worked as ordinary labourers in the vast Chinese hinterland.

I could smuggle one or two back into the fold, but not my old colleague Dr. Teng. I regretted the massive waste of expertise he'd worked so hard to attain. He was consigned to do manual work on a pig farm. Dr. Teng wrote to tell me he'd converted the pig-keeping into a scientific project by growing certain foods and experimenting with the findings of one diet versus another. By this sort of dabbling in the research that was once his normal work, and by occasionally pursuing the outdoor activities he so enjoyed, he managed to keep his sanity, hoping that one day the madness would be over and he would return to his hospital to look after people who needed good doctors.

Dr. Teng had been China's leading haematologist, a young man from the Hakka minority, whose childhood was so impoverished that he suffered from malnutrition while attending middle school and was almost blind.

He was a Wenham[4] scholar who went on to complete his post-doctoral studies at Harvard Medical School and now must occasionally have questioned his decision to return home to China.

Jiang Qing was so powerful that, for no apparent reason, she could send you to prison. I soon realized she only wanted me for bangmang. 'Bang' means help and 'mang' means busy. I was selected to distract her and had reservations about her motives.

I was soon to discover that Jiang Qing wanted the best of everything for herself. If she wanted to play table tennis, she would call for the World Champion, Zhuang Zedong, who would come and play with her even when she summoned him at midnight, and he would not leave before 3.00 a.m. This was a pure ego trip, because she was not a particularly good player. She also liked to play the piano, despite her lack of talent or ability to make herself a successful pianist. So, she had the best piano in China brought over to her in the vain hope that with the best possible instrument at her fingertips she would play better music.

People suspected she was having affairs, but there was no opportunity for infidelity because everyone was being watched or spying on everyone else.

Jiang Qing had been diagnosed with cervical cancer and sent to the Soviet capital for treatment in 1962. Unlike many people who lost their hair as a result of chemotherapy, she retained hers, which was very nice so she didn't need to wear a wig; but she wore one anyway.

One difficulty I had with Jiang Qing was that she seemed to be unaware that she might be hurting someone, or that others were hurting her. It was as if she did not register mental or physical pain. She could react without showing *subjective awareness*. She was very suspicious of people and sweated a lot, as if she was going through the menopause.

And she wanted the best doctor. That was me and I resented being her plaything. She claimed to want my special expertise for therapeutic purposes, but I became annoyed when I discovered she only really wanted me to help her to kill time. Jiang Qing seemed to sense this and reminded me, "I am the Chairman's wife and First Deputy Director of the Cultural Revolution Committee. Who are you?"

---

[4] The Wenham was the ultimate prize, given to the student who had made the most progress in their studies from Year 2 to Graduation. Apart from the prestige, all medical school fees were reimbursed to the student.

CHAPTER TWO
TRANSPORTING SILVER IN 1914

Dr. Wu:

My family was headed by medium-level officials; fairly well-to-do scholars in the late Qing dynasty, which ended with the Revolution of 1911.

My father and his two brothers were classified as Xiu Cai, as a result of their rank in the Imperial Examinations, equivalent to the Civil Service exams in the West.

> There were four levels to these exams – local county, provincial capital, Beijing and Forbidden City. The local county level was the first step, Xiu Cai, and before the brothers could take the next step, at the provincial level, the system was abolished; but they were always respected for having taken the first step.

Dr. Wu:

My family came from Jiangsu province, (where Zhou Enlai's family moved to when he was a boy) and the Wu brothers were allocated posts in different parts of Central and South China. In those days, it was common practice to send officials to distant provinces where they would be less likely to engage in corrupt practices away from friends who might try to influence them. Life was circumscribed by Confucian values, loyalty to the Emperor, family and village life.

In around 1910, my father befriended a very important high official, Sheng Xuanhuai, who was promoting the introduction of foreign technology to China.

The founder of Tianjin's Beiyang University and the precursor to Shanghai Jiao Tong University, Sheng served as Minister of Transport of the Qing dynasty and in 1897, opened the first Chinese-owned bank, the Imperial Bank of China. Sheng and my father were both from Changzhou and so in 1914, out of brotherly loyalty, Sheng asked my father to help him transport a quantity of silver dollars from Hubei to Shanghai. My father enlisted the help of his two brothers and the Green Gang, probably the most notorious secret society of the day, not unlike the Mafia, through his father's connections. He had decided to use the dollars to buy American petroleum in Hubei, as it was less likely to be stolen.

At the time, the only roads were mule tracks and man-made waterways in the countryside, and in the cities, carriage lanes and canals, as railways had not been developed throughout the country. Most transport was by canal or river. As pirates patrolled the waterways and bands of robbers were everywhere, my father arranged to transport the oil via mule train from Hubei to Shanghai. This took several months and, by the time the caravan arrived, the petrol was worth two hundred and fifty per cent more than the original dollars because of the war in Europe.

Father was rewarded with sixty thousand Mexican silver dollars, the equivalent of approximately US $600,000, and decided it was enough for the whole family to retire forever, since they didn't know what life would be like after the revolution that had ended imperial rule with the collapse of the Qing dynasty. In 1914, my father was not quite forty and he and his two brothers showed real Confucian solidarity by sharing the reward equally.

As many of the imperial institutions had been abolished, including the civil service examinations, and the brothers no longer had real occupations, they agreed to retire to build a family mansion in their ancestral home, Changzhou in Jiangsu province, to house their three families, with a courtyard each and one for their parents, unmarried children and other relatives.

> Changzhou was built on the southern bank of the Yangtze River and had been a walled city for 3,000 years since the time of the Western Zhou dynasty. It housed the soul tablets of the Wu

ancestors for many generations. Jieping's grandfather had started out rather humbly as an apprentice in a pawnshop. He was industrious and had excellent calligraphy. He eventually became the head of the pawnshop and in due course owned and expanded it. In China at the time, a pawnshop would have had similar status to a bank today.

Place names change frequently in China, and Changzhou had previously been known as Yanling and Wujin. It was renamed an ordinary prefecture in 589, to become a canal port after the Grand Canal was constructed in 609. Fish and rice were so plentiful that early on they spawned trades in bamboo, fruit and tea, leading to the development of a safe inland trading port for the flourishing silk and tea trade. The city soon developed into a trans-shipment point for local grains.

The Wu family's imposing, two-storey house was built near the bamboo-lined riverbank, its grey tiled roofs curving upwards on each corner. Past the red lacquered gate, the entrance was screened by a wall inlaid with marble. Visitors then turned sharply towards the moon gate (to obstruct ghosts who only travel in straight lines). There were five courtyards as was befitting the life of scholarship imagined by Old Wu, Jieping's father. Attaining the Chinese ideal of "four generations under one roof" put the brothers in an enviable position.

The traditional house, *siheyuan*, had four walls surrounding a courtyard, and several houses were connected by a series of covered verandas and pergolas, all inside a twenty-foot high wall. The area surrounding the archways was decorated with Confucian and Taoist characters and, under delicately carved arches, recounted fables of the past. In each courtyard dwelt a son with his wife and family, and unmarried siblings lived in the parents' large courtyard. Etiquette made it impolite to intrude into another's courtyard and family harmony was preserved by each one, knowing that manners were the essential ingredient in all human relationships.

Jieping proudly pointed this out, as we approached his old home many years later, and told me a story about the decision to build the kitchen outside the wall next to the river, in case of fire. He chuckled as he recalled this.

Dr. Wu:

It proved to be a smart decision for when a fire started a couple of years later, my uncles turned away those who came to help put the fire out. They would only have robbed the house and it was simpler to rebuild the kitchen than have those unwanted visitors in the compound.

> The population of Changzhou (from where many of the educated young revolutionaries came) rivalled that of Liverpool, the second largest port in the world at the time, and its inhabitants hailed from all over China. It had developed a reputation as a site well-known for industry and learning.
>
> Life carried on comfortably throughout the years of World War I in the idyllic mansion, but Old Wu recognized that the money would not last forever; and, having spent three-quarters of the funds on the construction of the traditional home, the three brothers realized they would have to seek paid employment somehow. Luckily, the bright young man who had purchased the petrol had left an impression on business mogul Sheng. He introduced Jieping's father to Liu Bosen, who owned the Baochen Spinners cotton factory in Shanghai and was also a tycoon in the shipping business. Old Wu now became manager of that cotton factory.
>
> By now, the winds of change that had driven the brothers into seclusion in the first place had gathered the force of a typhoon, leading to Sun Yat-sen's republican revolution, which failed eventually – in one sense – because it gave rise to the Warlord Period. The family continued to live at the mansion while Old Wu worked in Shanghai, but he would go home at weekends and sometimes took his young son Jieping to the factory with him and kept him in Shanghai where he stayed with cousins.
>
> In the early 1920s, the family relocated to Shanghai.

Dr. Wu:

The entire family finally left the mansion in Jiangsu at the beginning of the Japanese invasion in 1937 and the house was taken care of by my older uncle. He was responsible for the local cotton mill at that time, and when he left, his administrators decided to use the mansion as a warehouse.

Apparently, they stole everything and ultimately burned the house down to cover their theft. Most of the family records were burnt with the house.

All his life, Jieping was proud to be associated with Shanghai. He and many others felt it was the most "progressive" and commercially aggressive city in Asia.

Large Chinese cities were typically administrative centres, but Shanghai was a commercial hub, a Western city superimposed on a Chinese village. It could be compared with New York in that it was a city and not a government centre. Shanghai was not even a provincial capital, although it was by then the most international and colourful city in China, the 'Paris of the East'. In the course of his business day, Old Wu mixed not only with a variety of people from other provinces but with Russians, Indians, Jews from everywhere, and the dominant Americans, British and French.

Because of its location at the mouth of the Huangpu River, on the east coast, Shanghai was the most convenient location for the British to establish a commercial port. By the 1920s it was the most glamorous city in Asia, where merchant tycoons were carried in sedan chairs over the dead bodies of countless beggars and opium addicts. Modern banking and finance started in Shanghai, as did the Westernization of business in China. Shanghai became a replica of a Western city, except that gangs and secret societies penetrated even the foreign concessions and these gangs infiltrated the police, banks, brothels, schools and dancehalls. According to the geographer William Rhoads Murphey[5], "…there, more than anywhere else the two civilizations came together – the rational, legal-minded, scientific, industrialist, efficient, expansionist West, and traditional, intuitive, humanist, agrarian, inefficient, [sic] and seclusionist China". There is no mention of either the native work ethic or exquisite cuisine.

Foreigners considered Shanghai the most comfortable and civilized city in China, as Murphey reported in 1893 on the 50th anniversary of its establishment:

---

[5] Rhoads Murphey III, Shanghai: *Key to Modern China* (Cambridge, Massachusetts: Harvard University Press, 1953.)

"Shanghai is the centre of our higher civilization and demonstrates Christian influence for all of China. We are here in the midst of a people proud and prejudiced in favour of their ancient line of doing things, and what have we produced amongst them, for their benefit as well as our own? We might well point to the English homes we have formed here. In short, look at the *tout ensemble* of the Settlement – houses and streets lit with gas and electricity, streams of pellucid water flowing in all directions, and sanitary arrangements according to the best medical advice. We have steamers, telegraphs and telephones in communication with all the world; there are cotton and paper mills and silk fabrics of foreign invention and, last but not least, railways in the north as pioneers of what will yet be found all over China. Law and order are admirably preserved, in the midst of two hundred thousand people, at the instance of our own judicial and municipal authorities."

This underscored the cultural differences, but did not take into account the almost three million Chinese who lived without the benefit of sanitation, or the protection of the law. Nor did it mention the child labourers who handled the silk fibres, whose hands were so burned by the boiling liquids used to separate the cocoons, that they were disabled for life.

In the wake of the Russian Revolution, thousands of White Russians made their way to Shanghai and following the First World War, Shanghai offered stability and opportunity for the disenfranchised. Certain Chinese also found it a refuge from communist uprisings, while some well-known communists took advantage of the relative anonymity of the International Settlement.

Jieping's father was fond of reminding his children, "In 1861 we had submarine cable links between Shanghai, Hong Kong and Nagasaki. In 1881 the telephone came to us and by 1923 we had our first radio station." However, this family lived among the top one per cent of the city and could not have guessed at the hardship of the lives of menial workers, who slaved away beneath the surface to maintain the illusion of civilization.

Sun Yat-sen finally returned to China in 1921 with the hope of leading his struggling republic, when Jieping was just four years old.

At that time, Old Wu was achieving great success with the cotton mills. Sun's triumphant return sent a strong message to the Chinese people, but his popularity worried Western diplomats when he was reported as saying, "The foreign vampire will not give up its bloodsucking," and promised, "Henceforth we turn our faces away from the West." The international diplomats now turned against him.

Sun and his supporters feared that, just as the foreign merchants had found opium to offset the trading imbalance a century earlier, they now needed a Chinese stooge who could be manipulated and controlled by the West.

Sun's independence stunned his foreign supporters. He had raised much of his finance in the West, but as Western "diplomats" still controlled Chinese Customs and the Salt Tax, (as a result of the need to service the Boxer war indemnities and foreign loans) he now risked making enemies on several fronts. Old Wu was a great admirer of Dr. Sun, and his friends advised caution to the rebel President who had not lived in China since boyhood. But having trained and practised as a medical doctor, he was idealistic and ill-equipped to understand the political machinations that surrounded him.

Sun had inherited an economic system in which what remained from customs' duties collected all over China was reserved for the coalition of northern warlords in Beijing. These warlords had long been a part of Chinese history; in areas of weak government, strongmen with bands of supporters often emerged to take control. And now, with a weak central government and the disappearance of the Qing dynasty's 'official' class, former provincial governors increased their power and, depending on the size of their armies, exercised control over a growing number of districts as provincial warlords. The governors spent the proceeds of forty or more taxes on their provincial "defence" and there was no national civil administration to manage the nation's infrastructure. The foreign powers took advantage and associated themselves with their preferred province or warlord.

It was the dream, and some thought even the God-given right, of early travellers, businessmen and adventurers to introduce Western ways, religion and customs to enlighten the Chinese heathen and make trading arrangements simpler. Educated in America, Old Wu had more democratic values than his contemporaries.

Jieping's father ran the Shanghai factory for only two or three years before he was promoted to construct and manage a new cotton mill in Tianjin, in 1920. It was a time when other factories were sometimes crippled by strikes; and Liu congratulated his young manager on his ability to get along with the factory workers and thus avoid dissent.

Factories in China in the 1920s operated on two twelve-hour shifts, which Old Wu found was both inefficient and unreasonable. When he proposed changing the system, the factory owners argued that it would lower productivity, but Old Wu countered that he would take the consequences. He advocated that shortening the workday and giving a rest to the workers would improve efficiency and increase productivity. He successfully introduced the eight-hour shift, his profits grew, and it was for this innovation that he was recognised in *Who's Who*.

Jieping's father maintained the eight-hour shift system until he left, four years later. But after he was gone, the owners resumed twelve-hour days.

By the mid-1920s, three separate groups of strongmen controlled the major provinces in North China, South China and West China. The former general Yuan Shikai[6], who had famously persuaded the Empress to abdicate her son's claim to the throne, now stepped back into the limelight and took the reins of leadership into his own hands.

Sun Yat-sen was soon out-manoeuvred by Yuan Shikai, and obliged to restrict his sphere of influence to civil power, relying on the provincial warlords to protect his civil government with military power. He had a weakness for young ladies that was fully exploited by his "supporters". Among the ladies who attracted his attention, Soong Ai-ling (daughter of bible salesman tycoon Charlie Soong) became his Personal Assistant and managed his relationships as she saw fit. He later married her second youngest sister, Soong Ching-ling who, as his widow, became Honorary President of China.

---

[6] A few years later, Yuan Shikai ordered Imperial robes for himself; but was obliged to resign as President when his followers realised that he wanted to reinstate the Monarchy, with himself as Emperor.

Jieping knew these people only as 'Auntie' or 'Uncle' and could never have guessed at their later glory.

By the late 1930's, stateless European and Middle Eastern Jews found that Shanghai was one place they could go without a passport or visa. Sassoons, Hardoons, Epsteins and Kadoories thrived, establishing indestructible and commercial empires that would grant them world fame.

Shanghai was the centre of China's Industrial Revolution. The Chinese businessmen had taken the advantage during World War I, when European trade declined, and Chinese industry and commerce grew to fill the void. A modern Chinese business class gradually developed. It still had ties to the countryside, and many businessmen continued to receive some of their income from land rents from tenant farmers in their home villages. Now, they increasingly became involved in modern industry, finance and foreign trade.

Between 1910 and 1940, this urban business class became more and more important as a political force. The Shanghai business class represented by Old Wu and his brothers regarded the instability of the warlord system as inimical to its interests. They recognized that the unequal treaty system (imposed during the Opium Wars) could never be overturned as long as China lacked a strong government. The Chinese people craved stability and the business class shared the nationalist fervour of the 1920s, and came to identify with the Kuomintang (KMT) or Nationalist Party.

Defeated by Yuan Shikai, Sun Yat-sen was soon to acknowledge that what China actually needed was military strength. He chose the young and ambitious Chiang Kai-shek, heir-apparent to Yuan Shikai, to send to Russia to study their military academies. When he returned, Chiang was made Director of the Huangpu Military Academy in Guangzhou (known by many in the West as Canton). Chiang was a reformed womaniser who, before his travels, drank and whored with his Green Gang cronies, but now zealously embraced the disciplines he encountered in Japan and Russia.

Chiang's position as Military Commander gave him enormous power and the respect and complete allegiance of a new generation of officer corps. Zhou Enlai, who had earlier co-founded a branch of the Chinese Communist Party (CCP) in France, was named

Head of the Political Department and Mao Zedong became alternate member in charge of KMT propaganda. Never before had this generation of businessmen and academics felt they were part of a change for the good of China.

Having orchestrated this structure, Sun Yat-sen had begun to feel weak and exhausted and tried to concentrate on regaining his health.

As he learned of the coming changes, Old Wu was heartened to read the resolutions that dominated Sun's First Congress of the Kuomintang:

Entente with Russia;

Admission of communists into the KMT;

Social progress to improve the condition of workers.

Jieping's father admired and supported this early attempt at unification, when he could understand it, but warned his children, "All politicians are self-motivated. Better do something you yourself can be accountable for."

But Sun died of his illness at PUMCH in March 1925, leaving the way clear for Chiang to assume his mantle of authority. China had inadvertently found what Sun and his supporters had once most feared, "a Chinaman who could be manipulated and controlled by the West".

Dr. Wu:

After those few years in booming Shanghai, Father was sent to Tianjin to open a third factory, the Tianjin Baochen Spinners. I spent my middle school years in Tianjin from about the age of five, but went back to my childhood home in Changzhou quite often, to visit my grandparents.

My mother was born in Chenzha, between Nanjing and Shanghai. She was sold as a child-maid by her father into the wealthy Liu family. The first Liu wife could not have children and really liked my mother and tried to teach her to write characters, read, sew and embroider like the young ladies of her friends. But my mother didn't pay very much attention to the schooling side of her upbringing. She was very pretty and, along with another girl, was sent as a concubine to two rather influential families. My family was one; and the other maid went as a concubine to a very important man who later became Minister of

Legislations in Beijing, with whom she had two sons, who became professors at Tsinghua University and my mother, who became my father's concubine, always had a little rivalry with her "sister" child-maid, the Minister's concubine.

Mother and Father of Wu Jieping

So, we knew from an early age what our mother's expectations were: Tsinghua University, was the standard. Even then it was recognized as the Harvard of China.

My father was already very successful and when his first wife died, he became the nominal son-in-law of this highly respected Liu family, the adoptive family of my mother.

So, I was born to a concubine. Father lived with his first wife, whom we children all called Mother, until she died at the age of fifty-six. Then four years later, on what would have been her sixtieth birthday, my father did something very special – he commemorated his first wife by elevating my mother from concubine to wife and "rectified" the situation.

I believe Jieping meant that his father now strode into the 20th Century having cast off his feudal heritage. When I asked why the Liu family would give up two beautiful girls, Jieping replied matter-of-factly that it was to gain social or commercial advantage, because the girls were not needed by the Liu family and they had very tiny bound feet. With a wry smile, Jieping acknowledged with belated pride what was then regarded as the yardstick for measuring beauty, 'tiny Golden Lilies', as the bound feet were called, despite his repugnance for the practice.

Dr. Wu:

These girl maids were often beautiful and capable, and usually this qualified them to be sent to a wealthy family, as a secondary wife or concubine. In this way, alliances were forged between the wealthier and more powerful families. Marriage was a family transaction, not a matter of personal feelings.

> Clearly, little had changed at the heart of Chinese values, if this educated man could rationalize exchanging a human being for some other advantage. In China the tradition of having concubines had none of the pejorative overtones understood in the West. In those days, there were few of the derogatory connotations associated with the position in China, whereas in the West it was regarded as comparable with the role of mistress or courtesan, which to the Europeans meant being a "kept woman".
>
> Concubinage was practised at the highest levels of society. An emperor would have at least sixty and with rare exceptions, these imperial concubines were much more the servants of their mothers-in-law than the wives of their sovereign. But it was one thing to be an imperial concubine, with precedent firmly established by which a concubine could become an Empress if she gave birth to a son, and quite another to become the pawn in one's adoptive father's game of fortune. In Jieping's mother's case, the Lady Liu who took her as a child-maid adopted her and arranged for her "daughter" to go and live with the Wu family.

Dr. Wu:

By then, my mother had learned and adopted all the ways and manners of an old wealthy family and raised her children and grandchildren in the same tradition. She was very capable and gave a really good education to all her sons, daughters, step-children and grandchildren, with remarkable success.

> Jieping did not comment on his mother's failure to educate her daughters as her husband proposed to do with his sons, because in those days it would have been unheard of. There were only a couple of schools for girls and they were discouraged in China and the rest of the world. Between the three brothers at that time, there were nine sons and Jieping was the ninth.
>
> Our friend Chenny explained: "When people were lined up to be punished or criticized during the Cultural Revolution, the ninth person was always the intellectual at the bottom of the Red Guards' list. Soldiers were looked down on as *Qi Ba*[7] seventh or eighth, and very close to the bottom or lowest on the rung, but above the scholars, in the 1960s. This was a reverse of Chinese tradition where nine was associated with fortune and a long life, because the word for nine is pronounced like the word for long (duration of time)."
>
> To this day, the Chinese consider the number nine as lucky.
>
> I asked whether there were any girls in Jieping's family and learned that there were eight daughters; but it was a thorny subject with him as his otherwise faultless father did not educate his daughters outside the home.

Dr. Wu:

I was my father's favourite child. Before I was born, he and his brothers had eight sons between them. I was the ninth male child and was expected to be a model of fidelity, upholding traditional values and honour while improving the status of the family.

---

[7] Since the Yuan Dynasty, 'Qi Ba' referred to the lowest in society, manual workers and prostitutes; but even lower were beggars.

> In such a close Chinese family, first cousins were treated like brothers and sisters. The house was always full of "uncles, aunts and cousins" because no matter how distant the relationship, the elders were called uncle and aunt and even if someone was a distant nineteenth cousin, he or she was still called 'cousin'. The father was obliged to offer room and sustenance and if necessary, borrow money to aid whatever distant relative needed help or education.

Dr. Wu:

I was home-schooled by private tutors, with my brothers and cousins. There were usually eight to ten children studying quietly at their own level in the schoolroom with one or two tutors in charge and girls participated in some of our classes.

Our study was broken up by nature walks, ball games and sewing practice, as well as food breaks and rest times.

In the evening, we might go to the theatre and watch a Mei Lanfang[8] performance, for example, *Heavenly Maiden Scattering Flowers*, or *The Will to Live*, in which a father drove his son from home for having a love affair, then forgave his son and daughter-in-law when he saw her illegitimate child.

Or, we might have watched *Drama at Sea*, in which a girl refused to marry her parents' choice. She pretended to commit suicide and haunted her room as a ghost; but when she emerged and found her love was married, she actually committed suicide.

> Jieping recalled that these films provoked commentary on social problems and relations between the sexes, that neither Old Wu nor his wife was willing to engage in with their children. Today sex education is still taboo in China, even between educated parents and their children, and Jieping developed a determination to do something about this oversight.

---

[8] Mei Langfang (1894-1961) was a well-known Peking opera artist in modern Chinese theatre. He was known exclusively for his female lead roles and, particularly, his 'verdant-robed girls': young or middle-aged women of grace and refinement. These led to him being known as 'Queen of Peking Opera'.

The sons of Old Wu's older brother all became successful businessmen, the sons of his younger brother all became scholars, and Jieping's brothers all became medical scientists.

The four brothers of the Wu family, all Doctors and graduates of
Peking Union Medical College

*L – R: Paediatrician Wu Ruiping; Surgical Specialist Wu Weiran;
Urologist Wu Jieping and Immunologist Wu Anran*

There was neither political nor economic security. China's gentry had a choice of aligning themselves with the progressives, represented by the wily Chiang Kai-shek, or the warlord who had nominal control of their province.

Dr. Wu:

Father knew from bitter experience that politicians could be as corrupt, if not more so, than the despised Qing officials, and bade his sons study Western science. This inclination towards Western science had long been advocated by the Imperial family and their progressive advisers in Peking. But without national security, or a relevant legal system, life was so insecure that people simply disappeared with no questions asked, in a country with several different national armies and dozens of private ones.

My father had a real interest in foreign technology and taught himself photography. He bought all kinds of cameras and developing materials from overseas. He was always trying to improve things to make them more efficient. For example, instead of grinding the inkstone as he went along, he made four ink-sticks with a mechanical roller and battery to grind it more efficiently. He persuaded the husband of his first daughter to go to medical school. This young man had already graduated from Suzhou University as a teacher. Father convinced him to give up his job and enrol at Peking Union Medical College (PUMC), much against the wishes of his own parents. They quarrelled with my father, who was gentle but persistent and eventually convinced them because he was willing to pay all the expenses.

We had moved from the family mansion to a small house in Shanghai, then finally to a courtyard house in Tianjin, (Heavenly Ford), on the cotton mill grounds by the River Hai. This was exciting for us children as Tianjin was an even more famous port city, open to foreign trade only forty years earlier, where I was to learn another Chinese dialect in addition to Changzhou and Shanghainese.

> After Sun Yat-sen's death in March 1925, the KMT government was run by a coalition of three in Guangzhou: the Left-wing representing those who were allied to the communists, led by Liao Zhongkai; the Right-wing led by Hu Hanmin; and the third faction led by the remarkably ardent patriot Wang Jingwei, favoured by the communists but who later sold out to the Japanese. The coalition did not survive the workers' strikes, crippling both Hong Kong and Guangzhou; and when Liao Zhongkai was murdered, Chiang Kai-shek clamped down, initiating military rule. He also installed his men in the trade unions and assumed control of Guangzhou. Hu Hanmin was fired and the province and city were ruled by KMT leaders, Chiang Kai-shek and Wang Jingwei.
>
> An era of confusion, propaganda and misrepresentation was about to begin.

CHAPTER THREE
CHINA UNGOVERNED

The population of Tianjin in the early 1930s was under one million, with the international community making up more than twenty thousand. The city is situated in the great fertile plains of the north and had been opened to Western trade as a result of China's defeat by Britain in the second Opium War of 1858, when ten additional ports between Taiwan and Manchuria were opened for foreign trade. The cause of the first Opium War was the imbalance of trade between China and Great Britain. In the end Great Britain forced China to allow the sale of opium in exchange for their purchases of porcelain, tea and silk. The treaties resulting from the Opium Wars are what the Chinese refer to, resentfully, as the Unequal Treaties.

Shanghai, on the other hand, was a commercial success long before it attracted the Europeans, who should not have found it appealing as hot humid summers give way to bitterly cold winters and frequent flooding. The Wu family considered their move to Tianjin would be more advantageous than the competitive atmosphere of Shanghai.

Dr. Wu:

My father became general manager and this new compound was even more exciting for a little boy than the family mansion. It was outside the city wall in what was then called the Chinese Territory. It had its own electricity and an independent water system, at a time when there was no central city sanitation. We had a big house, and the assistant general manager and some engineers also lived within the compound.

My father did not want his children to follow the example of loyal court officials and filial sons of feudal society. He wanted us to be independent, to forge ahead with a sense of creativity. He thought like a modern scientist, but was trapped in a society where order and tradition were essential to stability. He recognized the need for both and tried to guide his family accordingly.

At dawn we heard the shrill whistle signalling the start of the workday; at dusk we watched exhausted factory workers trudge home, having earned barely enough to feed themselves. In the textile mills the workers were mostly women and children. No child could be denied the right to work and their nimble fingers made them ideal workers in the silk factories where most suffered a lifetime of pain as a result.

A couple of years after the move, I was impressed and excited by the arrival of an American engineer and his two sons. We studied together in my home on alternate days and at the factory with managers, who taught us maths and science. Later I understood that Father had purchased the latest American machinery for the cotton mill, which should have been fully repaid by this time, but was not, so the American manufacturer sent this American, called Mr Burton, to observe the manufacturing process. I was six or seven when Thomas and Arthur Burton arrived.

> Old Wu was unable to continue hire purchase payments on the equipment he had bought from the US because although manufacturing had improved several-fold and the quality could compare with the best Egyptian cotton, the changing tariff system made the agreement unsustainable. Old Wu tried to explain to his American colleague how the Treaty Ports worked: goods exported by foreign manufacturers were shipped tax-free on their manufacturer nations' ships, whereas Chinese-manufactured goods were subject to Excise Tax to add to shipping costs. Old Wu, therefore, decided to enter the shipping business.
>
> Luckily, Old Wu was fluent in English, which was very rare among Chinese businessmen. Most communication between Chinese and foreigners was conducted in what was known as Pidgin. Pidgin English was based on Chinese pronunciation of

English words (like "pidgin" for "business") mixed with some Chinese, Portuguese and Indian vocabulary, using Chinese word order and grammar. Portuguese contributed "joss" from Deus (God). Thus "joss-house" meant temple or church, "joss-stick" meant a stick of incense, and "joss-pidgin-man" meant a missionary. Chinese words included "taipan" for boss.

Chinese managers of Western companies gradually adopted Western ideas of business and its role in society. Many of Old Wu's colleagues came to reject the Confucian notion that business was something lowly, and they envied the legal protection that businesses enjoyed in the West, where there was a substantial body of commercial law.

Dr. Wu:

Between the ages of five and ten, I lived in the factory grounds adjacent to Tanggu Port. Our home nestled in one corner of the compound, with the cotton mill beside the River Hai. There were also a tennis court and a few houses for other employees. Sometimes we watched football and played it in the British concession.

Father was very determined and his attitude was persuasion rather than force. He liked the saying, "The tongue is soft but constantly remains; the teeth are hard, yet they fall out."

> When Jieping was nine years old, the campaign for "reunification of China" with Chiang Kai-shek as Commander-in-Chief was announced on 11 June and launched in July 1926. This "reunification" was Chiang's public agenda – his private one was to wipe out the communists.
>
> From Guangzhou, Chiang's Northern Expedition proceeded with the officer corps of the Huangpu Academy in control. Old Wu was aware that China was beset by contradictions, because the cotton spun in his factories was used for military uniforms. Without a central government, the warlords showed a surprising willingness to side with the disciplined, well-turned out National Revolutionary Army, the KMT army. An alliance with the KMT threatened their own armies and their independence, but the warlords had recently been subjected to unrest and revolt staged

by communist agitators in villages and entire districts opposed to them, so they joined the KMT.

At that time, Tianjin had several special zones called concessions. The Russian concession had been the most important zone before the Russian Revolution and its subsequent return to Chinese sovereignty, then the British, French, German and Japanese concessions. Distinctly Western in architectural style, each concession usually had a couple of churches, one Catholic and one Protestant, whose differences were largely lost on the native population.

The bells chiming in the early morning carried over the water to mingle with the ships' horns blaring in the morning fog. Only students and academics had any understanding of their relative status. Although the Wu family was not Christian, it was decided that Jieping should attend the Methodist school in the Chinese territory, which was funded by missionary sources. Jieping learned mathematics and English from both English and American missionaries.

Dr. Wu:

It was not the best school; Nankai, Zhou Enlai's old school, was more famous, but I couldn't make it into that one. I was ten years old and all my classmates were fourteen. I stayed at the missionary school for four years. My mother hired a big, strong young rickshaw puller and dressed him in double-layered coats and gloves that winter to save his hands. I got up around 5 a.m. to get into the rickshaw, and the puller took me through the German, French and Japanese concessions to get to the school. It took two hours to get there. The puller waited all day and then towed me back home for another two hours.

> Sitting in a wooden chair with an attached, pivoting desktop, the young boy studied history and gradually became aware that the foreigners lived according to their own customs in their own isolated colony in the centre of Tianjin city.
>
> The students were mostly Chinese and their Chinese teacher frequently became overwrought and would shout, "The future of China is *our* responsibility!"

Dr. Wu:

I learned from our teacher that it was the Treaty of Nanjing, opening up the ports and giving foreigners their own legal rights outside of Chinese law that made China a colonised state. This was not a subject discussed at the family table.

> At home during the summer holidays, the ten-year old could be found on the tennis court within the factory compound, which was rarely used by the executive staff for whom it was intended. They were massively busy as Chinese production soared while industrialization got under way.

Dr. Wu:

During these years I had no impression of China's problems. Mine was a trouble-free childhood, where we played hide-and-seek in the *godowns*[9], flew kites along the riverbank and devised our own games. We played table-tennis, football, badminton and tennis within the factory compound. There were calligraphy classes and my father was obsessed with American technology and was always checking his gadgets.

> One can easily imagine the well-to-do businessman dispensing with his business clothes, changing into a long silk gown, relaxing with his family amidst his astronomy collection, magnifying glasses, microscopes and cameras, a gramophone playing in the background, or poring over the catalogues that Mr Burton received from the States.
>
> Burying himself in the cocoon of family life enabled him to ignore the chaos and contradictions in the latest news headlines, such as:
>
> **100 Communists Beheaded in Public By Order of the KMT Commander of Changsha, Hunan Province**
>
> Unaware of what was happening in the outside world, Jieping did not even recognize danger when his mother took her children into the Japanese concession where his half-sister lived.

---

[9] Warehouses.

The country was beset by peasant insurrections, quelled by KMT brutality or hordes of warlord forces. Most Chinese were mortified at the very existence of foreign concessions and many groups organized revolts to undermine them. Jieping's father was aware that massacres on a grand scale were happening on the streets of Wuhan, and those who joined the revolt numbered hundreds of thousands. They stormed the British concession and refused to leave.

"The British," reported Eugene Chen[10] who had joined Sun's Canton government and become Minister of Affairs, " 'voluntarily' gave up that concession in 1928." This was the first foreign enclave in China recovered by the Chinese people and it exalted the prestige of the KMT, who immediately claimed credit.

The nationalist army impressed the warlords to such a degree that the old Manchu warlord Marshal Zhang Zuolin, then in control of Peking, pulled back his 150,000-strong army. The KMT army also attracted those warlords who wished to "surrender", including a share of undisciplined opium addicts.

It was well-known that Chiang was planning to march on Shanghai with the KMT army, but the target was unclear to most Chinese. The foreign concessions amassed forty-five thousand troops and had five thousand White Russian guards patrolling the streets to protect their interests. Foreign gunboats were moored at the Bund. Shanghai was then under the "protection" of warlord Sun Chuanfang when a general strike of the Shanghai General Union to protest the presence of the foreign troops was announced. A number of clandestine meetings occurred between delegates of Chiang and warlord Sun, whose army numbered two hundred thousand men. Others participating in these secret meetings included Huang Ching-yung, a gangster living in the French concession, and "Benevolent Gangster" Du Yuesheng with a personal army of fifteen thousand men. Together, these men contrived to "save" Shanghai for the foreign interests.

Chiang Kai-shek could not decide which he hated more, communist Chinese or colonizing foreigner; but in time he threw his lot in with the foreigners against the Chinese communists.

---

[10] Grandfather of our friend, Chenny. Eugene was an overseas Chinese, born in Trinidad.

With the help of the city's "protectors", Chiang machine-gunned the striking, unarmed students and workers, in February 1927. ("Mowing the grass" was a local euphemism for removing troublesome agitators.) The armies were equipped by the international concessions and it was reported in Tianjin that:

"Chiang attacked Shanghai, and neither the Japanese nor the Manchu warlord Zhang moved. In Wuhan, the Communist Party criticised Chiang, but he was supported by Marshal Zhang, who raided the Russian Embassy and hanged Li Dazhau (the liberal founder of the CCP, the grandfather of current Premier Li Keqiang) and nineteen of his colleagues."

There was no mention of civil war – just the usual warlords' conflicts.

But this Shanghai news finally worried Old Wu, who realized it would only be a matter of time before the same problems reached Tianjin. He was powerless and could only build up his business so that he could afford to send his sons to PUMC to become medical doctors. His anxiety abated a little when Chiang Kai-shek "retired" to spend his life in contemplation at his old hillside home. This alleged retirement lasted several months, before he was induced to resume control.

Since its naval victory in 1895, Japan had been flexing its muscles in Korea and Manchuria and in June 1927, Chiang Kai-shek had sponsored a league for the "Rupture of Economic Relations with Japan" and fined merchants for violating his boycotts. Chiang instigated other reforms, but was also reputed to have shared profits with racketeers from the Opium Suppression Bureau. He instigated the collection of "registration" fees from known addicts.

At about this time, Chiang travelled to Japan to ask Charlie Soong's widow for the hand of their daughter Meiling (following the introduction by Soong Ai-ling). Old Wu's friend Liu Bosen wrote that:

Despite the fact that Chiang was still married to his first wife, it was rumoured that Meiling agreed to a bigamous marriage with two ceremonies: one Christian in the Soong home, conducted by a Joss Pidgin gentleman and one Chinese, in the Majestic Hotel attended by among others, H.M. Consul General, the Japanese Consul General, and the Commander- in-Chief of the American Fleet. Her sister, Soong Ching-ling (widow of late President Sun Yat-sen) sent a telegram saying, "Don't marry that Bluebeard!"

That was a summer of drought, when locusts ravaged the plains and millions of peasants died of starvation. But Chiang's philosophy was that money buys everything, even warlords and armies. He was after all the "adoptive son" of one of the city's most notorious gangsters and the blood brother of Du Yuesheng, or 'Big-Eared Du', leader of Shanghai's Green Gang.

Old Wu hesitated to provide the KMT army with uniforms, but his American colleague questioned, "Are the other army's leaders more reliable?"

Chiang was elected to the Standing Committee of the nine-man KMT Central Executive Committee and was named Commander-in-Chief of the KMT army.

By March 1928, allegiances had changed and Chiang was en route with the Northern Expedition to fight Old Marshal Zhang Zuolin, the Manchu warlord. In Shandong province, some troops provoked the Japanese soldiers and fighting broke out with appalling atrocities on both sides; the castration and blinding of innocent prisoners was widely reported. On 11 May, the Chinese were driven from Jinan, capital of Shandong. Because Tianjin had five key foreign concessions and their business interests, Chiang could not think of attacking the city to destroy the railroad and cut off Zhang Zuolin's escape route. The Japanese told Zhang that if he retreated to Manchuria, they would prevent the KMT army passing the Great Wall through the Shanhai Pass. But the Japanese double-crossed him and bombed Old Marshal Zhang's luxury railcar on its re-entry to South Manchuria.

In a completely contradictory move, his son Zhang Xueliang (soon to be known as the Young Marshal) was immediately elevated to the State Council of the nationalist government at Nanjing, on 10 October, 1928. Under pressure from the Japanese, he agreed to maintain the "autonomy" of Manchuria.

Old Wu realized at once that he had more serious reasons to be worried. His older children were still only teenagers and Jieping was eleven, while his mother had produced several more babies since his birth.

The Quanyechang department store became a favourite haunt for his mother's shopping expeditions and Jieping was riveted by the vast array of products on show. He was tempted to spend his hongbao (the little red envelope of lucky money given to children at Lunar New Year) on fireworks and innovative distractions. Old Wu's businesses were thriving despite the civil war. His rivals were disadvantaged by disruption at the power station and the inability to transport goods because control of the railroads switched from time to time.

Dr. Wu:

It was nerve-wracking for my parents, but quite exciting for me, riding through the concessions and seeing so many different uniforms and trying to figure out who was a friend and who the enemy. A year later, Father rented a house near the school for myself, my older brother Ruiping and my sister. I believe I experienced my first intimation of racial discrimination at school. Our teachers told us of foreign oppression, which reminded me of a sign I had seen with my father in Shanghai.

Jieping recalled thinking back to the age of five, when he already had some knowledge of characters, his father helped him read a notice in the Bund Park in Shanghai that read:
"huaren he gou bude runei" –
"Chinese and dogs not admitted"
Without realizing it, Jieping was already aware of his country's subjugation. Only gradually did he come to understand that China did not have the power to protect itself, because of the family's need for refuge in the foreign concessions.

There was no central authority governing all of China. The northern warlords controlled Beijing, and each warlord controlled his own and one or two surrounding provinces. Chiang Kai-shek was Chairman of the State Council, with its capital at Nanjing. The founder of the Republic, Sun Yat-sen, had insisted it now be located in Nanjing in order to reduce the power of the northern warlords. But Chiang and the KMT controlled only four provinces, and the communist forces moved as guerrillas throughout much of the countryside.

In 1928, the Japanese invaded what they identified as Manchukuo, Manchuria, made up of the three provinces of the north-east.

While the communists were winning supporters in the countryside, they were being massacred in the cities by the British-aided KMT. When the well-equipped Japanese air force successfully bombed Shanghai in 1932, the Chinese people were proud of the efforts of the 19th Route Army. There were several armies in China at this time. Each warlord had his own army and the 19th Route Army was an army of the Republic of China, led by General Cai Tingkai, which later sought an alliance with the communists against Chiang Kai-shek.

Despite constant warfare, industrialists like Old Wu continued to drive the industrial revolution ahead full steam. Power stations were built, trains moved faster on newer tracks and steamer transport made regional trade cheaper. Air transport was beginning. Old Wu decided it was time he concentrated exclusively on the shipping business.

Warfare was again avoided as the Old Marshal's son, Zhang Xueliang, unified the three northern provinces of his father's territory, Heilongjiang, Jilin, and Liaoning, with the KMT. In recognition, the KMT gave him Rehe (Jehol) as part of his North-east Political Council. The Japanese pressured him for the "reunification of Manchuria", but Zhang decided to try to oust the Russians and take over the Soviet-controlled China East Railroad. Stalin's response forced his retreat.

Instead, Zhang Xueliang extended control south through the Shanhai Pass giving him control over the northern stretches of the Beijing-Wuhan and Tianjin-Pukou Railroad.

The Young Marshal, Zhang Xueliang, could not forgive the Japanese for double-crossing and bombing the train his father was travelling on in 1928. He was determined to oust the Japanese from his homeland.

Tianjin customs' revenue now went to him and the city benefited from his "protection". His North-eastern Border Defence Army numbered four hundred thousand.

Now, the able Young Marshal Zhang was arguably the most powerful warlord in China; but he was hampered by an opium addiction, which his enemies exploited to the full.

CHAPTER FOUR
FAMILY LIFE

Dr. Wu:

My brother-in-law graduated in 1929 from PUMC, paving the way for the rest of us. Then my older brother entered PUMC. Father admonished all the boys in the family, "Don't go into politics, which is dirty. And business has a lot of cheating and eventually you become bankrupt. The only safe career is in science. To be sure you will have a job, it must be in medical science." We didn't object. Father was so convincing that we all followed his advice, as did everyone locally. My three brothers and I all became doctors. My older sister was a housewife, married to a doctor, and my second sister married the Personal Secretary of Chiang Kai-shek. The next sister also married a PUMC graduate and my younger sister is a pharmacist. As all the family was involved in medicine, our devoted allegiance was to PUMC.

Grandfather used to say, "Never let your emotions control you; you must employ reason to control emotion."

My father was very liberal in teaching us about science and self-reliance; he taught us Confucian solidarity and loyalty to our brothers, but I'm afraid he was not progressive in regard to my sisters and neglected their education.

> Jieping neither criticized nor apologized for the treatment of women; he explained his family in its own historical setting. He was completely unabashed as he told me these facts.

His daughter later recounted, "Grandfather wrote to me during the Cultural Revolution and offered to take photographs at my wedding because he felt it was all he could do to make up for my lost decade serving the Party."

"My grandfather was incorruptible", she went on, "and never gained any advantage for himself. He was not in favour of a benign mother and strict father."

Jieping told me his father used to warn the family, "If a mother is too kind, she will dote on the children or help them lie, and cheat a strict father. If the children are spoilt or make mistakes, mothers should be blamed first." Jieping had occasion to feel both sadness and guilt when his mother was criticized for his mistakes.

Dr. Wu:

During the 1920s I went back sometimes to visit Changzhou; my uncle still lived there as an associate of the cotton factory. The twenty-foot high white walls, with their curved grey tiled roofs, surrounded the compound; with its tired, unused vegetable garden still producing yams and watermelons, and its two deep wells nearby where I remembered the servants lowering baskets of food to keep it cool and fresh.

> Jieping did not recognize, for many years, what a privileged childhood he enjoyed in the factory compound quite removed from the interesting heart of Tianjin. Jieping's father tried to guide his children in a very insecure world as the threat of warfare surrounded them. He advised tact in all aspects of life.

Dr. Wu:

My father often reminded us about what to do when crossing a one-plank bridge: "Try to persuade the other person to let you cross; but if they don't listen, there is no point in two crossing at the same time as at least one may land in the river." Later on, in the '50s and '60's, I realized that this could be misconstrued by the then-leadership: we could be criticized for not sticking to our principles.

In February 1929, the US officially recognized the KMT as the national government and renounced its right to extraterritoriality. China would now decide the tariffs on foreign imports. But America still excluded the Chinese wives of US citizens from residing in the US. Old Wu fully understood the significance of this, but did not share his disappointment at this time because it was a better business climate.

During his middle school years from the age of ten to sixteen (1927-33), despite the turmoil all around, Jieping's life was quiet and peaceful. He watched football in the British concession, played with his friends and read a lot of novels. By 1931 his father already had a prominent position in Tianjin as head of the state-owned steamship company, which ran routes between Tianjin, Shanghai and other ports.

Dr. Wu:

My father was the administrator of the steamship company in Tianjin from 1930 to 1936, and from 1930 to 1931 he was concurrently general manager of the cotton factory. The family moved to the British concession in 1930. Situated on the right bank of the River Hai below the native city, the concession controlled almost two hundred acres. We had lived on the other bank and now moved to a house on Victoria Road. It was a very unusual house in that area, which had mostly large buildings, and it had a large garden. The Methodist school I attended was in the adjoining Chinese territory, to which I could now ride my bicycle.

> Like Fleet Street or Fifth Avenue at the time, Victoria Road was lined with banks, clubs, hotels, a small park and the city's administrative, trading and financial centres. Turbaned Sikhs, the Indian police employed by the British, gave a dignified, international air to the district. Their station was directly opposite Jieping's house. Because his home was next door to the city's best hotel, the Court Hotel, Jieping knew the comings and goings of the foreign dignitaries who visited Tianjin. He'd sit huddled at his father's desk, daydreaming in a cane-bottomed revolving chair, with celadon green cushions plumped at his back, gazing out at the scenes below.

Dr. Wu:

Our new house was a three-storey, European-style red brick building, near the main office of the Tianjin Steamship Company. Coolies would be sent, when a trip was planned, to help carry the luggage to be loaded onto the steamship bound for Shanghai. On one of those occasions, while waiting with my mother to board a Shanghai-bound steamship on a sticky, humid June morning in 1931, I popped home to get a drink, passing the Sikh guards protecting the British concession. I noticed that, unlike the mutual contempt that usually characterized the exchanges between the Indians and Chinese, my relationship with the guards was easy-going and friendly; they were kind and helpful to me when I greeted them in English.

I was travelling to Shanghai alone with my mother, in the comfort of a first-class compartment. We were welcomed by the Captain and I was given a guided tour of Father's 3,000-ton vessel the following day, as we journeyed south passing junks, motorboats and foreign gun boats. Second class had ten compartments, and the third-class berths could accommodate several hundred travellers, as well as whatever fowl, produce, or work implements they would normally require. It would take the steamship three days to reach Shanghai.

I did not question my right to first-class travel. I had been raised in the natural expectation of convenience and luxury, but I did feel a little awkward being given a guided tour of the ship. I found the food delicious and decided I loved to travel. We passed close to the fishing junks, decked out with lines of early morning washing blowing in the breeze.

> Jieping gazed at the naked children on the fishing boats, unaware that their swollen bellies told a tale of hunger rather than satiety. Close to the city of Shanghai, he saw the filthy shacks almost washed away in the torrential rain one day, only to be shored up by the time of his return journey with pieces of cardboard, bamboo and old door handles.
>
> While international literature and arts flourished in Shanghai and, to a lesser degree, in the other Treaty Ports, the KMT forbade Westerners from teaching Chinese children (circa 1933). This was a setback for the Missionary schools that were then obliged to employ their own graduates. How could Jieping's sisters possibly get an education, when no girls' schools existed then in Tianjin? In Shanghai, the progressive educator and reformer Tao Xingzhi

set up private education, and some girls used correspondence schools. In 1932, the Private Shanghai Experimental School[11] opened and Soong Meiling (second wife of Chiang Kai-shek) attended the opening of the Shanghai Life Education Association & Children's School.

At that time, Old Wu would take his family to teahouses to watch American comedies. The idea had been introduced to Shanghai through the entertainment company of his associates at Ramos and Ramos Amusement Company.

Old Wu wanted the best schools, but did little to push his children academically. Jieping's teachers were the first generation of Western-educated Chinese graduates, whose example and encouragement set a standard of expectation that conditioned the students to achieve the highest results. Most of this was lost on Jieping at the time, as his main interest in life was to have a good time. That Jieping's teachers were graduates of Yenching, and the best universities in China, did not interest him.

Dr. Wu:

I played football and rugby and really enjoyed doubles in tennis at school, but I'm afraid I did the minimum homework when I got off my bicycle on Victoria Road and pushed it the fifteen yards up to our own red gateway. A favourite dish of Chinese fried noodles usually greeted me, so I was probably a little spoilt.

> Having eaten with his siblings, Jieping would struggle out of his long gown and into the kind of common cotton pyjama suit favoured by the majority. On winter days, Jieping would take his tea-jar and a Chinese novel and read until his younger brother was free to play chess with him. He later said that he learned all he ever needed to know about human relationships from *Dream of the Red Chamber*[12].
>
> There were five hundred thousand soldiers in the city, (for whom Baochen Spinners supplied cotton uniforms), many gaunt from

---

[11] The opening took place in Chongqing, because of the war and the School moved to Shanghai in 1946.

[12] The classic novel written by Cao Xueqin during the Qin dynasty. Precise, detailed observations of life and social structures typical of 18th Century Chinese society. Printed 1791.

famine, as well as a mass of crippled beggars. Both the Central and Eastern Railroad were guarded by foreign soldiers with bayonets fixed to their rifles. Jieping couldn't guess whether the shots he heard in his father's study came from the foreigners' rifles, or whether the warlords were shooting their rebellious, communist-inspired employees. Daily, he watched poverty and hunger strip the poor of their dignity as they lay dying by the riverbank. But that was normal life, which the boy was obliged to take in his stride.

Nobody cared, not the Europeans in their white summer topees, not the Chinese in their long silk scholar's gowns as they strolled through Gordon Park (where Jieping later sat the Cambridge Overseas Exam in Gordon Hall) and not the mass of Japanese military. Cycling carefree, whistling a tune through the concessions, a myriad of languages and cultures assailed him; the White Russians patrolling some concessions spoke a little Chinese. And he marvelled at the Japanese Emporium, its tower strung with necklaces of electric lights.

As Jieping lay under his mosquito net on airless summer nights, he could hear the strains of the orchestra at a restaurant nearby, to which the diners danced between courses. On the bridge was the home of the Tianjin Volunteer Corps, which the Wu brothers were invited to join. Old Wu was accustomed to host banquets for Tianjin businessmen at some of the best hotels and restaurants, when they returned from their summer holidays at Beidaihe. There were cinemas, and music blared through the city from radios and gramophones, to which everyone seemed glued. Young men sported either cloth caps or Derbies and smoked an astonishing number of cigarettes.

Dr. Wu:

We had offices in the Japanese concession, but I had no real impression of the state of our country until Japan took the north-east in 1931. The student strike of 18 September, 1931 really woke me up. I was already in my first year of senior middle school and was made aware by my teachers of China's latest humiliation.

I began to know what patriotism meant at that time. The day the Japanese took the north-east with Pu Yi as puppet Governor-Emperor (named heir-apparent by the dying Cixi), I was fourteen.

When a teacher explained the Treaty of Shimonoseki, I accepted what I had long suspected: we were enslaved to foreign powers, particularly to Imperial Japan. I was filled with a sense of national degradation. Our teacher wrote some lines from the Father of Taoism, Zhuangzi (c. 369 B.C.), on the blackboard:

> *Steal a hook*
> *And you hang like a Crook*
> *Steal a Kingdom*
> *And you're made a Duke*

One day on my way home from school, I witnessed Japanese sentries forcing my brother Ruiping and his friend to pull down their trousers and bow in their underpants. I felt humiliated on Ruiping's behalf and couldn't look at him when he came in. He never told our parents.

> Japan had made itself the "custodian of democracy" in Asia. It propagandized its own interest in China to suit the alleged fears and concerns of the powerful Western nations. Japan claimed it would withdraw once the so-called 'threat of communism' was annihilated. As he dealt with their shipping needs and demands, Old Wu was unaware that Japan had its own plans for the future of the Asian peoples.

Dr. Wu:

My parents did their best to protect us from their concerns and we all thought our father was very progressive as he was so admired by workers and business leaders in the community. They saw that he was always trying to improve productivity and was very inventive and caring. We just assumed we'd be fine whatever happened, but Father's fixations should have been a warning.

> China had experienced one revolution or war after another, for almost a hundred years, and Old Wu concluded, "Whoever wins or loses, everyone needs good doctors." And that was that.
> When I questioned Jieping about how his father would have reacted had one of the sons chosen another profession, he told me,

> "We were happy to follow his direction. He was well known for his good judgment."
>
> "And how did your mother feel about that?"
>
> "My mother followed Father's guidance and did so very well."
>
> "Were there any doctors in the family?"
>
> "No, my paternal Grandfather's success as a pawnbroker was probably because of his excellent calligraphy."
>
> One can imagine those small, neat fingers clasping the brush and covering a page with neat calligraphy strokes, as Jieping rhapsodized about his father's ability to improve things.

Dr. Wu:

My maternal "grandfather" was so wealthy he did not need a profession. But he was not my blood relative and we all felt the need to prove our branch of the family.

> I could see that even in old age Jieping was still star-struck by his father's inventiveness and expectations. He still wanted to get everything right, as if his father were looking over his shoulder.
>
> I was astonished that this medical scientist, with his excellent command of English, easily accepted all the contradictions he faced in life, and while he seemed to forget his Confucian heritage, one could see by his actions that he was bound by its precepts. In a household like Old Wu's, a clear division of hierarchy and responsibility prevailed, yet Old Wu was an anomaly. Jieping's mother was an elegant, diminutive young woman with bound feet who instilled in her sons a sense of purpose and pride. His father enjoyed the company of English and American colleagues as friends and had several hobbies. He felt that the technological advances of the West and scientific thinking were essential to the development of China, despite his reservations about certain other Western customs. Yet he lived in feudal grandeur, in a lifestyle beyond the dreams of most Chinese.
>
> Jieping went on regular fishing and family trips with his brothers and cousins. He recalled one Mid-Autumn Festival when he was young, where the cousins placed the round, white, shiny moon cakes in the moonlight with melons and buns; his favourite *yuebing* (moon

cake) was pork and onion and he sneaked out and consumed one when the others weren't looking. Luckily, he wasn't caught. The young man grew up in this apparently benign, traditional household, surrounded by uncles, aunts and cousins who joined together to be schooled by private tutors in the Chinese classics, blithely unaware of the century-long chaos into which China was spiralling.

In Jieping's childhood, there were eighteen universities or institutions of higher learning, sixteen Protestant missionary colleges, twenty-seven private colleges and sixty Catholic missionary schools where the two per cent of China's 475 million population was sent for a new education. This highly-educated elite was to be challenged in ways they could not imagine. They were trying to make sense of the conflict between the modernizing influences of science and democracy on the one hand, and ethics and morality underpinning ignorance and slavery on the other.

Because of his position as head of the steamship company, Old Wu's name was proposed as an industrial adviser in his thriving province. He learned a great deal from ensuing meetings and interaction with foreigners.

Like many of his other advisers, Chiang Kai-shek's military and economic adviser was a foreigner. Max Bauer was a German arms broker who spent much time in China from 1927 to 1929. Following his death, Chiang chose General Hans von Seekt and invited him to become Senior Military Adviser at the expanded German Mission, on a colossal stipend of two thousand US dollars a month.

China was pushed from within and without in its industrialization. The initial exchange organized by von Seekt was of antimony (to harden lead alloys used in munitions manufacturing, especially shrapnel shells and cartridge caps) and tungsten (which has the highest melting temperature of any known metal) to make armour and armour-piercing shells. Hunan and Jiangxi provinces had fifty per cent of the world's tungsten supplies. The German Military and Finance Ministry cooperated with the National Military Council directed by Chiang and exchanged weapons for ore. Old Wu was aware of the irony that Chinese labourers mined the products used to manufacture the guns that would slaughter their brothers in the army. All of this trade required transport and the Tianjin Steamship Company benefitted accordingly.

Old Wu was torn between his desire for peace and the on-going orders for military uniforms that kept his factories producing the best cotton in the country, while he expanded his fleet of steamships to accommodate the demands of these new industrialists.

German industrial strength contributed substantially to China's industrial development for a time. Old Wu marvelled to his children that Otto Wolff had completed two stretches of strategic railway with great speed and efficiency. Krupp was credited with developing rolling stock, Daimler-Benz ran factories for truck assembly, Junkers' factories made bombers, Siemens provided docks and Farbens led in chemical plant production. But the KMT-German plans were foiled by Hitler's fear of the Comintern[13] and the Soviet Union. He began to promote German commercial contacts with the Japanese in Manchuria instead. Old Wu saw that Chiang had been double-crossed and his great industrialization efforts curtailed. He would be forced to cut back accordingly in his production.

Old Wu was painfully aware that Chiang Kai-shek allied himself with the warlords in the cities if he couldn't defeat them. He infiltrated the labour organizations and the industrialists paid secret society members to discourage the CCP. Old Wu was torn by the need to keep his workers safe and his gradual inclination towards the values of communism. At this time, Chiang Kai-shek's success was mostly in the cities. But his chief opponent and sworn enemy, Mao Zedong, was now embedded in a base in the Jinggang Mountains, between the provinces of Jiangxi and Fujian. Mao had little difficulty channelling the fiscal discontent of the peasants into class warfare. His supporters initially were bandits, robbers, soldiers and prostitutes.

"They lead the most precarious existence of any human being, but they are all human; they all have five senses and we are therefore one," Mao told his followers.

Mao's lifestyle could not have provided a greater contrast to Chiang Kai-shek's. The latter was married to a pretty, American-educated millionaire. She had persuaded her husband to adopt

---

[13] This refers to the Communist International advocating and supporting world communism. It was sponsored by Stalin and Lenin, who advocated world insurrection led by the Workers' Movement.

Christianity before marrying and had secured the support of the American government to provide financial aid to the KMT. The couple confiscated fortress-like mansions in the various KMT bases they called home, whereas Mao Zedong abhorred such trappings and lived with his peasant supporters in makeshift mountain cabins and caves, until they were discovered and forced to move on.

Old Wu lived between the excitement of a developing economy, led by Chiang on the one hand and the egalitarian idealism of Mao's communist philosophy, on the other. He could not keep his excitement to himself and discussed the mores of greater productivity, leading to greater personal freedom, with his family.

Wu Jieping (back row, centre) surrounded by his family

CHAPTER FIVE

SUBMITTING TO AN ARRANGED MARRIAGE

The Wu family continued to live in feudal harmony. Wu Jieping demonstrated to all his family that he was a dutiful son observing appropriate filial piety when he accepted, without question, his father's decision that he should study medicine. But he was spirited enough to make it known that he did intend to protest if, when an "arranged" marriage was being considered, he thought his prospective spouse was unsuitable. Despite adoring his father, he told him as much. It did not take him long, when he did marry, to recognize that such arranged marriages should not be the province of parents and advised his younger brothers against it. He seemed to have righted a wrong when he told me, "I was the last in my family to accept such an arranged marriage."

While he too admired much about the West, he was also appalled by it. Attending a Harold Lloyd comedy at the International Settlement, he observed that the film represented the Chinese as a race of gangsters. Some people he knew stood up and denounced the film and were arrested for their impertinence. Jieping had to control his rebellious spirit and try to channel it in the right direction.

There was so little family discord that Jieping remembered the few occasions very clearly.

Dr. Wu:

Once, when Father returned from a very successful trip to Henan province, he brought gifts for all members of the family. To his daughter-in-law, his elder sister-in-law and my mother he gave gold bracelets. His sister-in-law was convinced that she had been given something inferior to the other two. Later on, to satisfy her curiosity, she asked Father to bring the other two and proceeded to measure them in his presence. They were identical, but Father's pride was hurt.

> The sister-in-law had nine "Blood-sisters", friends from like families with the same interests and ambitions, who often held *mah-jong* parties together. This sister-in-law, Jieping's aunt-in-law had earmarked the daughter of one of her "blood-sisters" to marry *her* son, who was number eight in the family and therefore senior to Jieping.

Dr. Wu:

For some reason unbeknownst to me, Father decided that he wanted this girl for me. Such an overture was a most unusual gesture on the part of my usually-considerate father and a serious breach of family etiquette. It was tantamount to stealing the fiancée of his older brother's son. But Father clearly had heard something he liked about the girl and although he didn't know the family personally, he persisted. Her family originally came from the same city in Jiangsu province and were distantly related.

> Old Wu had looked long and hard for the ideal spouse for Jieping. He planned a direct hit and, in 1931, Jieping was steered in the direction of this distant cousin.

Dr. Wu:

In my adolescence there was a conflict between feudal and modern ways. I felt I wanted to choose my own spouse, but I understood that my father wished to find the most suitable match, engineer things effortlessly and allow the young couple to meet and then leave everything to nature.

> Jieping was not party to the intense negotiations on the part of both families, nor to the elaborate plans his father was making for this seamless introduction.

Dr. Wu:

Father arranged a trip to create an atmosphere and then told me, "You are free to choose." In searching among our distant relatives and family friends, he chose the girl from Shanghai who was promised to No. 8. He instructed my older brother Ruiping and his wife to accompany me to stay at the home of "cousin" Zhao Junkai and then, if we got along well, they should take us to Hangzhou where he had rented a luxury houseboat.

I was well aware of the purpose of the trip and so was Junkai (Di to her prospective spouse) and there was a moment on the boat when we both knew we would be compatible.

> The correct Confucian upbringing did not permit the young couple to question how a twelve-year old girl and a fourteen-year old boy could have such a responsibility foisted on them.
>
> His older brother favoured Jieping most in the family and had already submitted to an arranged marriage. His was a happy marriage and he dutifully agreed to take his younger brother to Shanghai. The role of matchmaker, or go-between, has long been a respected position in Chinese society and Jieping trusted Ruiping's judgement.

Dr. and Mrs. Wu Ruiping

Jieping and Junkai spent a few lovely days together on the West Lake. Left alone with a pretty girl in a romantic setting, Jieping found that nature gently fanned the exposed embers and he confessed his attraction to his distant cousin, Junkai.

Dr. Wu:

My brother and sister-in-law accompanied us back to Shanghai and left me there, to become more acquainted with her family. I was fourteen and she was twelve and, following the houseboat trip on the West Lake, we happily acquiesced to our parent's wishes. I believed my father when he said that I could have rejected the plan if I didn't like her; but basically, Father knew I would yield to his decision. Junkai was pretty and as the eldest of her family, she was very self-confident and pretty bossy towards her two younger sisters.

> The courtship continued for the next two years, while Jieping was still at middle school. He hadn't a care in the world and was a very useful little forward on the football field and, because he was much younger than his classmates, he was treated with amused tolerance by the older players.
>
> In the midst of the courtship, Old Wu fretted that his wife would have no grandchildren to clean her grave and care for her parent's spirit tablets. The Japanese attacked Shanghai in January 1932 and he quickly summoned his son home, to be sure he was safe. Reports of the bravery of the diehard 19th Route Army, possibly the toughest fighting force in twentieth century China with a number of German-trained divisions, inspired the nation by their defence of Shanghai against the superiorly numbered, trained and equipped Japanese army, showing the world that China would not be cowed.
>
> Students and business leaders insisted that the KMT armies fought back against the Japanese; but Chiang Kai-shek firmly refused and signed the disgraceful Tangku Truce with the Japanese in May citing, "internal pacification before external resistance". This was tantamount to admitting he would fight a civil war against the Chinese communists before a war of resistance against the invading Japanese. Thus, the nationalists' recognition

of Japan's annexation of Manchuria empowered the Japanese. The communists were being advised by the USSR who knew little of China's vast hinterland and its peasant population who had been enslaved to the good earth from time immemorial. Divisions among the communists rivalled those between the KMT, warlords and secret societies, who were all loosely united in their fear of communism.

Dr. Wu:

Our school got priority in the Yenching University entrance exams because it was a Methodist school. I felt sure I would not pass the normal entrance exams, but they only tested me in English, Chinese and IQ. I remember enjoying that part vividly. I thought I did quite well, and Yenching rated it very highly as a measure of intelligence. Arthur Burton was the only other boy from Tianjin who took the exam and would have had even more advantage as he was an American Methodist.

> Yenching University was already regarded as the Oxford or Harvard of China. It was formed by merging four Christian colleges, including the North China Women's College, over the course of four years. Yenching formally opened in 1919 and was therefore almost the same age as its youngest student by the time he enrolled. Designed in a traditional Chinese architectural style, it is one of the loveliest university campuses in the world.
>
> In 1919, John Leighton Stuart became the first President of Yenching University. He was born in China to missionary parents, but educated in the US. Through his creating partnerships with Harvard, Princeton, Wellesley and the University of Minnesota, students were exposed to an international curriculum and their degrees were recognised by these American institutions. Leighton Stuart was popular with his students for almost three decades; but when the Civil War raged, he was made US Ambassador and his reputation suffered as a result of his attempt to serve two masters.
>
> Yenching University has since boasted some of the most dynamic men and women in Chinese history. Author Han Suyin was a student while Jieping was there: as was Huang Hua, who later became Foreign Minister and Vice Premier.

Old Wu recognized this university as the necessary stepping-stone for PUMC, Peking Union Medical College. Jieping had to attend Yenching in order to get into the best medical school, which got its degrees jointly from the USA. The fees at PUMC were one hundred silver dollars a year, which meant that only wealthy industrialists and gentry could afford to send their children there. One of Jieping's friends and later colleague, a haematologist called Dr. Deng, told me, "Dr. Green, the then head of PUMC, loaned me the money and was repaid when I won the Wenham Prize."

Before Jieping married Zhao Junkai, he had experienced the disappointment of a love that could not be. He had become very attached to his cousin-in-law. They were about the same age, but the girl was the niece of his brother-in-law and daughter of a widow.

Dr. Wu:

She could correctly have addressed me as "Uncle" and although I was very fond of this girl, I realized that marriage between us could never have come about because I had already been promised by then, and in any case, I was made aware that her family was not quite good enough. Someone once explained to me that you could "marry down" only for beauty or brains, otherwise "the door must fit the door jamb".

Father's weakness was that he looked down on girls; boys got a good education, girls got very little. He wanted his sons married young, in case love affairs distracted us and ruined our lives. By my childhood or young manhood, the world had modern ways where boys could choose their own companions. But my parents did not subscribe to this innovation.

Finally, we submitted to Father because we worshipped him. I married Junkai on an auspicious day Double Ten. (My brother had also married on 10/10, ten years earlier).

By the time we married in 1933, I was sixteen and had been enrolled at Yenching University for just a month. Father arranged everything at a smart hotel in Beijing with both Western and Chinese menus and hired a jazz band. After the marriage, I appeared to be all right, but I had a nagging suspicion that I hadn't really had a free choice, although I had no particular objection to my wife.

How Junkai must have felt about her spouse's attitude one can only guess at, but Jieping was in no position to dispel his disappointment. He was stuck.

Dr. Wu:

Yenching had a very open and free form of education, unlike anything we Chinese students had experienced before. As well as the required Pre-Med courses, we also had the opportunity to study English, Chinese, Philosophy and History: a wonderful menu that very much appealed to me.

> The first Chinese university in Beijing, the Imperial University, was founded in 1898. It was during the Reform Period of the late Qing dynasty that officials recognized the need to encourage and promote talent and open the educational system to Western thought and practices. It was to that end the first university dedicated itself.
>
> A second University was opened, using the funds paid to the US by the Boxer Indemnity compensation, extorted from China by eight nations who co-operated in a joint expedition to protect their nationals from the Boxer Rebellion[14]. The President of the University of Illinois, Edmund James, proposed a plan[15] to establish scholarships for Chinese students to come to the US, believing that a centre focusing on intellectual development and moral education would contribute to the nation's commercial development. The fund created Tsinghua University in 1911. James saw this as a prep school before students went to the US to complete their education.
>
> After Mao swept into power, Peking University moved its campus to the Yenching site and these two merged and became the present-day Beijing University or Beida.

---

[14] The Boxer Rebellion, 1899 – 1901, began as an anti-foreign, anti-colonial, peasant-based movement in Northern China.

[15] The Boxer Indemnity Scholarship Program was regarded as reparation to help bridge the cultural gap between China and the USA. Between 1909 and 1929, approximately 1,300 Chinese students studied in the USA.

Dr. Wu:

In my freshman year, I was the youngest in the school, I was still growing but my schoolmates knew I was married. Some girls approached me, but I had no interest in them – yet I felt very lonely. My father and I were not close at that time.

The problem was that Father, unlike many parents, did not act in a superior manner towards his sons, but treated us more like colleagues. The loneliness I felt was due to the feelings I had developed for that girl relative in Tianjin, just after I had met and been promised to Junkai in 1931; but I was not old enough to express anything like that. And this made me unhappy, so for those three years at Yenching, I was lonely and didn't mix with anybody.

I lived on campus in the suburbs, a long way from our house and went home at weekends. Classes started at 8 a.m. six days a week and the failure rate was thirty-five per cent that first year. When my older brother was at PUMC, Father bought a two-storey house for his sons to occupy until they graduated; it was not very extravagant, but it permitted a good lifestyle. I was on good terms with my wife. We shared the house near PUMC with my brother and his wife. Ruiping had already completed his internship and was earning an excellent salary.

> With nothing exciting to look forward to each weekend, Jieping boarded the bus as it swung out of Yenching campus past Langrunyuan, a desolate garden of decaying trees, formerly the home of a Manchu Prince and a vivid reminder of the destruction and decay of the old order.
>
> The sense of frustration is evident in Jieping's lack of interest in going home for the weekends. He was too proud to share his feelings with anyone outside his family, and his adoration of his parents and sense of loyalty prevented him from admitting that while his parents did their best, they imposed values that drowned his free spirit.
>
> Jieping told me that in his first year at Yenching, as an immature seventeen-year-old, he and his fifteen-year old-wife had a little boy, but it was a difficult labour and the baby died a few days later. Although he was already a thoughtful student, he had not read biology or anatomy and admitted, without embarrassment, having

to ask his brother how to prevent Junkai becoming pregnant in future. Sitting on the bus together, Ruiping explained the rhythm of life, when the egg would be most receptive to the sperm. I sensed that the death of the new-born baby did not move him much, as his self-absorption continued for several years.

And in the meantime, Jieping's father grappled with reports of the infighting maelstrom, as China struggled against the ropes of tradition that were strangling her while over her hovered several nations with swords drawn, ready to slice the Chinese pie. Old Wu informed his sons of the undeclared civil war taking place in the hinterland.

Despite the annihilation campaigns at the hands of the nationalists, the Red Army, now led by Mao Zedong, survived the purges ordered by the USSR, and their own infighting, and set out from the Soviet base in the Jinggang Mountains. They were pursued from base to base, many of which were overrun and abandoned. They next settled at the Ruijin station and tried to attract local warlords to join them in a united front against the Japanese. But the negotiators halted when Chiang's armies caught up, sweeping into Jiangxi province. Many communist bases were destroyed and their leaders trapped on the advice of Hitler's German strategists, von Seekt and Falkenhausen, who now advised Chiang Kai-shek. This base was blockaded with the help of three hundred thousand conscripts and the communists were unable to obtain salt. Mao and Zhou Enlai held war councils with their military leaders, frantically searching for an escape route.

Finally, one of Zhou's suggestions was adopted – to abandon the base and evacuate their armies towards the Hunan-Hubei provincial border. Their USSR-designated German adviser opposed the plan, but finally saw they had no other choice.

All children under the age of twelve and their mothers, (including two of Mao's sons) were left with the twenty thousand soldiers to cover the exodus of the majority.

On a foggy morning on 16 October, 1934, with the acquiescence of the local warlord who hated Chiang Kai-shek, the Red Army marched out singing the Marseillaise to fight the Japanese, inviting all armies to join their alliance. More than one hundred thousand people, bearing red banners, marched in a ten-kilometre procession, named by one army leader 'the Scorpion'; two Corps in front of the main body and two behind. The doomed expedition was going according to plan, until the procession was strafed by German-piloted planes. Many died and others deserted. The remainder attempted crossing the Xiang River, where more than half did not survive. They were weighted down with guns, ammunition, sewing machines, medical equipment and all the excess material of conventional war. This was the start of what later became known as 'The Long March'.[16]

The next time, Mao's suggestion was adopted: to head for Guizhou province whose warlords were opium-consuming members of the Gelao minority. Two of the communist leaders were also members of the secret society, Brothers of the Robe. Safe passage was not guaranteed, as the local minorities had their own alliances and grain was scarce. Less than a third of those eighty-seven thousand who had set out arrived in Liping County, in misty Guizhou, in late December, where they halted to rest and put political wrongs to right. While the infighting continued, Mao suggested they plough north-west towards Zunyi, crossing the treacherous Wu River, where they would form another base. The exhausted remnants crept into the city where the local garrison surrendered and warlords disappeared. The local leaders waited outside and when Mao rode in on his white horse on 9 January 1935, the army's ringing ovation welcomed *'Chairman Mao'*.

In the meetings that followed, Zhou Enlai took responsibility for both political and military mistakes: "I am to blame. If we had consulted Mao Zedong, we would not have lost so many followers. I will now step down as commissar of the Red Army and the Military Affairs Commission. These as well as Party leadership should be united."

As a result of the Zunyi meeting, Mao became Chairman of the Politburo and the Military Affairs Commission, and Zhou became Vice Chairman and Political Commissar of the army. Zhu De was Commander-in-Chief.

In the intervening months, as news leaked out, Old Wu continued to apprise his sons in Peking of conditions between the

---

[16] See Map 5.

nationalists and communists. Old Wu wrote, "A reliable journalist shared his report with me":

"When the communists learned that Chiang Kai-shek planned to attack Zunyi, the twenty thousand remaining resumed their march and with guerrilla tactics dictated by Mao from Master Sun Tzu's, *The Art of War*, Mao exhorted his followers: 'The enemy must not know where I intend to give battle. If he does not know, he must prepare in a great many places.' And Mao proceeded to lead his followers in a not-so-merry dance, into the most bewildering marches and counter-marches, backwards and forwards, crossing and re-crossing rivers, going south in Yannan as if to capture Kunming, and then suddenly veering away from it. Suffering enormous losses, Chiang Kai-shek observed, 'The Red bandit remnants are in their death throes.'

Crossing the black, muscular waves of the Dadu River by moonlight is akin to crossing the Styx in Western mythology, but it was managed in boats hastily built of yak and goatskin laid over bamboo, while volunteers were strafed carrying planks along the single-person metal bridge that had been rendered useless.

It took ten days to cross, overcoming a garrison in the process. On they marched, through the Great Marshes and valleys in the Snow Mountains, clawing and fighting through bogs of slime. Tibetan marauders and clouds of insects also hampered their progress. They continued without food or water, climbing Liupan Shan, stumbling into the lunar landscape of yellow loess on 19 October, 1935. Those who led were driven by hope, hatred, hunger, desperation and fury to infuse their people with their divine obligation to wage a patriotic war of resistance against Japan. Their new base, Bao'an, offered shelter in the form of cave holes scooped out of the yellow earth that was once the cradle of Han civilization, close to the Great Wall and the tomb of their first Yellow Emperor. Those remaining numbered fewer than four thousand and were exultant to have stumbled 'home' at last."

It seemed to his sons that although Old Wu was a supporter of Sun Yat-sen, who had formed the KMT and appointed Chiang Kai-shek as overall commander, and Old Wu's factories were key suppliers of uniform fabric to the nationalist army, his sympathy was increasingly diverted to the communists.

A few months later, Old Wu sent them another report:

> 'The communist army and followers soon learned that Chiang had bowed to and accepted all of Japan's demands and had stated, "Japan is helping in joint-suppression of communism in China."'

The Wu family did not understand how Chiang could sell his Chinese brothers down the river, but sensed it was driven by American fear of communism and the fact that the US was supplying Chiang and the nationalists with hundreds of millions of dollars and modern weaponry. Old Wu continued to keep his sons in the capital informed.

On the Long March, Zhou Enlai was credited with raising Mao to the Party chairmanship and it was said of him, "Mao knows no heaven above him nor any of the rules of mankind." But by now, the diplomatic skills and exactitude of Zhou Enlai, his "Housekeeper", could smooth the middle path.

Within the next year, Zhou had persuaded KMT General Yang Hucheng, controlling Xi'an, to cede a larger area to extend their base to the town of Yan'an, on the Yan River, which boasted a Catholic church and a Song dynasty pagoda. This town was to become the Mecca for students, intellectuals, rebels, revolutionaries, writers and actors alike, for more than a decade.

CHAPTER SIX
POLITICAL AWAKENING

Dr. Wu:

On 9 December, 1935 a student movement started at Yenching to fight against the Japanese attempt to render North China a Special Zone as a preparatory step to taking all of North China. Despite KMT efforts to minimize public protest, a massive student rally was organized. These 'December Ninethers' were hosed and clubbed by police; but they'd struck a national chord and, in the following week, were supported by comparable rallies in the other main cities.

There was a heated debate between supporters of the communists and supporters of the KMT. Gong Pusheng and her sister Gong Peng[17] were active organizers as well as participants in the debate. Huang Hua, later to be New China's first ambassador to the United Nations and a Vice Premier of China, also took a leading part in the exchange, as did Shen Chang-huan, a future foreign minister of Taiwan. He, needless to say, was on the side of the KMT. Many of the students were involved.

> Jieping was being forced out of his self-absorption by his immediate environment. It was rumoured that a pact had earlier been hatched between General Ho Yingching, the pro-Japanese Defence Minister in charge of Beijing and the Japanese ambassador in 1935. Chiang

---

[17] Gong Peng was a pretty young diplomat who became official interpreter to Zhou Enlai. Her sister Gong Pusheng, also a diplomat, a graduate of Columbia University, was later named Ambassador to Ireland, following the untimely death of her sister. We became good friends through the introduction by Huang Hua's wife, Liliang.

Kai-shek had fought the Japanese in the beginning, but before long he compromised with them allowing North China to become a Special Zone, nominally still under the KMT government, but very pro-Japan.

Dr. Wu:

The debate culminated in a decision to strike the next day; to stop all academic activities and join the students in Tsinghua and Beijing Universities to fight against Japanese aggression and Chinese collusion. Striking was difficult and solidarity with other students was even harder because the Japanese had closed the city gates. But the strike went ahead and the students of Yenching went around the city walls in order to join their comrades from other universities. At Yenching, groups of students stood outside each building to prevent others attending lectures. Despite the highly charged climate of the times, some students were indifferent to the fate of China and keen to get on with their education.

I rode my bicycle around the campus to see what was going on. Nearly thirty students had broken through the blockade and were attending class. I watched them through the window, thinking they were entirely wrong. PUMC had sent a biology professor, Alice Boring, to be in charge of the pre-medical group. On the day of the strike she intended to carry on her class as usual, but a Chinese professor named Hu interceded on our behalf and persuaded her to stop her lecture.

I regarded the episode with Professor Boring as significant; a Westerner, seeing the anger of the students and the deteriorating situation in China, had been persuaded to cease her duties and stand aside while the students fought their fight.

I was a very average student at that time and looked down on the swots and felt especially contemptuous of girls who memorized everything. I played a lot of tennis. Then I had my first awakening. One day, I realized I didn't know anything. It took me a long time to understand myself. Nobody ever summarized, 'How one grows up,' or 'What is my place in society?'

> So, Jieping read widely to try and figure out a philosophy by which he could live his life. During his three years at Yenching, Jieping was a quiet member of the student organization, unlike many of

his politically active chums, who organized important student activities. But he was anti-Japanese as early as 1931.

Dr. Wu:

Only at Yenching did I really learn that the Japanese and Chinese were very different; under the Meiji Restoration[18] Japan had moved from a feudal to a capitalist society at any price. While I burned with indignation, there was nothing I could do but democratically support the student revolutionary leaders Huang Hua, Gong Pusheng, Gong Peng and others. There were both low-key communists and nationalist sympathizers striking. But it became evident who some of them were when they denounced those who wanted to appease the Japanese by agreeing to a Special Zone. In the mornings as we entered the campus, we often heard shots and one Monday morning another student was gunned down right beside me. When I enquired what he had done, I was warned, "He did not kowtow to the Japanese flag representing the Emperor!"

After that, I always tried to find a door where no sentry was on duty, otherwise I was bound to comply with the obligatory kowtow. It was in the midst of this total insecurity that Wu Xing was born at PUMC in 1935, when my wife was 16 and I was 18.

That strike got international coverage because it was led by the diminutive Lu Cui, who was so thin she was the only one able to crawl under and open the locked gates on the second strike, where she was beaten and then arrested for her trouble.

> The *Herald Tribune* labelled her "China's Joan of Arc". Later, when I met Lu Cui myself, I was struck by her beauty and total assurance that she had no other choice but to stand up and do the only thing she could do.
>
> These political actions followed along the lines of the famous Student Strike of 1919, when the protesters rioted against the terms of the Versailles Peace Treaty. That treaty had revoked the promised end of extraterritoriality and the monopoly of salt

---

[18] The Meiji Restoration: in Japanese history, the political restoration that brought about the final demise of the Tokugawa Shogunate (military government). The Meiji Restoration came to be identified with the subsequent era of major political, economic and social change; the modernisation and Westernisation of the country, 1868-1912.

and customs. The new terms accorded the Japanese the right to take over the former German "possessions" in China. Those infamous Twenty-one Conditions, the students then claimed, "would make China a colony of Japan". And now they were witnessing the fulfilment of their prophecy by the creation of a Special Zone. Jieping and his fellow students were determined to take a stand once more against Japan, but they were frustrated.

Dr. Wu:

The strike did not achieve much, other than being commemorated by a plaque in Zhongshan Park. But its timing was apt because the following month, the Red China base sent an appeal to all Chinese urging unity and cessation of internal warfare, in an effort to launch a united front against Japan.

> Seemingly a world away in the elegant confines of PUMC, Jieping continued to make fun of those who succeeded in memorizing the countless formulae that is the language of science. In preparation for an exam one day, he joined a group of students who were carefully examining bones.

Dr. Wu:

We were required to recognize and name every bone in the human body, including the metatarsal bones in the foot. Some students kept bones in their pockets to become familiar with them by touching them. I also kept a pocketful and would learn by touch. Then, in the company of classmates, I would pick up a bone at random, toss it in the air, catch it and name it. I showed off, juggling the bones, and broke the monotony.

> This was followed by a juggling exhibition several times and invariably, he got the name right each time. After dazzling his friends, he admitted that he'd practised hard while rote learning. Yet he considered this talent quite useless. His class-mates could forgive their mischievous little brother, as he was still the smallest and youngest in the class. The friends he made at PUMC were to become life-long companions.

Dr. Wu:

On Sunday mornings, we had the opportunity of attending church together and could further enjoy exposure to Western thinking and values from the various speakers who were invited to present a lecture on a favourite subject; the joys of mountain-climbing vied with Moses' parting of the Red Sea in the minds of the credulous young men and women.

We were lectured not only by Western academics, but also by China's greatest scholars. The former President of Tsinghua University and economist, Zhou Yichun, came and talked to us about budgeting our *lives*.

> Life on campus was full and exciting and life at home, no less so, for in 1936 his second daughter Wu Bing was born. Their home was just a few blocks from the Forbidden City, closed to the public but where Junkai could push the perambulator while her sister-in-law and maid looked after Wu Xing.
>
> Jieping was not yet in his twenties and still a student at pre-medical school, so he had to be diligent for the first time in his life. He was developing a growing awareness that his country was going through a major political upheaval that he could not blithely ignore. Through the challenges of his studies, his early marriage and fatherhood, Jieping reluctantly became an adult in war-torn China, still strangely sheltered from the surrounding chaos. The characters for his name, Class, Prosperity and Peace, were a constant reminder that he had inherited with his name the weight of his family's expectations.
>
> In an apparent lull, the Japanese seemed satisfied with Chiang's secret agreement, while Zhou Enlai reached out to Zhang Xueliang, known as the Young Marshal, ousted from Manchuria by the Japanese. His army was now installed at Xi'an, capital of Shaanxi in which Yan'an was the new communist base. The Young Marshal realized that Zhou Enlai was right when, after a failed attack on the Red base by the Young Marshal, Zhou wrote, "Inhuman is he who slays his own brother to feed the Wolf."
>
> For half a year Zhang Xueliang tried to convince Generalissimo Chiang to join the Reds instead of attacking them; and when Chiang announced another annihilation attempt against the Red base, the Young Marshal lay siege to the city of Xi'an and kidnapped Chiang.

Unseemly gossip circulated of Chiang escaping in his nightshirt without his dentures. Telephone wires hummed.

While the towns of Bao'an and Yan'an are in bordering provinces, it took Zhou Enlai a day and a half to ride to Yan'an airport so he could then board the Young Marshal's plane to Xi'an. Zhou did not wish for Chiang to go on trial, as this would distract the army and the nation from the object of the united front against the Japanese. In the confusion, the KMT ministry ordered Xi'an to be bombed and only on the intervention of Chiang's wife, Meiling, were these orders rescinded in favour of negotiations.

The negotiators included the Soong sisters, Sun Yat-sen's widow, Soong Ching-ling, Chiang's wife, Soong Meiling, and adviser W. H. Donald, who tried to reason with his former charge, the Young Marshal, who retained the kidnapped Chiang Kai-shek as his negotiating weapon. But the Young Marshal would not relent until Chiang agreed to a united front against the Japanese.

In the fiasco that followed, Chiang turned the tables and the Young Marshal was taken captive by Chiang on 26 December, when he flew off with his prisoner without signing any agreement. The Young Marshal was sentenced to ten years for insubordination, but remained under house arrest four decades later.

About a decade later, Zhou Enlai arranged for Xueliang's young mistress to leave China and move to Taiwan, to look after and comfort the Young Marshal. They married in 1964. When the Generalissimo died in 1975, the Young Marshal travelled to the US to visit his family, eventually settling in Honolulu in 1995. He died there in 2001, aged one hundred.

Chiang Kai-shek was now forced to move against the Japanese more by their arrogance than by agreement with the communists. "We can take all of China within three months," the Japanese boasted. Many in China believed they could, including Wu Jieping.

In Shanghai, in August 1937 the Japanese bombed hordes of refugees, while Europeans still combed the antique stalls and markets for the Song and Ming artefacts the Chinese cared little about. In the afternoons, the hotels in the international concession still held tea-dancing and at night, "respectable" European men and wealthy Chinese drew up in their Ford convertibles at "girlie" bars, to while away their cares. Despite these well-orchestrated meetings, the Europeans regarded the Chinese as "forever unable to rule themselves, because they are weak, devious, volatile and timid"[19].

Old Wu wrote to his sons that the Japanese warships on the Bund suddenly made Beijing seem a more neutral and attractive base than places like Shanghai, Tianjin or Nanjing. Reports of the Japanese murdering schoolchildren made mothers sick with fear as they said goodbye to their children in the mornings, not knowing if they would see them again. By now the population of Shanghai was over six million. While Old Wu was still useful to some of his old customers, in the autumn of 1937 many colleagues were dispossessed and helpless. Poverty was rampant and the poor peasants took the brunt of it, just about surviving on acorn-meal and sorghum, both of which are almost indigestible.

Despite his well-advertised marriage, Jieping was popular with the girls in his class; but he was not interested. As he left Sage Hall in the shade of a gold leafed gingko tree, he now planned his weekends with a precision that was to serve him well in later life.

Jieping was to be drawn closer to communism during his remaining university years. On a visit to Sage Hall with him sixty years later, I saw that the gingko tree is still majestic and the statue of Li Dazhao (1889-1927), the spiritual father of Chinese communism, stands erect.

Dr. Wu:

When the family left Changzhou, Father lost everything in the fire set by the employees to burn down the house. Then the Japanese took over the shipping and requisitioned all other transport. Soon after, the cotton factory was bombed and Father was left with nothing but the two apartments in Shanghai and no business to run.

Only on 7 July were we finally given the right to fight the Japanese. The war had formally started because of aggression at Lugouqiao, later known as the Marco Polo Bridge Incident.[20] The Japanese claimed they

---

[19] Han Suyin, *A Crippled Tree*, 1972, Triad Books.

[20] On July 7 1937: the conflict between Chinese and Japanese troops, near the Marco Polo Bridge, developed into the warfare between the two countries that was the prelude to the Pacific side of World War II.

lost two guards who entered the garrison town of Wanping and the Chinese guards had the temerity to respond by shooting them dead. The Japanese army then took this as a signal to enter Wanping. They did not even bother to declare war, but all Chinese knew the occupation had begun in earnest. We had no reliable news in China and came to depend on the BBC radio news and foreign publications to learn about what was happening in our country.

Chiang Kai-shek's hand was forced and he announced publicly that the KMT government would resist. But in his discussions with Zhou Enlai, he made it clear that he wanted the Red Army under his leadership.

On Tuesday 27 July, 1937, *The Guardian* reported:

'After fierce fighting yesterday at Langfang, the railway centre midway between Peking and Tientsin, from which the Chinese were finally driven out, Japanese soldiers last night entered Peking.

They had previously demanded entry into the city at the conclusion of fighting a short distance outside, and had been repulsed by Chinese guards when trying to occupy the suburban railway station just outside the west wall.

Twenty Japanese are reported to have been killed inside the Changimen, the western gate of Peking, when three lorries were blown up with hand-grenades. One Chinese policeman was killed and another wounded.

Ten lorries full of Japanese troops had passed through the gate when the fighting broke out. The Chinese allege that the Japanese opened fire, and that the Chinese guarding the gate then dropped the hand-grenades. The Japanese say that the grenades were dropped first.

The majority of the Japanese soldiers took refuge in a temple inside the city walls, where they are now surrounded by Chinese troops and by about 1,000 armed plain-clothes policemen. The entire section of the city near the Changimen gate has been cordoned off.

The fighting at Langfang continued for eight hours until noon yesterday. A bombardment by seventeen Japanese aeroplanes finally forced the Chinese troops – who, suffering heavy losses, had already resisted one aerial attack and heavy fire from field guns – to flee, leaving the Japanese to occupy Langfang. This materially strengthens their grip on all the railway system of North China. General Katsuki, the Japanese Commander-in-Chief in North China, last evening presented an ultimatum in the name of the Imperial Japanese Army, demanding the withdrawal of the whole of the Chinese 37th Division – the soldiers involved in the original Lukouchiao [Lugouqiao] clash – by noon tomorrow, under threat of 'military measures.'

> *Precisely at this time, Jieping had a "minor surgical procedure" from which he lost 10kg.*

Dr. Wu:

I remember lying in my hospital bed and thinking PUMC would soon be taken by the Japanese; so as soon as I could walk, I travelled to Changzhou to rest for a time. In August, there was a great battle in Shanghai; but I went south by steamer to Changsha in Hunan province, to see if I could join their 'Yale in China' programme.

I no sooner got there, in October, than I was informed that PUMC had opened despite the Japanese occupation. I had to travel from Changsha to Hong Kong and board a ship for Beijing. I arrived on 18 November and found I had missed my entire third year course in pharmacology. I also had an exam in pathology, but had not attended even one class. My Professor advised, 'Why don't you take just the oral exam now and defer the practical until next semester.' I had five hundred pages to read in two weeks and I just managed to pass.

> Appalling tales of atrocities in the December attack on Nanjing terrified young Chinese. In the days and weeks that followed, many of Jieping's fellow students reported the loss of a loved one while others were moved to join the volunteers as Japan expected the Chinese to sue for peace. Old Wu worried that each time Junkai went out of the apartment in the French concession in Shanghai a Japanese might be insolent to her and that she would not stand for that.

Dr. Wu:

My family and Ruiping's family returned from Shanghai at the end of 1938. Because of the constant interruptions, by 1939 I had a backlog of courses from my second year and a very tight schedule.

During that period of hospitalization (for adenoidal surgery) and travel, I had had the time to reflect and decided that I could not be a doctor, not to mention a good doctor, unless I really paid attention to practical work. I did not like to study and was just average and relaxed about it, but in 1939, I changed.

With this in mind, I tried to get the necessary knowledge from books; but I finally concluded that to be a mature doctor with the ability to solve problems, I must be allowed to practise what I was studying. I had gleaned that people with an opportunity to practise were better able to apply their thinking.

CHAPTER SEVEN
'OPPORTUNITY FAVOURS A PREPARED MIND'

Dr. Wu:

My third year at PUMC became very important for me. I began to be involved in clinical medicine. I was now observing students a year or two ahead of me and I realized that they knew how to handle patients. I felt like I knew nothing, yet I was there to learn medicine and how to solve patients' problems. This recognition made me worried and my studies took on a new meaning. Up to that point I had been an average student and rather self-satisfied, but now I wanted to change.

> Jieping's self-reflection made him realise that he did not want to be a good doctor, he wanted to be a *great* doctor – and not only to please his father. When he awoke to his own inadequacy, it sharpened his focus. It also coincided with a self-diagnosis of renal tuberculosis. He needed one kidney removed and knew then that if it spread to the other kidney, the chance of his becoming a great doctor and doing his father proud was less than even. In his gentle, enthusiastic voice, he ruminated:

Dr. Wu:

That year I unconsciously tried to integrate thinking, knowledge and practice while developing the ability to become a good doctor. But at the same time, I was ill and the only cure in those days for TB was sunshine, cod liver oil and rest. So, I had plenty of time to read biographies of eminent doctors like John B. Murphy[21], William Halsted[22] and others; and this benefitted me tremendously.

When I was twenty-two the TB affected my lungs, but they healed. I then suffered from haematuria and acute abdomen pain because of blood clots in the urethra.

The Japanese were here so there was always tension in the air; Junkai had headaches and threw up a lot. There were food scarcities and we were too terrified to take the children out, so they, too, were housebound.

After the successful removal of one kidney, I feared the TB had returned, but my professor consoled me that the discomfort I felt was probably just a stone passing. I felt doomed, but I survived.

> One can well imagine the trauma in Junkai's life, with little children and a nervous husband with a cloud hanging over them, in a city occupied by demonstrably brutal Japanese.
>
> Jieping reminisced, many years later, about his fortune in attracting excellent teachers and students as friends and his good fortune in getting along very well with the mostly foreign faculty. He recalled William Brand at Yenching, a playful lecturer who lightened the prevailing sombre mood by tossing chalk at the students and teasing them.

Dr. Wu:

Brand left Beijing in 1941 after Pearl Harbor, when I was twenty-four years old. He knew he would be taken by the Japanese sentries who had been parading around the college for some time and went to the guerrilla-occupied area. I was sad to see him go, but felt great relief that the Japanese would now be answerable to the Americans.

> Jieping recalled a Chinese idiom, "Don't read dead books, don't read books to die, and the dead don't read books", the individual phrases of which use the same four characters in a different order. He reeled off ten different words suggesting that China knows

---

[21] John B. Murphy revolutionised abdominal surgery and introduced Murphy's sign, a diagnostic technique to identify gallbladder disease and Anastomosis [Murphy's] button to join segments of the intestine without sutures.

[22] William Stewart Halsted revolutionised general surgery with the introduction of general anaesthesia.

very well the importance of analytical thinking over rote learning. Recognizing for the first time that he had obediently followed his parents and teachers' leadership, Jieping made a point of learning to think for himself.

Dr. Wu:

After I returned from my nephrectomy, in just one trimester I became the best student in class. During that year, the eminent Professor Isadore Snapper, a renowned clinician, joined the faculty. At PUMC we were allowed to attend any and all lectures outside our curriculum; so although I didn't know much, I attended all his lectures and learned a lot about the ways of clinical scientific thinking and presentation. He gave me an oral exam about one patient at the end of that year. His questions taught me more than any book had ever done. He was apparently satisfied, because that year I got the highest marks.

> The most outstanding student during Jieping's first and second years at PUMC was Huang Guo'an, from Fujian province. Due to Jieping's illness, which delayed him for half a year, and the fact that Huang did not return to Beijing in 1939 (because he, too, thought the Japanese would requisition PUMC), they were still in the same class for their fourth and final years. In the spirit of healthy competition that prevailed among both faculty and students, Jieping invited Huang to share his room. They were friendly competitors who got on extremely well, although they were both vying for the same laurels.

Dr. Wu:

Another turning point had been the Commencement Address given by Isadore Snapper in 1940. It was entitled *Opportunity Favours a Prepared Mind*. He had taken this expression from Louis Pasteur who had observed, "In the field of observation, opportunity favours the prepared mind." His example was Alexander Fleming's accidental discovery that staphylococcus colonies were impeded by the growth of fungus. This had been observed for many years, but only when Fleming asked, "Why does it stop the growth?" did he discover the anti-bacterial properties of the penicillin fungus. That was in 1928, but usable penicillin was not manufactured until 1943 because its molecular composition was so unstable. It took teams of expert chemists from all around the world to establish this conclusively[23].

Snapper's lecture opened me up to a question that had never been put to me before: "What is a prepared mind?" A mind that thinks about all you've done, summarizes the experience and expects to meet something more challenging in each new experience? People with the same opportunity achieve different results in practice. Louis Pasteur felt that in order to pursue any study, one needed a specific thinking process. This leads to a rational understanding of man.

The thinking process is not just reflecting on things. You develop a rational understanding of the process. With each opportunity and each experience, you face the future in a different way – that is the prepared mind.

For anyone involved in any kind of work there must be some integration of practice, thinking and knowledge. But only when you can consciously integrate these three can you really proceed.

> By the time I met Jieping, his thinking had also been affected by his embrace of socialism; and the writings of communist thinkers is evident in his examination of his personal development.
>
> During his forced isolation with TB, Jieping had read the medical papers of famous specialists and applied them to his own education as a clinical surgeon. And he was determined to follow in their footsteps, to the American medical schools that had produced them. Both doctors had also studied in Europe and returned to America with greatly refined techniques.

Dr. Wu:

I felt I was beginning to understand, but I was just an intern, and I had been observing the diagnostic technique of different doctors. For example, at that point I was studying with books and anatomical charts and models precisely where the appendix was located. I saw hundreds of cases of appendicitis in those days; sometimes it was hidden or difficult to find. When it was found, it could look or feel different. I decided I would try and predict whether it was easy to locate, whether it was inflamed, whether it was small or large.

---

[23] I told Jieping that Dorothy Hodgkin, who featured in my book 'For Our Daughters', shared the Nobel prize for using crystallography to determine the chemical structure of penicillin biomolecules.

So I made observations and took extensive notes throughout my fourth and fifth years. You must palpate the least painful side first and try using just one finger. I would gently test with the patient's legs extended, then with the legs drawn up. I'd check the temperature and blood count to see if I could predict where it was located and how badly inflamed it was. I discussed it with the other students and wrote up and summarized my findings. That also impressed my professors.

I began to sense that my dedication to just four or five cases might be more effective than someone else who had only superficially investigated ten or more cases. I came to the conclusion that if I committed totally to clinical practice, I could be better after just five years than those who had practised for ten years more casually. I invited fellow student Huang to study and compete with me.

> I asked Jieping what he did to be sociable and relax. He laughed, as if at a misspent youth, and told me that in his fourth year he was still the best bridge, table tennis and badminton player. Jieping went on to win the prize for the best student of his class.

Dr. Wu:

The highest prize the university awarded was the Wenham prize, which went to the best student overall for the five years. My older brother and several of his friends were Wenham scholars. Apart from benefiting from the prestige of winning the award, the successful students would also have all their medical school fees paid back. This permitted professors to take a chance on particularly bright but poor students, lending them the fees with reasonable expectation of being repaid.

> Old Wu sent word from Yan'an. The Politburo gossip was that Mao Zedong had divorced his wife (who had given birth on the Long March) to marry a pretty young actress whose name he romantically changed from Lan Ping, Blue Apple, to Jiang Qing, Limpid Stream. Mao's closest associates supported the marriage, on the condition that she have absolutely no political involvement.
>
> While Jieping grappled with his studies, his father did everything he could think of to secure his business in order to support his family. His children's education had to be paid for while the Japanese encroachments continued. The Japanese took

Guangzhou in October, causing massive disarray, with both the KMT army and Red Army apparently fighting for supremacy, instead of fighting the Japanese.

Old Wu was accumulating outstanding debts as the KMT bases moved and the bills for the uniforms remained unpaid. While he awaited payment, the KMT and communist armies debated who would lead the defence of Wuhan. Chiang would not fight the assault on Wuhan and retreated in another long, ponderous and dangerous trek from Wuhan to Changsha to Guilin and finally, to the hilly city with all the KMT government machinery, Chongqing in Sichuan province. Zhou Enlai participated in the retreat while Mao Zedong directed operations from the cave city of Yan'an. It was said that while Zhou maintained the appearance of a united front, the Red bases were expanding both north and south of the Yangtze.

At the onset of war in Europe, the German Ambassador to China suggested that China sue for peace with Japan in May 1940. But instead, the communist army in North China prepared for a major guerrilla offensive against the Japanese. Unfortunately, they were led by conventional warriors and suffered immense losses, while the Japanese followed success with a 'scorched earth' policy.

It was becoming clear that the communist army bases were worrying to Chiang and his KMT armies. By the end of 1940, relations became tragically clear when a Chinese communist garrison commander, besieged by the Japanese, appealed to the KMT HQ. The Commander was taken prisoner and his nine thousand remaining troops were massacred by the KMT on 7 January, 1941. This was later referred to by Chiang as a "disciplinary" measure and invited international criticism particularly from the US, which was pouring money and arms into China to benefit the KMT.

Old Wu was reassured by the Soong family that the KMT was adequately funded to pay their debts. He worried about his involvement with the KMT, when they were reportedly doing nothing to fight the Japanese. If the Japanese succeeded in annexing China, life in future would be unbearable and the family would all have to learn Japanese – if they survived.

While Zhou Enlai had predicted Japanese expansion into Asia, the world was taken aback by Japan's surprise assault on the American fleet at Pearl Harbor on 7 December, 1941. As this event brought the US into the war, Jieping's American friend Arthur, and many of the visiting professors, were obliged to make a quick exit.

Students were motivated to resist and learn. Jieping's progress was so apparent to his class and Faculty that he was elected Student Marshal in the fourth year. Jieping felt confident that despite being behind in the first couple of years, he had made up the lost time. But at the rushed graduation, just after Pearl Harbor, no evaluation was made – the Wenham scholarship was not awarded at all that year, to Jieping's continued regret. Everyone acknowledged it was his by right.

Dr. Wu:

The PUMC diploma was a grand parchment made up by the Chinese Medical Board in New York, but after Pearl Harbor they couldn't get through. So, my graduate colleagues and I received a typewritten sheet instead. Its only merit was that it at least had all the professors' signatures as usual. A diploma was not enough to practise medicine; it required a licence issued by the municipality of Beijing, which was controlled by the puppet government. As Student Marshal, I was sent to organize the licences on behalf of my graduating class.

> Jieping went to the Chairman of the Union of Medical Doctors in Beijing. Student Marshal Wu told the Chairman, "I've come to pay my respects as a recent graduate of PUMC."
>
> The Chairman was very impressed by the standards of PUMC and had himself graduated from Beijing Medical University (under Japanese control). The medical school had been under the influence of Japanese returned students since the early 1930s. When Jieping's classmates received their licences, they were surprised by Jieping's diplomatic skills. He told them, laughing, "Remember, I learned about human relations from 'The Romance of the Three Kingdoms'!"
>
> Jieping was finally awarded the Wenham Prize a year or so later and felt grateful to be able to relieve some of his father's financial pressure, as both the cotton mill and steamship company had been commandeered by the Japanese. By the time Jieping was awarded the prestigious prize in his final year, it was the equivalent of five years' fees at PUMC, and he still had two younger brothers to be educated.

CHAPTER EIGHT
QUESTIONS OF LOYALTY

Dr. Wu:

Several decades later, I was informed that I was to travel to North Korea with a Dr. Huang to treat the leaders. When we met and I recognized my former roommate, he confided, "When we were at PUMC, the Registrar Dr. Ferguson said to me one day, 'You were the best student in the first and second years, but if you come up against Wu Jieping, you will be second'."

The change in my attitude had caused something of a sensation at PUMC. I received my B.Sc. in 1937 and M.D. in 1942.

> The Registrar felt that tuberculosis had taught Jieping some surprising lessons. A Chinese proverb translates as, "Failure is the mother of success". Jieping's academic improvement surprised everyone at his college, including the Registrar.

Dr. Wu:

My wife took very good care of me even while she was pregnant. I had my kidney operation in March and our son, Wu Desheng, was born on 22 April, 1939. I resumed college in September.

Over the years Junkai had a number of unwanted pregnancies, but I managed to terminate them quite early. However, on one occasion, she haemorrhaged so badly I had to call a friend and get her admitted to hospital.

We were generally happy, probably because we were no longer teenagers and spent much more time with family. We had a nanny and my brother had a family cook and housekeeper; so my wife and sister-in-law stayed home looking after the children and relaxed by drawing and painting. My father supported my studies throughout those years.

> But now Old Wu was broke and really appreciated that Jieping was able to return the investment in his education and stand on his own two feet. After all, his brother was very well paid; and everyone expected this to be the case for Jieping and his younger brothers coming along behind him.

Dr. Wu:

After Pearl Harbor, my brother was committed to finding a private space for critically-ill children and the most obvious place was our home. Both families moved and rented smaller homes and my brother continued to support me financially. I needed to live up to Father's expectations and was motivated to work hard, in order to repay my debts and start providing for my own family.

My ambition took hold in 1940 and continued to spur me on when I was invited by Zhong Huilan, Dean of Central Hospital, (later known as Zhonghe Hospital), to practise general surgery during the Japanese occupation. Everything was going according to plan, but I needed a little more money to put into the family. My brother had become very prosperous, so naturally I felt that I personally should do a little better.

At that time Wu Xing was being looked after by my parents in Shanghai. As the first granddaughter of my mother, she had that expectation and we brought our second daughter, Wu Bing, back to Beijing.

Private medical practice in China was the norm and did not change either in times of war or with political parties. All graduates got licences to practise private medicine, but I never actually practised privately because it was becoming socialized by then and the Government was already paying our fees. Because of inflation I received payment in kind, 500 catties[24] of millet on paper. My brother received 1,000 catties and another 1,000 catties' compensation for giving up private practice.

---

[24] A cattie is approximately 500g.

Before long we were able to exchange our 500 catties for cash. At Beijing Medical College, on the first pay scale grade, my salary was RMB 240, or $25 per month. On the second grade, it was RMB 280. Ten years later, I qualified for third grade at RMB 330, or $36 per month.

All this time my brother and his colleagues were on much higher salaries and receiving compensation for loss. We always had to pay for our own food and a nominal amount towards housing. I could rationalize that it was a sign of the times and that it would revert to normal as soon as the war was over. I also had my career to look forward to and the challenges were a great distraction, whereas Junkai scraped and scrounged while her sister-in-law enjoyed the benefits of my brother's advantageous position. Our circumstances were a lot worse for my wife than for me.

I had already completed my studies when PUMC closed in January, 1942. We got by on a very sparse diet and sometimes got rewarded with extras from our association with American institutions; but the Japanese took over many of those institutions and that was the end of those privileges. I went from PUMC to Central Hospital, a period that would turn out to be very important and beneficial for me. It helped me become a mature surgeon. At Central Hospital, I laid down practices and advances for later years and strove to progress and gain self-confidence. From Central Hospital, I went on to Beijing Medical College as Assistant Registrar, then Registrar, then Chief Resident.

On 1 July, 1945 I became Visiting Surgeon and on 15 August, when the Japanese surrendered, I re-joined PUMC. It was shocking to contemplate the devastation of Hiroshima and Nagasaki and I briefly wondered if we would be called upon to treat the injured; but I had my hands full with war victims from the Japanese occupation and near-conquest of my country. I was also very conscious of the need to provide for my wife and children and that required me to concentrate on my career.

> As the peace charade was played out in Nanjing, Chiang flew additional battalions in American planes to the places where Mao planned eventually to encircle the cities and cut the nationalist forces to ribbons. The undeclared civil war that had gone on throughout the Japanese occupation could no longer be disguised; and Jieping realized there would be an urgent need for hospital care.

Dr. Wu:

I wanted to work for my own interests and those of my country. We did not distinguish our patients by whether they were red or blue. I was aware that I had treated some of Chiang's Blueshirts in the past. I was approached by communists through a relative of my wife, in 1943, when I was House Surgeon. He gave me a list of wounded people who needed care and I got on my bicycle, not knowing the dangers I might face. I did this for patriotic reasons and because my wife's relative turned out to be a member of an underground communist movement. Attending to those men changed my life. China was transformed by the war in ways that were not always visible.

> Both the US and Great Britain had signed treaties with China that effectively ended extraterritoriality. After the fall of Japan, France also signed a treaty with China. Finally, Shanghai became a Chinese city under Chinese administration where the foreign community no longer enjoyed as many of their past privileges and now lived in Shanghai at the discretion of the Chinese. Many still enjoyed the good life during the civil war, but when in May 1949 the Chinese communist army took the city, the remaining foreigners, accompanied by many wealthy and successful Chinese, left forever. Jieping had studied under some of the most distinguished medical scholars from the USA. He was well aware that he was not interested in becoming just the best surgeon in China, but one of the best in the world; and visiting China's best hospitals honed this ambition.

Dr. Wu:

Families were divided, with some members accompanying Chiang Kai-shek to Taiwan, including some of my close relatives. Others moved to Singapore and Hong Kong, while whole swathes relocated to the US, UK, Canada and Australia. Since childhood I had had quite a lot of contact with Americans – the friends I played with in the factory compound, living in the foreign concessions, at middle school and university – so it had always been my intention to see for myself what America was like. At PUMC, we frequently had professors on sabbatical leave visiting from America. Some would stay for as long as two years, and I admired these scientists very much. I had a clear impression that medical science in the US was of a very high standard. The standard at PUMC was very good, but I often wondered how much better it would be in the USA, the place I considered the motherland of medical science.

After VJ Day in August 1945, a friend and I were eager for any opportunity to study abroad. There were open examinations to apply for overseas study, but unfortunately there was no exam in general medicine, only veterinary medicine or anaesthesiology.

My department head at the Central Hospital was a surgeon with the rank of Brigadier General at the Army Hospital. He was recruiting doctors to go to America and asked me to join him in 1946. But I did not want to be involved with any kind of military activity for the National Chinese Government. I was not that sure the communists were any better than the KMT, but I felt they couldn't be worse. I regarded the nationalists as one of the greatest misfortunes in Chinese history. I was not a communist, but I held the nationalist government responsible for every betrayal to the Japanese, especially the loss of the north-east in 1931. My understanding of the activities of both the nationalists and the communists came mostly by word of mouth from my father and the student intellectuals I met at Yenching University.

> His philosophical readings had given Jieping a healthy scepticism for all views, especially second-hand ones; but it was clear to everyone that not only had the KMT not been fighting the Japanese in the north-east, but that North China could have become a special (Japanese) region: and the nationalists were prepared to sign that pact.

Dr. Wu:

When I left the Central Hospital to go to Beijing Medical College, the promise was that I would be given the opportunity to go abroad. I was finally sent by the Chinese government, but it was actually paid for by ABMAC, the American Board for Medical Aid to China.

A very close relative of mine was married to Chiang Kai-shek's chief economic adviser and closest friend, but this did nothing to endear Chiang to me.

What impressed Jieping initially was the behaviour of the People's Liberation Army, the PLA, and the fact that so many former nationalist KMT soldiers now joined that army. The Red armies were all united now under one name, the PLA, People's Liberation Army. In fact, between 1945 and 1948 more than 1.75 million KMT troops joined, or rather submitted themselves, to the PLA, although they really didn't have much option.

Dr. Wu:

As the PLA released Japanese Prisoners of War (POWs) in Manchuria in 1945-46, Russian troops marched in to secure the north of China for the CCP. And in the south, the US air force held the southern port cities for Chiang and the KMT while their ambassadors met with Zhou and Mao to negotiate a peaceful transition to a coalition government. Observing the planes, Mao was reported to have said, "The sky cannot cover both of us."

After thirty-two years of war, the people craved peace and each side had representatives, ambassadors and international newsmen to promote a coalition government. But the US Ambassador Patrick Hurley talked of peace while the US transported KMT troops to Manchuria. He was accused of deception, resigned and was replaced by the much-admired John Leighton Stuart, former Chancellor of Yenching. He brought along a number of translators, including Huang Hua. President Truman also sent General George Marshall to help sue for a coalition government. In one exchange between Marshall and Zhou Enlai, Zhou said, "You talk of democracy while lavishing hundreds of millions of dollars on the military dictator, Chiang Kai-shek!"

The fear of foreigners, examples of PLA/communist fairness and the rallying call of egalitarianism opened the eyes of many divisions of KMT soldiers, accustomed to the corrupt ways of their nationalist leaders.

Soon, fighting erupted between these divisions in Manchuria and the PLA generals put down their weapons and declared, "Chinese do not fight Chinese."

The Japanese had been defeated, with each side claiming responsibility for the defeat; but the fighting had not ended and life in the capital seemed even more precarious. I decided to spend the year, 1945-46, getting better prepared and gaining additional status.

Better prepared for what? Jieping wanted to know everything there was to know about general surgery, so that he could improve people's well-being and restore their health. He taxed himself with becoming the most knowledgeable and renowned doctor in his field, so that when he faced his peers, he would not feel he had let his patients, himself or China down.

Jieping spent his life proving that it had been worth saving.

CHAPTER NINE
FIRST CONTACT WITH THE USA

Wu Jieping was finally selected at PUMC to do a post-doctorate in urology at the University of Chicago. He left China in 1947, not knowing when a return to normality might begin, because at that stage Chiang had promised to return and resume control. If that happened, the communists would probably be slaughtered.

Jieping arrived by ship in California. He was in his early 30s, armed with an optimistic outlook, a little money and a good command of English.

Dr. Wu:

I was an immature idealist, open to absorbing whatever *Meiguo*, the beautiful country, had to offer. I was supported by the ABMAC. I had left my wife and three children, with the hope of returning better informed about many other aspects of life, as well as medicine. The year before my departure, inflation had risen from 100,000 per cent to 2.8 million per cent and most of my salary was a millet allowance in any case.

> When he arrived in America, Jieping boarded a Greyhound bus for the long journey from California to Chicago. After dozing for a couple of hours, he awoke to find the bus full. Soon, an elderly black man got onto the bus and the young Chinese visitor rose to give him his seat. This was greeted by an almost audible hiss on the part of the other passengers. Jieping was unaware of the cause

of the transgression. There were no other Chinese or blacks on the bus, so he had to wait to find out.

Dr. Wu:

Somewhere further on, I requested directions to a public convenience. When the conductor explained there were two, I stood looking at the signs, trying to decide if I would be regarded as "coloured" or "white", but the memory of the park sign in Shanghai barring entry to "Chinese and dogs" directed my footsteps.

My mentor and teacher was the most famous physician in medical science, Dr. Charles Huggins. He had a brilliant Filipino surgical assistant, Dr. Manuel, who one day, caused a minor accident. The humiliating tirade he was subjected to for this human error appalled me.

It was my first personal exposure to racial discrimination among the scholarly fraternity around which my life revolved and it made me very uncomfortable that the other students seemed to take it for granted. When Dr. Manuel finally left Dr. Huggins, he joined the American Red Cross where he had a very distinguished career.

> Jieping's gentle upbringing had protected him from the coarseness and brutality of his fellow men. When one day, some months later, the humiliation had been forgotten by the Filipino doctor and he offered an opinion in the operating room, the famous Professor immediately cut him off yelling, "Enough!" with the implicit suggestion that he was not qualified to participate. Yet Huggins had always been kind to Jieping and had invited him to his home when he entertained his post-doctoral students.
>
> When his wife sent him a copy of the studio photograph of their wedding day, Jieping was moved to write how much he missed her. His daughter, Wu Xing, told me that although he didn't have much money, "He sent Mother a magazine each month and folded a pair of nylon stockings inside, as an expression of his love."
>
> Jieping also sent her some of the latest fabric fashionable in America at that time: "Father's very good taste was evident in his selection and Mother made a cheongsam from it and looked exceptionally beautiful." At a time of shortages and restraint, it is easy to imagine the excitement an American postage stamp inspired.

Dr. Wu:

I never had the feeling that China should become a modern democratic country because I had no experience of one – until I went to the US. I was not motivated to go to the States to write a special thesis or to study a particular situation, but to see what the US was like, how good its science and technology really were and how it had reached its current stage of success so quickly. I wanted to see for myself just what it was that accounted for its success and openness.

I still didn't have a focused interest in a specific subject. But what I gained was an in-depth knowledge about how scientific research should be carried out. I helped Dr. Huggins in some experimental work, but I did not work on a subject or problem of my own thinking.

Huggins used to say, "Science is simplicity." He'd come in early and work in the laboratory. From 4 to 5 o'clock he'd sit and reflect on what had happened in science that day. When you have a research subject, you may conceive some preliminary ideas of what you want to arrive at but miss those things that are not on your schedule, which come up all of a sudden.

Clinicians rarely have a research interest so when I came back from the States in December 1948, the Chinese Society of Biochemistry asked me to join because they knew I had worked with Huggins and that it had influenced me greatly in scientific research. I explained that I had learned how one must consider things and have an open mind: results may not be what you wish, but they could indicate something more important because you are actually looking for something new.

Dr. Huggins wanted me to stay to take care of the clinical side, because his urological operations were actually not very good and he used to say, "You have three hands." Because I had much smaller hands, I was much better at operations than he was. But I learned a lot from him.

> Jieping realized that while he might well make Assistant Professor right away, if he stayed on in the US, and become a full professor a few years later, he would eventually be stopped by his yellow skin and probably not qualify for tenure. His life could have been better in a sense, and unquestionably more comfortable, but the intellectual compromise was one he could not consider. He decided to return home to serve his country, recognizing that in his case, he really had no choice as he wished to be reunited with his family.

Jieping might have stayed in the States, had it not been for his sensitivity to racial prejudice and revelations concerning the Truman-Dewey Presidential election from his year in Chicago.

The press in Chicago had firmly supported Thomas Dewey for some months prior to the 1948 election. Then, on the eve of the Election, they did an "about face" and supported Truman. Jieping was at a complete loss to understand how such a transformation could occur. He asked within his circle of friends and faculty and found, to his complete surprise, that some horse-trading had taken place and that in essence, President Truman had allegedly bought off the press. Jieping's view of democracy in action was a disappointment. He found its professed egalitarianism to be surprisingly superficial.

Trained at the Rockefeller-funded PUMC, and armed with his postdoctoral education in America, Jieping was now a highly educated young man. Yet thinking of Francis Bacon's teaching about using science to combat ignorance and prejudice, he could not equate the scientific advances of this great American nation in which he was now a guest with the socially regressive inequalities that surrounded him. While his surgical training progressed, his social conscience also developed and became more affirmed.

Dr. Wu:

When I went to the States, there was nothing to stop me staying; but Huggins' racist attitude affected my decision to return. There was little communication between China and the US, and what there was consisted mostly of KMT propaganda on the tenets of communist practices and beliefs: for example, that communists would have a common wife, that their children would be switched about and given a number instead of a name, and worse.

> Jieping realized that whatever awaited him on his return to China would be better than attempting to make a life for himself and his family in the United States. He travelled west to see his old friend Arthur Burton and was appalled to find that the family was under investigation for "Un-American Activities" during the period of Joe McCarthy. At one point, Arthur unobtrusively passed

him an envelope, on the outside of which he had written, "Walls have ears". Inside was a letter detailing what his father had been subjected to. He was accused of being a communist sympathizer and had his home ransacked. The accusations contributed to a complete nervous breakdown.

Jieping reported to the ABMAC the result of his year studying and his intention to return home as planned, but he had a surprise response.

Dr. Wu:

I was very disappointed to find, at this crucial juncture, that ABMAC had withdrawn its support of medical education to mainland China and switched allegiance to the small minority of nationalists who had fled to Taiwan with Chiang Kai-shek.

I returned to China with the clear intention of developing urology as a discipline in Chinese hospitals and while awaiting the natural sequence of events, involving both research and setting up the hospital departments, I would go about setting up a private medical practice.

> When Jieping left America, he said goodbye to a host of friends who accepted his explanation that he owed a certain allegiance to his motherland. He confessed that he had written a request to ABMAC asking if they could provide the equipment to set up the first Urology Department in a Chinese hospital and was enormously disappointed when it was refused. But undaunted, Jieping took with him some medical instruments, including a simple cystoscope, which he had proudly bought with his own hard-earned money. It was the first cystoscope in China and can be viewed, to this day, in the small urology museum attached to the Wu Jieping Medical Centre.

CHAPTER TEN
CHINA HAS STOOD UP

Jieping had walked smartly down Nanjing Road to the Bund and sailed out of Shanghai in 1947 for America. The city he was leaving was the most international city in Asia – well-kept and clean – with most people oblivious to poverty and trouble. It was, after all, the "Paris of the East", its European inhabitants engrossed in private clubs, orchestras, museums, dance halls, racing, casinos and opera. Few bothered to see the large gap that had always existed between the wealthy and the poor.

On his return in December 1948, Jieping bypassed Shanghai and made straight for Beijing to be reunited with his beloved family, Di, his children and parents.

In the secrecy that surrounded the new leadership, it was not publicly known where the new seat of government had established its headquarters. It later emerged that Mao Zedong and those close to him were in the Western Hills and moved, from time to time, as if they were still using guerrilla tactics and had not won the right to rule.

Eventually they settled within the Forbidden City and, while the Party leadership comfortably nurtured the secrets of its past, a new order emerged from the caves of Yan'an, armed and ready to exercise the refined tortures of antiquity on the corrupt practices they anticipated, which characterized earlier dynasties. Thus, Mao ensured the establishment of the Red Peasant dynasty.

The gossip in the capital was that the walls of 'The Purple Forbidden City' had turned red in anticipation of the new Red dynasty. Because ancient astronomers believed that the purple star Polaris was the centre of heaven, and the heavenly emperor lived there, the seat of the earthly emperor should be the Purple Forbidden City, its walls reputedly painted with a secret formula including vermilion, egg white and cinnabar. The new leaders saw no reason for socialism or communism to diminish the expectations of the masses. The walls of the Forbidden City are not in fact purple, but a dark vermilion red.

The northern section, Zhongnanhai, would now become the seat of power, where the emperor lived with his family, and the southern section, the Outer Court, now also known as the Palace Museum, would be where he or she exercised supreme power.

Mao Zedong was full of contradictions. His centre would be the Emperors' former home and his Outer Court would be Tiananmen Square, in the great outdoors, soon to be enlarged, where the peasant could rub shoulders with the knowledge-bearer. Mao was a keen reader, particularly of history, politics and warfare. To his bitter disappointment he had not been admitted to study at Beida, Beijing University. Resentfully, he found work in the library and read for himself the textbooks he would have studied as a student. He was keenly aware of the truth in the maxim, "He who reads and writes, rules. He who does not, obeys and labours."

The intellectuals, or knowledge-bearers, subscribed to the exalted tasks of the Common Program[25] in 1949. This was defined by Zhou Enlai, and approved by Chairman Mao, in order to put China back on its feet and guide it into the modern age.

This literocracy later suffered the humiliation of guidance and supervision by Party apparatchiks, frequently uneducated but loyal Party members. They rarely saw eye to eye with the intellectuals, who now virtually had to kowtow to them. China suffered then, as now, from social differences created by the lack of educational opportunities.

---

[25] The Interim Chinese Constitution contained the guiding principles and philosophy for the new state. 'The Common Program and Other Documents of the First Plenary Session of the Chinese People's Consultative Conference' (CPCC) was adopted in Beijing on 29 September 1949.

Dr. Wu:

In the confusion between my own values, those I'd left behind in the US, the propaganda put out by the nationalist press and the little I knew about communism from my Yenching days, I read all I could lay my hands on to help develop an understanding of socialist and communist doctrine.

These readings greatly influenced me and I began to doubt the faith I'd had in Father's capitalist values. From that time on, I began to believe in communism. My confidence was bolstered considerably by the actions of communists I observed, educated, young volunteers who were helping to create order in the hospitals, and many soldiers of the PLA, who had a modesty and sense of gratitude I had not encountered with the KMT soldiers.

I knew I could depend on my own ability as a medical doctor, that I could rely on science and technology, but I didn't get sufficient answers to the philosophical questions to serve as a bedrock on which to base my life in New China. What was my future? I soon realized that my future was not just in myself, nor in my decision to return to China, but essentially lay in co-operation with my fellow countrymen. I had left China a private citizen, but returned to a country that was embracing a new ethos. Raised in a culture of each person for himself and his family, I needed to prepare my mind for this transition. I was still struggling with the questions of "thinking" and recognized the need still to learn "how to think in this new society".

I felt that if I could follow the advice of prominent Marxists and "integrate practice, thinking and knowledge," I could gain an understanding of socialist principles. But the way of thinking was something I had not considered. I had never considered the philosophical question raised by Chairman Mao of how to think. I read somewhere that China needed a new political theory to revitalize and change the country. Somehow, I had to develop an understanding of political theory, in order to facilitate the changes. We had to conquer our own weaknesses.

On my return from the US, I found Junkai had studied accountancy in my absence – she was a very determined girl and succeeded in getting a job as a Certified Public Accountant in the Ministry of Agriculture Film Department.

Reunited physically and philosophically, we felt the exhilaration of the movement that was sweeping across China and embraced this fresh era with total commitment. We started to attend the YMCA in the evenings to study Russian. We were excited, as we were young, energetic and very optimistic. When the People's Republic of China was established in 1949, a few months after my return, the Communist Party warmed the hearts of millions of people. Old foot-soldiers of the PLA set a fine example, wanting nothing for themselves and everything for the country. They gave confidence to the young people of China and to me personally. For me, that was a very important year. I had grappled with socialist principles in such a way as to make myself a willing convert, and in doing so had developed an understanding of the language and ethics that helped my scientific mind accept that there was a different way of looking at life.

> As thousands of banners fluttered in the early morning breeze, Jieping felt carried along on a magic carpet of hope and optimism. He and Junkai were among the hundreds of thousands who crammed Beijing for Mao's address in Tiananmen Square following the end of the civil war and Chiang Kai-shek's departure for Taiwan.
>
> When Mao spoke the words, "Ours will no longer be a nation subject to insult and humiliation. We have stood up", many present were moved to their very depths. Mao awakened a long-suppressed pride in Jieping, which was to develop its own responsibilities. He felt privileged to know China's past, as well as her present. Those words motivated and prepared the young Chinese to give themselves wholeheartedly to the development of their country. Had they overheard the conversation between Mao Zedong and Zhou Enlai, they might have been forewarned. Mao confided, "What we have inherited is a blanket full of holes." And when Zhou agreed, he recognized that as China's "Housekeeper", Mao charged him with "patching up the holes and one day providing a new blanket".
>
> Many Chinese who were studying overseas were inspired to return, following a call by Zhou Enlai welcoming the intelligentsia, regardless of their political persuasion, to return in October 1949. He told them that the motherland needed their expertise, since China was in almost total disarray following a half-century at war. He contended that with their return, she would recover both heart and soul.

PART TWO

CHAPTER ELEVEN
HOME INTO HOSPITAL

Dr. Wu:

In late 1949, about six months after my return from the US, I attended a symposium on socialist philosophy organized by the Educational Workers Union. It covered the subject of the gradual development of society from slavery to feudalism, from capitalism to communism; and the writings of Mao, *On Practice*[26] and *On Contradiction*, were very influential.

Although I didn't completely understand them at the time, these essays would become the foundation stones on which I would build a modus vivendi that was compatible with my own ideals. Mao's theory was that "knowledge comes from doing the thing rather than reading about it and that one corrects a problem by finding the inherent contradiction, curing the root of the problem and not its symptoms. The principal contradiction in Chinese society is between the proletariat and the bourgeoisie; between the socialist and capitalist roads."

I was aware that Mao claimed to be a peasant with simple tastes, and understood from local gossip – of which Junkai was a great source – that Mao conducted even Cabinet affairs from his bed. When he finally got up and dressed, he preferred his worn old clothes and canvas shoes to formal attire. Of course, this made a positive impression on all of us.

But questions circulated inside the family and among my colleagues: How long would Mao live an imperial life inside Zhongnanhai, protected by armed guards, while claiming to be a peasant? What was the threat

---

[26] Mao Zedong's philosophical work; essays as part of lectures given in 1937 in Yan'an.

that required Wang Dongxing, a Vice Minister of the Ministry of Public Security, to supervise the guards?

We observed that these guards were placed at all the entrance gates to Zhongnanhai and changed frequently. It was also well known that Mao held his meetings and received foreign dignitaries in Longevity Hall, but resided in another building, Chrysanthemum Fragrance Study, separated from Jiang Qing's bedroom by a large dining room. While my brother and I lived in two rooms convenient to PUMC, our homes and hospitals were in the same district as Zhongnanhai and we were curious to know more about our self-proclaimed Red Bandit peasant leader.

> In the secrecy of the new regime, nothing was leaked to the outside world; there were no press conferences and apparently, no accountability.
>
> It was known that Zhou Enlai had honoured Mao by tasting his food in public, before the defeat of the nationalists; and this now continued on a grander scale and extended to all ranking leaders and even distant provincial leaders.
>
> Doctors who visited Mao reported to Jieping and his brothers that they were obliged to check in with Mao's bodyguards and were frequently made to wait for hours before being accompanied to his enormous, airless bedroom where the windows were shuttered so he couldn't tell if it was day or night.
>
> It was rumoured that Mao warned his doctors they could discuss his condition and treatment with him alone; and neither reveal his condition to, nor consult, other doctors.

Dr. Wu:

We learned that when Mao complained about indigestion and was recommended to cut down on pork belly, he declined this advice claiming, "I've eaten it all my life and I'm not stopping now…. It's good peasant food." This was in 1950, when millions of peasants could not afford even a bowl of rice.

While I was still at PUMC, my brother, Wu Ruiping, had donated our house at 13 Dongtangzi Hutong to become Beijing's first private children's hospital. I had mixed feelings about this, while Junkai complained that it was our home full of the children's dreams and childhood memories. But Ruiping persisted and he and Dr. Zhu Futang, Paediatric Department Director at PUMC, ran the little paediatric hospital together, joined by Dr. Deng Jinxian in 1942.

While she was looking for a home to rent, Junkai learned that the Beijing Housing Administration had asked for the full deeds to be handed over to them. I could not show her the sympathy I felt as this last, cosy refuge disappeared. It was no consolation that our bedroom became the main patient's private room. Yet our patriotic spirit was so high that we put the feeling of personal loss aside and only considered how it would help the motherland.

My brother's partner Dr. Deng wanted me to join them, performing circumcisions and other small operations, but I was not prepared to give up the chance of practising at a large hospital for work in a 3-bed private clinic. I willingly gave up my house and piano, but not my opportunities to practise what I had trained for. Besides, circumcision was not a common procedure and even if I were also to perform other small operations for chronic infections, this work could not possibly become my full-time occupation.

I helped with relevant cases, but wanted a broader range of experience and was keen to continue my urological research. My brother and his partners were among the most influential practitioners in Beijing; the three doctors were relatively affluent and Ruiping was able to continue to support me until I found a position at Beijing Medical College.

> Many years later, Jieping was reluctant to admit the reason why he could not find a hospital readily willing to employ him. As the Wenham Scholar of his year, his credentials were very high, following his four years of medical practice before spending a year working under a Nobel laureate. The problem was that nobody would risk having him on their staff, lest he show them up. He was perplexed and had no choice but to take consultancy work, here and there, throughout the city.

Dr. Wu:

Nowadays, endocrine surgery falls under urology. But at that time, there were no specialist endocrine surgeons. That work was handled by general surgeons. At Beijing Medical College a surgeon, whom I had known in Chicago, was furious when I operated on the adrenal gland of one of my patients. "This belongs to General Surgery not to Urology!" he accused. As there was no definite designation, I told him, "If you wish to take care of these patients, do so. I will practise adrenal surgery in the other city hospitals."

The first hospital I consulted at was an ENT hospital. I developed adrenal surgery there because the chief physician had been our Professor of Biochemistry at PUMC and he trusted me. With my help, he became the first doctor to start urological surgery there.

> Some months later, Jieping's reputation as an adrenal surgeon led to an interesting turn of events. The General Surgeon, his former colleague at the University of Chicago now practising at Beijing Medical College, admitted, "I have never actually operated on the adrenal glands." He apologized for his outburst, so Jieping returned to the hospital to take over adrenal surgery there. He later had to operate on his colleague's prostate and, by then, was on very good terms with him. There was no triumph in Jieping's voice as he recounted this.
>
> Luckily, Junkai did not rely solely on her husband for her entertainment; her love of life had not diminished and, as a Shanghainese, she knew how to get around and find pleasure in life. Her dress style had changed, as had her hairstyle, and from time to time she now sported the Sun Yat-sen style suit, baggy pants and matching green jacket with mandarin collar and boyish hairstyle then fashionable in Beijing. On the weekends, she took the children to the bird and snake market, then to enjoy their fill of local dumplings before heading to the jade or pearl market. If Jieping had the day off, the family might go to a movie instead. But he was often busy, trying to find appropriate work in a city that had changed remarkably in the year of his absence.

Dr. Wu:

Neither my brother nor I had enjoyed any "family time" back then. We lived at the hospital and, in keeping with the times, our families lived in small apartments. We considered ourselves fortunate to take a half-day off at weekends to see our families and maybe go to the cinema.

For millennia, China's sages had decreed that manners were the essential ingredient in all human relationships, characterized more by ritual than by genuine courtesy. But with the change to a socialist philosophy came a radical change in traditional manners and rituals. Mao was aware that Confucius had said "A virtuous ruler is like the Pole Star which keeps its place while all other stars do homage to it."

Old Wu confided in his sons that he worried that Mao did not repudiate his personal deification as Zhou did. While Zhou Enlai had publicly tasted Mao's food and drink to be sure it was not poisoned and to give Mao "face", it was a cue to the sycophants among his followers that they should similarly prove their obeisance and homage.

Jieping's father was now a keen mah-jong enthusiast and visited friends to play, hearing rumours that passed for news when there appeared to be none. He revealed, "Ye Zilong, the head of the Office of Confidential Secretaries, has become Mao's chief steward with responsibility for supplying food and has installed a food station at Beihai Park. The food has to pass through two laboratories, one testing the nutritional value and the other testing for poison. Mao makes sure that his food is tasted by others before he touches it and virtually the same tests are conducted throughout the provinces for the provincial leaders. Why is Mao so obsessed?"

Old Wu was discomfited that while Mao insisted that China remodel its feudal heritage and adopt socialist and communist values, some of those around him bowed low as in Imperial times, without being chastised by Mao.

Jieping was disappointed that Mao deliberately set a lower tone that would undermine the status of the intellectual and official. He exercised his theory that more could be achieved "with a fart than a conference", to the discomfort of all but the sycophants. Mao had an affable manner and could disarm his intellectual advisers with witty sarcasm. But privately, he called intellectuals "poisonous weeds". He later admitted, "I told the rightists to criticize us in order to help the Party. I never asked them to oppose the Party... not to make trouble." Jieping was beginning to feel uncomfortable with the contradictions from the Leader.

Dr. Wu:

It was my bad luck that I could not hide the fact that I was the son of a wealthy industrialist, part of the hated bourgeoisie. We heard rumours that Mao allowed himself to be pampered and flattered. Among the dishes brought to the Chairman was the so-called choicest food of the imperial dragon, swallows' flesh. But Mao was superstitious and believed that "He who dined on swallows' flesh never tempted the dragon by riding afterwards in a boat"[27]. He rested in his large bed, frequently receiving guests and advisers while surrounded by his favourite books. When introducing the communist philosophy to the people, Mao had insisted, "The Party committee system is an important Party institution for ensuring collective leadership and preventing any individual from monopolizing the conduct of affairs."

> This confused Jieping's scientifically-trained mind; he was fully aware that research required individual focus and thinking. He now faced daily contradictions and was consulted by the Western-trained medical team in charge of Chairman Mao's well-being. They were challenged by the Traditional Chinese Medicine (TCM) team, which prescribed teas, potions and soups to boost the Chairman's virility. "Dragon blood", rhinoceros' horn and a hundred virgins were among their other recommendations.

Dr. Wu:

If Mao was now the dragon, Jiang Qing was his phoenix empowered by the spirit of creation. She stood firmly by his TCM team, although her daughter Li Na received treatment at the Paediatric Hospital that was my former home.

> The one and only Paediatric Hospital in Beijing was still very much in demand. As a home, it had been comfortable; as a private hospital it was minute. Located on one of the narrow alleys a couple of blocks from PUMC, it had two floors and by the time Jieping and I visited it together in the 1990s, it housed eight families. We came

---

[27] Mao did not wish to fall prey to the dragon, the ruler of the seas who, according to Chinese legends, could smell swallows' flesh and raise a storm to drown the boat.

unannounced, and the National People's Congress chauffeur parked in the street outside a garden gate. Behind the gate was a stucco and wooden European-style house about a hundred years old, slightly tilting on one side, probably from dry rot and neglect. Somebody was repairing a bicycle puncture in the front yard and spare parts littered the entranceway. Jieping's bodyguard explained who the guest was and why we had come. A very obvious change came over the few people present. There were embarrassed apologies for the state of disorder, as though they held themselves responsible and had known that one day, someone would appear who had known the house in different circumstances. The bicycle repairman clearly lived there and asked Jieping which room he wanted to see.

Not to discomfort anyone, Jieping said that his old room was downstairs. When the repairman knocked on the door, it was opened by a diminutive little woman with wispy grey hair and shiny baby gums. Although it was midday, she wore thin cotton pyjamas and we had clearly roused her from her bed. When she heard who her distinguished visitor was, she pressed us to stay awhile and offered cha; but the famous Dr. Wu Jieping said quietly, "We must be going, thank you, thank you", squeezing her arm affectionately as he declined the polite invitation. Jieping was then about the same age as the lady who now occupied his bedroom. He was dressed in a pale green textured linen suit and immaculate white shirt and tie. With his black hair, thick and shiny above his unlined face, he looked young enough to be her son.

As we departed, he commented on how tall the trees had grown in the garden and on the cheaply built porch that now shaded the entrance to the house. In my own mind, I couldn't help comparing the former occupant of that bedroom with the present one and wondered which quirk of fate made their lives so different. I concluded it could only have been their education.

Dr. Wu:

What established my position as a leading urologist in China was my unique specialty in diseases of the kidney. Having had my own kidney removed – and some trouble with the remaining one – I was able to focus my attention in ways that my fellow students could not.

Jieping knew his place in society was established by his fate and the hard work that followed his early brush with death.

One patient referred to Jieping had undergone the same operation as he himself, namely removal of one kidney, but then the patient was diagnosed with TB of the remaining kidney. Jieping decided to remove only part of the adrenal medulla, leaving some of the kidney to function. Luckily for Jieping, his gamble paid off and the patient improved and recovered.

Jieping then concluded that TB of the kidney was curable if it was unilateral. In the 1950s there were many deaths due to TB of the kidney, so Jieping tried to devise a conservative surgical approach. The work was interrupted by the war on the Korean border.

Dr. Wu:

On 25 June, 1950 the Korean War started. On 25 October China went to the rescue of the North Korean forces with a "volunteer" army, as the Americans approached the Yalu River.

Intellectuals, among which were the returned students from American universities, both admired and feared the US. We had coined the term Qing-Mei to describe that special feeling of closeness between America and China. But we worried that the Americans (only a step away over the Yalu River) would use the North Korean base to invade China and support Chiang Kai-shek and restore the nationalist government. On 9 March,1951 the first voluntary medical team left Beijing. The decision to stand against the Americans greatly lifted the spirits of the Chinese people. Nobody would have predicted that the Chinese would stand up to the US. We got weapons for the defence of Korea from the Russians. Stopping the Americans crossing the Yalu River was one of the most courageous decisions my country has ever taken.

Although I felt initial conflict because of my continued admiration for the US, I joined the Voluntary Medical Corps as captain and chief surgeon. My younger brother also volunteered. I had been very impressed by the medical team of the PLA, who, although not remotely as qualified as they should have been, demonstrated a humane ability to relate to the injured soldiers as comrades, creating a rapport that made me question my own approach.

I used to look on the men I treated as "soldiers", but this experience showed me that understanding between all people is possible. I began to re-evaluate my doctor-patient relationship and question whether I was developing the right connection with the sick and wounded I had been treating.

> Over the years, I witnessed Dr. Wu Jieping's extraordinary ability to communicate with patients regardless of age, gender or education. Mindful of a patient's vulnerability, he sometimes sat on the edge of their bed or on a chair beside it. He always looked them in the eye and explained who he was and why he'd been consulted. Then he'd ask, "How are you?" with genuine interest and made sure of the patient's privacy while holding their arm reassuringly. As he conducted the exam, he would speak quietly but audibly so the patient could hear, even if they did not understand completely the language of medicine.
>
> Jieping's elder daughter, Wu Xing, also decided to "volunteer" for Korea. She had just graduated from Middle School when the independence of China was threatened. She was very patriotic and Jieping felt he should support her in joining the movement "to resist America and assist Korea". But her mother was so distraught, she spoke to neither husband nor daughter for a whole day and refused to help Wu Xing with her packing. Wu Xing was planning to attend medical school and postponed her application until her return.
>
> Her father was sympathetic and it was he who in fact helped her collect the necessities and pack them neatly. Wu Xing saw her father as a hero and tried very hard to please him. She did not return for six years, yet her father was not concerned as to her security. Her mother was devastated but could not complain, because Chairman Mao's own son, Anying, had died at the hands of an American gunner, shortly after his arrival at Headquarters, which had been set up in a gold-mining settlement. His body was not flown home and Mao wrote[28],
>
> "In war there must be sacrifice. Without sacrifice there will be no victory. To sacrifice my son, or other people's sons,

---

[28] Chairman Mao's Revolutionary Family. Red Book Publication, Nov. 1950.

is just the same. There are no parents in the world who do not treasure their children, but please do not feel sad on my behalf… There are so many common folk whose children have shed their blood and were sacrificed for the sake of the revolution; they are in need of consolation. We ought to pay more attention to showing them greater concern."

This was no consolation to Junkai and she directed her anger and frustration at Jieping.

I was aware of many contradictions in Jieping and wondered how he could optimistically rationalize so much of what life had thrown at him.

Dr. Wu:

My father supported us, but after my graduation he had lost everything. My brother then assumed that responsibility, which was not a very heavy burden. As the New China era dawned, my father was just a medium-sized capitalist. He still owned the family apartments in Shanghai and, technically, owned the house in Beijing.

Wu Xing came back from volunteering in Korea in 1956 to study medicine, but the entrance exams were very tough. I thought it better if she were to study a subject she was more capable of passing.

> What Jieping didn't say was that he was in a position to pull strings on her behalf, to get her into medical school, but would not do so as a point of honour in the new egalitarian society. Jieping's wife was furious with him and criticized him, saying, "You never lifted a finger to help anyone in your own family", causing her and her family lifelong regret. Wu Xing was told that she was too old and struggled to get into any institute of higher education. She eventually accepted that she should study Russian and became so proficient she interpreted for the Bolshoi Ballet when they visited China as soon as she graduated. Wu Xing married Li Feng, who was also a teacher in the language school and had interpreted for Chairman Mao. After 1960, the end of the Soviet period, she resumed her study of English.

Dr. Wu:

Before Korea I kept all my patients, including members of the family, at arm's length. What I saw of the relationship between the medics and soldiers made me want to join the Chinese Communist Party. The officials who needed to approve my application said I was okay, but they needed to evaluate my "social relationships".

They found that in the 1920s, my brother-in-law, (Gao Chi Chien's father), had been very close to the KMT. He was Personal Secretary to Chiang Kai-shek and Consul General for the nationalist Government in Singapore. His intimate friends actually founded the KMT. But he fell out with Chiang Kai-shek and lived in the US after the Japanese were defeated.

My brother-in-law was a member of the delegation with the Soong clan to attend the Coronation of Queen Elizabeth II[29], headed by Soong Ai-ling's husband, H. H. Kung, who was Minister of Finance. (Soong Ai-ling's dress was said to rival that of the Queen, as it was studded with genuine diamonds and pearls.)

This connection branded me as suspect, so the communists suggested I join the Jiusan Society instead, in 1952 (of which I was made President, in 1994). I became their delegate from Shanghai to the National People's Congress. The Society had the same goals as the Chinese Communist Party and there were no contradictions. Both strove for long-term co-existence, proclaiming, "We will share glory and shame equally."

> It would be some years before Jieping admitted to himself that it was easier to believe this kind of propaganda than challenge it.
>
> From the beginning of the New China era, several so-called democratic parties, like the Jiusan Society, existed alongside the Communist Party, mostly a watered-down version of democracy along communist lines. At the Chinese People's Political Consultative Conference (CPPCC), groups from each party are represented. For example, the Jiusan Society (founded in Chongqing in 1945) had about 185,000 members in 2019. They send delegates biannually to the National People's Congress (NPC), where all policy decisions are presented and discussed. Gone are the 'egalitarian' ways of modest cadres representing their village,

---

[29] On 2 June 1953 at Westminster Abbey, London.

unit or organisation. The members now arrive at Beijing's best government hotels in chauffeur-driven cars, while streets are closed and whole districts blockaded to allow them priority.

In time, Jieping became a Vice Chairman of the NPC and enjoyed both the status and trappings associated with the position. By its very nature, the NPC had become the kind of elitist organization Mao had once despised.

Before Jieping left China in the summer of 1947 to undertake post-doctoral studies in the US, he had grappled with the following question:

Dr. Wu:

I was not sure whether communists were better than nationalists, but I felt they couldn't be any worse. Previously, I had tried to ignore politics and bury myself in medical science. Reluctantly, I realized that this was a luxury I could ill afford. My political education began in earnest in 1954, when China had its border dispute with India and Jawaharlal Nehru, India's first prime minister, visited China. I unexpectedly learned some lessons from Zhou Enlai's handling of the situation.

> Jieping realized that in order to be accepted as a proper socialist, he needed to cultivate the language of propaganda that was relevant to each situation and he tried to understand the Five Principles of Coexistence[30] being talked of everywhere in Beijing. At the Geneva Conference in 1954, Zhou had said that Asian problems had to be settled by Asian countries. He was referring to the colonization of Vietnam, Laos and Cambodia by the French and of India by the British. Because Britain had arbitrarily created borders between India, China and Tibet, there were border conflicts. But Zhou Enlai held out a hand to Nehru, by emphasizing the bigger picture and long-term goals.
>
> I am sure Jieping wondered, later, what happened to the idea of "shelving differences" as real and imagined inequalities wreaked

---

[30] The Five Principles of Peaceful Coexistence were originally conceived by Zhou Enlai and Jawaharlal Nehru, India's first Prime Minister. The Panchsheel Treaty was signed on 29 April 1954. The Principles continue to be cited today, underscoring China's approach on foreign policy.

havoc on the lives of millions of his countrymen. One can sympathize with someone whose family had been steeped in Confucianism for centuries and become enlightened through his medical studies, but who had become disillusioned with the kind of democracy he experienced in America. In the early years following his return, Jieping didn't know where to find a *modus vivendi*.

Dr. Wu:

It was clear, even to me, that without "tactics or flexibility", it would be difficult to carry out the Principles of Coexistence. This later developed into what is now called "working for consensus and shelving differences, which make peaceful co-existence possible".

I didn't know philosophy and had little knowledge or interest in political systems. But, when two district cadre leaders who had fought against the Japanese and the KMT were caught for corruption and sentenced to death, that really influenced me in favour of the communists.

After Liberation, the three partners, Wu Ruiping, Zhu Futang and Deng Jinxian, had decided to hand over their private hospital to the people. On Children's Day 1952, Vice Mayor Wu Han[31] accepted the hospital on behalf of the Government. It was to become the precursor of the Beijing Children's Hospital.

> Jieping later admitted that this had been a far-sighted move on his brother's part, as it saved most members of the family being branded as "filthy capitalists" a decade later.
> Many years later, I asked Jieping, "Did Mao change the material work ethic of the Chinese people?"

Dr. Wu:

Those were transient changes. Chinese society changed tremendously. It could have been different, had Mao and the CCP given more thought and planning to material salaries as well as ideological thought. The Party could have lasted a long, long time. With socialism, people get what they need, people do as much as they can and get what they're worth.

---

[31] Vice Mayor Wu Han was disgraced and hounded out of office for putting on a play about former corrupt leaders, to whom Chairman Mao thought he was being compared.

The CCP said, "With Communism, 'You do what you can and take what you need' ideologically."

> He did not disagree when I commented, "Looking at China now, in a market economy, it seems more like, 'Take what you can get away with.'" Jieping reluctantly admitted that the system was too flawed to be sustainable. His embrace of the egalitarian ideals of socialism and communism soured some of his family relationships.

Dr. Wu:

My son was very bright, from an early age. He was a little spoilt by my father and of course I, too, spoiled him. My father wanted a grandson and adored him. He could repair anything handed to him at the age of only 7 or 8; but during his last year of middle school, he became very interested in a girl. That really distracted his preparation for the university entrance exam. He did not get into Tsinghua University for Engineering so he was recommended to enrol in a "normal" school for teachers; he had very low marks and they had very low requirements.

In the mid-1950s there were strict regulations. If you were accepted at a school, you had to enrol. This of course would affect your future. Junkai was furious and wrote to the government. She was very brave! She wrote, "My son could be a very good engineer if he had the opportunity to study at Beijing's Tsinghua University." This letter would normally have had no consequence, but she also approached the Vice Director of Beijing Medical College where I was working at the time. Our son was granted the favour of taking the entrance exam a year later and was accepted into Tsinghua University. That was very exceptional in those days; I never believed it could happen. He is now a top engineer for the Beijing Municipal Bureau of Engineering and Architecture.

My second daughter, Wu Bing, graduated from the College of Aviation Engineering and has a very successful career. She had an unarranged marriage to a man named Zhou, a metallurgy specialist in titanium and the son of a famous writer. Wu Bing is very happy and is good with people. She became very interested in politics and is now involved in administration.

Jieping's mixed feelings about arranged marriages were evident in some of our conversations.

I asked Jieping who he feels closest to. He replied, "Wu Xing is a very nice daughter, wife and mother."

I am friendly with Wu Xing and she provided me with a Mandarin teacher; and she once confided that her father in fact originally favoured her only brother, Wu Desheng, with whom he lived. But when Jieping married Gao Rui, his third wife, he moved with her to a large apartment. He rarely saw his son subsequently, because Wu Desheng did not get on with Gao Rui.

CHAPTER TWELVE
HAD I EMBRACED SOCIALISM AND COMMUNISM COMPLETELY?

During 1951-52 there had been many attempted reforms in China, particularly Land Reform, as Jieping explained:

Dr. Wu:

Peasants were accustomed to being exploited by landlords and they accepted this as normal. For a generation, Mao's article on *The Importance of Peasants in Hunan*[32] had made a huge impression. Mao wanted to make peasants aware of their birthright. They believed they were enslaved to the land *by right*; it was very difficult to raise their consciousness.

> Mao masqueraded as a peasant, even though he had grown up in a manor house on the family farm. Through this propaganda campaign and his hatred of intellectuals, he became a Chinese version of Robin Hood in the 20th Century. His campaign of land reform and redistribution broke up the estates of the gentry and redistributed their holdings to the peasants.
>
> Several decades later, this act has become a double-edged sword as local governments try to claw back the land for development, causing numerous peasant revolts, annually.

---

[32] One of his most famous and influential essays, the *Report of an Investigation of the Peasant Movement in Hunan* was published by Mao Zedong in March 1927. Also known as *The Hunan Report*, it was written at a critical time in the Chinese revolution.

Jieping kept his head down. He dealt with surgery in the mornings, saw his patients in the afternoon and continued his research in between. In the evenings, he attended self-criticism meetings, also known as 'struggle sessions'. But he felt the sense of unease that pervaded the capital.

Dr. Wu:

Within a few years, communism became firmly established in China, but Mao was disappointed with the growth of the economy and found his central planners too cautious. He decided to unleash the full force of human will to achieve his dream of an economic breakthrough.

Following his visit to the Soviet Union in October 1957, where statesman Nikita Khrushchev had treated him like a raw recruit to the high table of communism, Mao became aware of Khrushchev's ambition to negotiate formal relations with the US while sacrificing anyone who got in the way. Mao determined that China instead would show the world what could be achieved with "spontaneously-generated mass economic productivity" and challenged his people to beat the UK's steel production.

Spurred on by Khrushchev's claim that the Soviet Union would soon produce more steel than the US, Mao released the masses from the constraints imposed by the state and encouraged decentralization. He worked tirelessly with Vice Chairman Liu Shaoqi, announcing "sixty points on methods of work". He dispatched 1.5 million urban workers to rural areas in January 1958, to disseminate his enthusiasm for mass productivity.

Mao's determination went unchallenged by all but his bravest economic planners, who paid dearly for their presumptions. The race to beat the UK's steel production appealed to the entire population, who were instructed to set up furnaces in their yards and compounds and went about stoking the household stoves, with a new pride and determination. Mao did not need to remind them of the results of the Opium Wars.

The officials revered Mao as their saviour and went to absurd lengths to reassure him that his daft plans were illusions with promise. Jieping and his colleagues had the education to realize that his judgment was flawed, but nobody dared speak out and he confined his views to his family. As he said to his brother, "The entire population is subjected to a fantasy by dangerous and foolish leadership; and, added to a natural calamity…. we are courting disaster."

Ruiping had just returned from the countryside and admitted, "The country is in a frenzy… The whole country is building backyard steel furnaces… And what is the Chairman doing? He's dancing. I am embarrassed to tell you because I was invited to one of those dance parties the Chairman enjoys after dinner. His wife, Jiang Qing was not present, nor were his two usual nurses.

Somebody invited several young ladies and one behaved outrageously, arching her back and wriggling in step to the Chairman.

The writhing of their bodies was so embarrassing, I didn't know where to look: and this continued until the early hours of the morning." I thought, 'It's no wonder he can't get up before mid-afternoon.'

> Jieping buried himself in his work, travelling on a motorcycle from one hospital to another; with a lunch break which he used to review his morning's work, as he'd learned in America from Dr. Huggins. These reviews grew increasingly political, because he was obliged to attend 'class struggle' sessions at each hospital and found his work time reduced as a result.

Dr. Wu:

As ninety million men were mobilized as steel smelters, with little raw materials, I sometimes remembered how fortunate I was to have a profession that protected me from this call.

I thought I had embraced socialism and communism completely and joined the masses in praise of this new philosophy; but after many years I secretly agreed with somebody else's assessment that concluded, "The disguised polemics shrouded in symbolism could hardly be understood by the elite who conjured up these terms, let alone the masses." I felt disheartened when I read Mao's words, "China's 600 million people are, first of all, poor and secondly, blank." We were there for him to mould according to his whims.

Jieping did not try to make sense of the pronouncements that were being touted, in the Spartan language of communism, as 'The Great Leap Forward'.

When he moved to Beijing Medical College[33], he consulted and lived there from 1958 to 1973, but was not actually attached to that hospital. Jieping's parents, children and grandchildren had all lived at Jieping and Junkai's apartment, although Jieping slept at the hospital four or five nights each week.

"Home was my refuge; the only place where I felt I could be myself," Jieping told me.

Longing for some peace, Jieping went home one Saturday, but was disappointed when he arrived before Junkai and met his mother looking even more dejected than usual. He recalled their conversation.

"What is it, Mama?" he asked when he saw her face, "Is Baba…?"

"No, it's nothing *really* important, it's just that today the Unit's scrap steel collector came and took away all our metal-ware. So now we have no beds, because they needed the box springs from our bed and yours. We have to sleep on our mats, on the cold floor. And I have nothing to cook in, and not even a basin to wash in. My rice cooker is gone, even the tin teacups!"

"They've taken all non-essential goods from the hospitals too. But never mind, I'll get you some plastic bowls," Jieping reassured her.

"They won't be much good for cooking rice!"

"Mama, you won't need to lift a finger to cook ever again! We'll all be eating in the communal kitchen; we must do what we can to support our Chairman."

"I tried to stop them taking the children's tricycles," his mother said, "but they asked me if I wanted to be the one exception in Beijing who thought children's pleasure more important than the Chairman's wishes. I had to let them go, as well."

In the apartment, he comforted his grandchildren on their sacrifice as they listened to music blaring from loudspeakers:

---

[33] It had been the German Hospital in the Qing dynasty. It was demolished and the site now houses an apartment building.

Long Live the Great Leap Forward! Everybody Make Steel.

He helped his parents and grandchildren go down several flights of stairs, to the massive makeshift canteen that had been erected in the open courtyard of the apartment block. His mother looked around at the large cauldrons of rice, meat, fried bread and vegetables and said, "I can see now why people won't need their cooking implements anymore."

After a hearty dinner, the children started crying again as they would normally have been tearing around the compound on their bicycles following supper. "This will be a challenge to their imaginations. It won't do them any real harm," Jieping said, as he comforted Wu Xing when she arrived with her little girl.

Jieping was accustomed to travelling from his Unit near PUMC to the other hospitals on his most prized possession, a Royal Enfield motor-cycle, which he had bought with his first year's pay cheque. He was dusting it one evening, on the bicycle rack of the new Soviet-style apartment complex where they now lived, when he was approached by several colleagues.

One asked, "Why is your motorbike more important than your mother's wok?"

Jieping had a retort on his smiling face, until he heard another say, "We've given up everything, all our pots and pans to be melted down. Is it that you don't want China to beat England's steel production?"

An ambulance driver added, "We've come to help you. This reflects badly on our Unit, you going off on your steel motorbike when the rest of China is sacrificing every piece of steel they own."

"I need my motorbike to check on my patients and on the building schedule of the new hospital," Jieping said.

As his colleagues pulled the wheels off the motorbike, one of them said, "This is for your own good, Comrade Wu, and the good of *our* Unit. We'll just take the steel parts. Here, you can keep the tyres." As he said this, he wrenched the steel from the wheels and handed the rubber tyres to Jieping.

Years later, Jieping confided that he had taken the tyres, cleaned the dust off and held them to his heart, as one might hold a child or a favourite pet. Jieping had watched, unable to stop the tears welling in his eyes from streaming down his face, as the group bore away his pride and joy, gleaming and sparkling in the twilight glow.

Jieping put on a brave face when he recounted this event several decades later, but it still rankled with him.

Dr. Wu:

I used to get some relief from the gloom when I heard the Royal Enfield engine purring and then, with the wind in my hair, I was free for a few minutes every day and immune from the insanity around me.

> Jieping did not blame his comrades for destroying his Royal Enfield. The gesture was symptomatic of what was wrecking the economy, collectivization. He was developing strong doubts about collective thinking and reports of a failing economy were rife.

Dr. Wu:

Mao discredited negative reports. The weather was ideal in the summer of 1958 and we all believed the miracle of communism was just around the corner. Heaven was pleased and sent the highest yields and best crops of grain under the sun, yet the towns were seriously short of food.

> The honeymoon was over. An old school friend wrote:
>
> "Every able-bodied man and boy was seconded to steel production, with the result that women were left to harvest and could not because they did not have their menfolk's strength. They watched helplessly as most of what they had sown began to rot on their stalks. It was a bitter pill to swallow when they were celebrated for 'holding up half the sky'.
> "The officials had inflated the anticipated harvest figures to ingratiate themselves with the Chairman and then taxed the peasants accordingly. The only way to pay the taxes was with grain and produce and now the peasants had little, or nothing, with which to feed their villages."

Food had seemed abundant when the communal kitchens started, and the peasants gloried in their full bellies and in the absurd propaganda they imbibed alongside. For example, the friend wrote, "Provincial leaders would pile a ton of rice on a lane beside a rice paddy and claim that one mou (1/16 of a hectare) could yield ten thousand Jin of rice, enough to feed an army."

The fiction that Mao chose to believe worried some scientists and advisors, but Mao told them, "China has always suffered from natural disasters and subsequent famines."

The Great Leap Forward had been launched with the hope of galvanizing human life and the economy alike, "by eroding all distinctions of age, occupation, gender and skills". Together with his comment that "Women hold up half the sky", it allowed the Chairman to exploit the female population and get them out of the factories, homes and offices where conditions were considerably less harsh.

In a stirring campaign that excited and motivated the entire population, co-operatives were merged into immense communes managed by Party bosses. The peasants were told to put commune production ahead of private production and they would all be fed, in exchange. The local Party groups were given enormous local autonomy.

Exaggerated claims of record-breaking gains in agricultural and manufacturing production were announced and made headlines. Mao rode the tiger and scoffed at his Premier, "You said this was adventurism… You called it haste… But so was the Long March, so was our War of Liberation… Our motto should be, To Dare."

When the quotas were not reached, local leaders confiscated the peasants' grain, protecting themselves and those in their favour. The resulting famine coincided with the repayment of debts to Russia in grain. In Mao's Great Leap Forward, at least thirty million Chinese died of starvation.

Dr. Wu:

By 1959 China was on the verge of economic disaster. Yet the tenth anniversary of New China was fast approaching and the Chairman had commissioned the construction of ten monumental building concepts.

HAD I EMBRACED SOCIALISM AND COMMUNISM COMPLETELY?

This involved the formerly-reviled labour corvée[34] dressed in revolutionary fervour. The Great Hall of the People, housing huge reception rooms representing each province, and the Museum of Revolutionary History were constructed on the sides of the hugely expanded Tiananmen Square.

We had a really bad famine entirely as a result of wrong ideological leadership. People were out of their minds. Those people were the officials who slavishly followed Mao's directives and hid the consequences from the leadership. Mao eventually recognized the problem in 1960 and the hardship was corrected.

> Jieping was not joking when he made this comment, but the irony was not lost on me. That so-called *'hardship'* was a catastrophic famine, causing the needless deaths of millions. Although Jieping could not openly admit it, the communist propaganda meant that he deluded himself, as did much of the population. In his attempt to set the record straight, he still white-washed the facts with his use of the language, that certain misdeeds had been "corrected".

> State leaders went to the countryside to see for themselves. Chen Yun, who had been with Mao since Yan'an and foremost in responsibility, went to his own village near Shanghai, to find out the truth about the communes. He had been Vice Chair of the Eighth Central Committee and a member of the Standing Committee. His report, (for which Mao never forgave him) was followed by recommendations to the state leaders:

> "The thirty million peasants who had drifted into the cities since 1957 should be relocated back to their families in the countryside, and unemployed urban youths should be sent to work there as well."

> Following a provincial tour and unwelcome home truths from some courageous observers, Mao made a self-criticism in front of seven thousand people in Beijing. He then ran for cover, as had become his pattern, and handed the mess over to the economic planners, Liu Shaoqi and Deng Xiaoping, with the hope that they could engineer economic recovery.

---

[34] Unpaid, forced labour.

Dr. Wu:

In the aftermath, Mao was discredited and retired from the scene. The central planners, meanwhile, still had to come up with a programme for economic recovery and the restoration of national morale. The principle of the communes would remain, but six per cent of the land was to be restored to the peasants as private plots. The closure of twenty-five thousand enterprises saved the salaries of millions of unproductive city workers. Working in small communes of twenty to thirty households, with realistic quotas locally produced, the peasants were to be given the economic incentive of producing for the open market on their own plots.

> Several years earlier, in 1954, Junkai unluckily developed an overactive thyroid, Graves' Disease. It was difficult to operate on her and her surgeon suggested, "Why not take a break from your strenuous work?" It was not the time to ask for favours and their neighbours and colleagues chided them about Junkai returning to work. Jieping thought the budgeting pressures in the department affected Junkai personally. She was painfully aware of the national economic decline.
>
> China was cut off from the outside world, trying to find a socialist path and any citizen who did not toe the party line risked their life. To his great relief, Jieping told me, "I finally joined the Chinese Communist Party in 1956." Clearly it offered some psychological protection and Jieping felt better armed against criticism and those who were simply jealous of his success.
>
> But the mantle of protection that this provided him was ephemeral. One could be criticized for the smallest act of kindness and for lifting a finger to give another an advantage. Jieping was aware of the penalties of helping any member of his family:

Dr. Wu:

I found a way to help my wife by getting her a job in the Records room of PUMC. Because she was a little abrasive, I had to find a position that had minimal interpersonal contact. She did quite well and worked there until 1962. At that time, I was sent to treat President Sukarno in Indonesia, and while I was away, Junkai had a mild stroke. She had had high blood pressure, but the stroke was bad luck because she was rather young, only forty-six. Premier Zhou Enlai did not reveal this to me during my five-month trip. I only learned of her condition when I was leaving Indonesia, via a letter sent to the Embassy.

When I discussed this later with my wife, she accused me of waiting until all the Government business was taken care of before I opened the letter. After the stroke, she could still walk and I did my best to take her out to the cinema and accompany her on her early morning walks. But, regretfully, the next stroke paralyzed her.

My wife always grumbled that I took no care of the children – which was true. She also told me, bitterly, "You cried when Premier Zhou Enlai passed away, but never shed a single tear when my mother died, and even stopped people consoling me, telling them, 'She'll be all right.'"

You see, I am not very sentimental. When you cry, it costs you more sentiment.

> I was sorry to hear Jieping pride himself on being unsentimental, but I learned over the years that this was more his wish than reality. In the terrible Tiananmen Square incident in 1989, he cried, because he felt he had failed the students by not going there in person to reason with them.
>
> He told me his wife used to say, "You don't have to say anything. You have ten black marks," referring to girls he liked – he always told his wife everything. I thought, "Jieping, you didn't need to burden your wife with these unnecessary confessions."
>
> Jieping had found it difficult to be close to his wife. He was not very "sentimental" with her, but he never had any love affairs. And although it was an arranged marriage, it lasted over forty-five years, until Junkai died in 1979.

* * *

> Jieping rarely held grudges against other doctors and by the time we met in 1979, he was well versed in the art of concealing his expertise in order to avoid the cult of individualism; and almost as adept in concealing his contempt for dishonourable colleagues, and sycophants, alike.

Dr. Wu:

In 1957 I was invited to visit Georgia, the home state of Stalin, as part of a medical team. We were received by Premier Zhou Enlai. The leader of our three-man team was a Dr. Wong, who had operated on Zhou's arm years earlier in Chongqing in 1943. This man was a PUMC graduate who had moved from general surgery to urology. Later on, he was made Chief Surgeon of Beijing Hospital; he was a good man, but he was very conservative in the operations and not very good. He always invited me to "assist" him. He had been Zhou Enlai's surgeon for many years before Zhou received the delegation in the Soviet Union.

One of the operations Dr. Wong had performed on Zhou Enlai involved scrotal pathology, which he hadn't done well. When the disease recurred, Wong asked me to help, and that was the first time I was involved in a surgical procedure on the Premier. I subsequently became leader of Zhou Enlai's medical team.

In those days, technology was such that one could not be sure when there were cancer cells, but there appeared to be some evidence with Zhou that they existed. We had to report the diagnosis to the Central Committee of the Chinese Communist Party and seek permission to tell the patient and to prescribe the necessary drugs.

I went to see him, and Zhou said, quite calmly, "I accept your diagnosis and recommended treatment, but it must fit my work schedule."

Following the cystoscope investigation, we were able to confirm that he had carcinoma of the bladder. At the time, cancer of the urinary tract didn't seem as bad as other cancers, like cancer of the lung or kidney. I was able to say that it could be cured even if it metastasized. But there was also the possibility it could spread, to the point where it could not be cured. The lining of Zhou's bladder seemed to have cancer in a couple of places that might suggest a recurrence, but could also be a new cancer, because we found a carcinogenic substance in the urine.

In April 1955, Dr. Wong had operated on Zhou Enlai for appendicitis, just before the Bandung Conference[35] in Indonesia (following independence from the Dutch in 1949). It was a minor operation, but

---

[35] Indonesia was one of five key sponsors, mutually frustrated by the failure of Western governments to consult them on decisions affecting Asia. The Bandung Conference, held on 18-24 April 1955, was the first large-scale conference held to promote Afro-Asian economic and cultural co-operation. The Conference embraced twenty-nine countries, representing a combined population of 1.5 billion.

in those days one was hospitalized for a week and in this case, Zhou was travelling to the Bandung Conference within 6 days of surgery. That was the time Zhou escaped death, when the Taiwanese planted a bomb on the plane he was supposed to travel on. We felt that the appendicitis might have saved his life, because he missed the flight and all aboard were killed when the plane blew up in mid-air. The flight was to go from Beijing to Hong Kong to Bandung, Indonesia. Although I am not religious, I thought at the time, sometimes the dice roll that way for a reason.

> From then on, Dr. Wong asked Jieping to consult on many other patients in whom Zhou had an interest, until it was commonplace for Jieping to attend most of his consultations. It is unclear whether Zhou instructed Dr. Wong to seek Jieping's advice, or if it was Dr. Wong's initiative.
> These personal physicians had a difficult job; they were comparatively young, were not well trained and did not have the opportunity to improve themselves. They had no scientific or medical journals. Their responsibility was limited to the care of their charges and if they needed any help, their mission was to know where to find the right consultants to help them.
> At the Zhongnanhai clinic, the central government clinic, Jieping gradually became the consultant for the many people in whom Zhou was interested.
> Given his former mistrust of the Japanese, Jieping was obliged to consider the future relationships between China and Japan when he was made Secretary General of the first delegation of the Chinese Medical Association to visit Japan in 1957, at a time when the PRC did not have diplomatic relations with Japan. Those relations were not re-established until September 1972.

Dr. Wu:

The chief of the delegation was a very well-known Chinese doctor called Ke Ling, who had been director of the hospital in Macao. Because of his dapper appearance and his two cars, he was regarded as a bourgeois by many; but in fact, he was an old member of the CCP and well known to Zhou Enlai. He was later made Dean of Chung Shan University (now Sun Yat-sen University) in Guangzhou.

In the 1950s, Jieping was inundated with requests to prepare reports for the Ministry of Health for many of the delegations going abroad. He smiled as he told me this, saying he was unsure whether this administrative work had been authorized by a friend, or an enemy.

CHAPTER THIRTEEN
"MY GENITALS ARE SMALLER"

The shortage of scientists was a serious impediment to China's growth. There were barely five million "knowledge bearers" (university graduates) among a half billion Chinese and of these, fewer than one hundred thousand were doctors or scientists. The systematic self-criticism sessions were beginning to erode the confidence of the staunchest idealists.

Chairman Mao was intent on constant revolution, but the intelligentsia were benumbed by interrogations conducted in public by their academic inferiors and a subsequent loss of face left many disillusioned and depressed. The purported rationale of revolution was "to liberate productive forces, transform China from a medieval agricultural society to a modern, industrialized country, to raise the living standards and the cultural standards". But Jieping felt that for that revolution to succeed, China needed an educated, scientific base.

In the class struggle of the times, the educated were condemned to anything from ostracism by the communist workers, to imprisonment and death. Zhou Enlai had to steer his boat carefully in these troubled waters and announced, "Mental labour and manual labour are both necessary; by deploying mental labour, our intellectuals are part of the working class."

To be fair to both camps, and not knowing precisely what Chairman Mao had in mind, Zhou suggested a campaign for free discussion both inside and outside the Communist Party, hoping the intellectuals would approve and join the regime. Mao gave a long speech to the Central Committee on "The Correct Handling of Differences." Zhou Enlai approved the title of a campaign inspired by an old Chinese saying, suggested by the poet, Guo Moruo, "Let a hundred flowers bloom and a hundred schools of thought contend." Everyone was invited to write or voice their differences.

Nobody had any idea of the trap the Chairman was setting.

Dr. Wu:

The Hundred Flowers Movement seemed to herald an intellectual renaissance and there was widespread hope among intellectuals and students. But the secrecy among the leadership did not permit the underlying discord to be viewed or corrected rationally. Mao took his time and the campaign was only announced in February 1957.

Nobody was prepared for the barrage of criticism heaped on the Party, including one headline:

MAO ZEDONG, ZHOU ENLAI, IT'S TIME FOR YOU TO STEP DOWN.

On 14 January 1956, Zhou Enlai was giving a talk in the Central Government for the benefit of intellectuals. As the intellectuals as a class had been vilified and tarnished with the same brush as capitalists, Jieping thought it represented a change of heart in the communist leadership.

Dr. Wu:

The subject was the Communist Party View on Intellectuals. His talk lasted seven hours. I was very impressed with Zhou's energy. After four hours there was a break and I was amazed to see that Zhou did not leave the podium. He ate two bananas and then talked for another three hours. What impressed me most was the power Zhou believed intellectuals had in changing ideology in three main ways: first, involvement in social events; second, increasing general understanding through their own specialties; and third, their learning the theory of how to acquire knowledge.

Jieping's relief at the changed status of intellectuals was short lived. One evening his father mentioned, "This time the Chairman didn't give any warning of reprisals when he invited 'different thoughts to contend'. I think it's a trap, something has to be done." But before anything could be done, "a well-orchestrated counter-attack against the so-called Rightists" started and lasted from March to July 1957. As Chairman Mao had supported Zhou's initiative in allowing and even inviting criticism, Jieping felt let down by Zhou's judgement.

Newspapers, magazines and individuals became immersed in a movement of self-criticism that was to last for a long time. But Mao was not satisfied. He wrote his rationale in the Literary Gazette, then explained openly that the real purpose of launching the Hundred Flowers Movement was "to let the evil spirits and demons of all kinds 'contend freely' and let the poisonous weeds gain a luxuriant growth, so that the people will be startled at such things in the world and will take action to wipe out these low scamps." The tirade continued, "We told the enemy beforehand: demons can be wiped out only when they are let out of the cage and poisonous weeds can be got rid of only when they come out of the soil. Do peasants not weed several times a year?"

Four generations of the family had got together to celebrate Old Wu's 80th birthday with a Sunday banquet, when Jieping commented, "Don't you think Mao is a genius? He's written this very witty rationale in the papers, it's simply brilliant and very, very funny!" Jieping laughed, but his father replied sternly, "Anyone else writing a diatribe like that would be locked up. The man's gone mad." Junkai and their children gaped in surprise at the two who rarely differed.

In the days and weeks that followed, people stayed at home as fear of reprisals brought Beijing to a virtual standstill. As weeks turned into months, the Anti-rightist Campaign was transformed into a national reign of terror, together with a Rectification Campaign. When the criticism reached his own home, Old Wu was reported by a former employee for exploiting his workers. He was paraded around the neighbourhood with a tall, white paper dunce's cap and criticized for his bourgeois values of "national salvation through industry". This referred to a paper that Old Wu had written years earlier and which was now being used to strike him down.

Jieping was sick at heart. His father was depicted as a capitalist traitor and had no means of defending himself. He was humiliated and his children were invited to criticize him. "I can't think of anything bad to say about him," Junkai told her husband and mother-in-law. "You'd better think of something. We all have to," came her husband's reply.

When evening came and Old Wu was still being *struggled against*, Junkai got onto the podium and, pointing a finger, shouted, "You chose me as your daughter-in-law. You believed that higher education made men superior, yet you never educated me or your daughters. So, you didn't learn what our Chairman knows, that women hold up half the sky." When Jieping was asked what contribution he could make to his revered father's rectification, he felt sure his father would understand the bitter pill. Jieping told the Unit team where they lived that "He took jobs from the masses by inventing things like this automatic ink-stone". Jieping demonstrated painstakingly what everyone knew: how to grind the ink-stone by hand and mix it until the right consistency and colour was obtained. He then showed his father's battery-operated model, which instantly produced the right colour and consistency. This was immediately commandeered by the chief critic.

The Unit leader said, "Not only is he not satisfied with the educational choices we made for his grandchildren, he's started tutoring them himself, so that they'll be qualified for the same elitist lifestyle we all know he enjoyed in Tianjin and Shanghai."

Old Wu was beaten by his neighbours, as well as by people he didn't even know. He told his children, "You were right to criticize me, I deserved more, and I'm sure you won't make the same mistakes as I have."

For a few weeks he said he could hear a buzzing in his ears, but soon he was almost completely deaf.

Dr. Wu:

Father withdrew into himself more and more and lost interest in his grandchildren's homework. Mama worried that his spirit was broken and that he'd never return to the sparkling companion he'd been before. She, too, became quiet and withdrawn.

> Mao resorted to an age-old political trick and succeeded in distracting attention from his failed economic planning, by launching a reign of terror on his critics.

Dr. Wu:

Early in 1958, when I returned to Beijing from treating a foreign dignitary with a colleague, we found the streets of the capital full of colour, awash with red banners floating in the breeze. I had a sense of joy as I drove through them, until the driver explained, "You can't see the characters fluttering in the breeze." The characters read, "Long Live Chairman Mao, Long Live the Great Leap Forward."

> In the mid-1950s, in what Jieping felt was a spirit of openness and modernity, he agreed to help a group of graduates who had been told by a publishing house that it would not consider publishing any work on sexuality unless Jieping edited it. As most of the contents had to come from foreign publications, Jieping understood how helpful it would be for these students' advanced degrees to have the texts properly translated and edited. Because of his early contributions to both a psychological and physical understanding of sexuality, Jieping regarded his participation as a social responsibility and moral obligation.

Dr. Wu:

When writing a book, it is important to know who the intended readership is. If a book dealing with sensitive issues gets into the hands of people for whom it is not intended, there could be appalling consequences. In the case of a book on sexuality, I felt that if, for example, it got into the hands of delinquent adolescents who then committed sexual crimes, they could cite their reading of such a book as part of their defence.

Reading such a book could lead to sexual arousal and, as we learn by imitation, the risks were substantial.

The task of translating was beset with problems. A foreign publication might have chapters under various headings: married couples, cohabiting couples, sex partners, and so on. But in China, this was illegal. Under the heading 'Sexual Intercourse', the variety of positions the students wanted to include was disturbing; in China, even in the mid-1980s, not many people had experience or knowledge of oral or anal sex.

> Jieping was worried: on the one hand he did not want to be overly conservative and on the other, he did not want to go beyond the bounds of acceptable behaviour. This guardianship of sexual morality was a burden Jieping willingly shouldered because of China's entrenched view of sexuality as something dirty, complicated and immoral.

Dr. Wu:

My desire to enlighten my fellow human beings always had to be balanced by a recognition of the superstition and ignorance underlying sexual mores in China, and a regard for social order in the presentation of the material.

Zhou Enlai recognized the importance of sexual education. The State leaders had a tradition of addressing graduating students in the People's Congress Hall before they embarked on their careers, in an effort to prepare them for the real world. One year, Zhou gave the address and told the audience that he had been very fortunate because at Nankai Middle School, he had had a European teacher who explained adolescent changes.

> Zhou asked Jieping to take responsibility for introducing physiology and hygiene to the curriculum for students aged ten to eighteen. He also arranged for the publication of books to help teachers to interest the students in these important subjects. He then assigned Jieping the responsibility of finding out the results of this teaching over two years in the Beijing municipality.

Dr. Wu:

I had a meeting with the Director of the Bureau of Education and a number of teachers, male and female, to discuss the subject. It emerged that they had been using a depleted text of the book I had edited, from which the diagrams had been torn out. Realizing Zhou Enlai would want to know why, I questioned the teachers on this. They said that some boys had shown the diagrams to the girls with suggestions that made them uncomfortable, so they thought it better to remove the diagrams. When I reported back to the Premier, Zhou said, "Everything has two sides: for the majority it will be good, you must believe in the majority." Zhou advised, "If any of our senior leaders feel insecure about their sexual performance, you must be prepared to reassure them and extract agreement from the rest of the medical team." I did not try to guess which leaders he could be referring to. Patients with urological problems also talked of sexual dysfunction. I gradually realized that it was not enough to explain things just to the man – his wife should accompany him as well.

A complaint of sexual dysfunction was entirely different from complaints of other diseases. A lot of the symptoms were psychological. Some of my patients were very senior leaders. For example, a man would declare that he was impotent. I would ask what he meant and would rarely get a clear answer. Occasionally it would be, "I have premature ejaculations." Then I would ask what he meant by "premature" – how long should it last not to be "premature"? Other times, a patient would say his genitals were under-developed. When I asked one very important patient, a senior communist leader, how he knew, he replied, "I saw other men bathing." (The majority of people in China would not have baths or showers at home, so public baths were the norm.)

So, I had to ask, "What is the natural size?"

The response was, "My genitals are smaller."

I used a little psychology and told him not to judge by looking down at himself: "Next time you compare, you should look in a full-length mirror so that your judgment is based on the same visual perspective."

This was a very sensitive moment, as the patient was usually surrounded by a number of other people. He instantly responded, "I have nobody of a similar build to compare my problem with; but you are almost the same build. Why don't we compare sizes?"

Jieping felt obliged to comply. The leader's response was not consoling. He laughed, telling Jieping, "We both have the same problem. Your teapot is as shrunken as mine!"

Jieping had operated on one of the attendant medics in the group as a young boy, and had circumcised him; and when this leader pointed to him and observed his bulbous protrusion, he commented, "You see, his teapot is much bigger than mine." Jieping replied, "That's because he's much younger and has been circumcised."

The young medic asked later, "Dr. Wu, why did you tell the Chairman that I'd been circumcised?"

"Because it would reassure him, and it is true. Don't tell me you didn't know – you're almost forty years old."

"Nobody ever told me, and I assumed everyone was like me."

"You can't have studied your anatomy very thoroughly or examined the cadavers in the lab," Jieping admonished him. "The other student dentists or doctors never mentioned it and you assumed you were like everyone else. You must pay more attention to detail. As I've been your doctor and you've been in perfect health, there was no need to discuss this. Don't you recall my treating you in hospital?"

"Vaguely. I think I had my tonsils out at the same time and that hurt a lot more."

Jieping had brought a book along to show the patient what a normal "teapot" looked like and now had to educate a brilliant young medical doctor, who had been formally educated, as well.

CHAPTER FOURTEEN
CONFUCIAN SOLIDARITY

Dr. Wu:

"Comrade Wu, why are you late?" Wang Dongxing barked at me when I arrived one morning at Zhongnanhai to discuss the Chairman's health. Premier Zhou Enlai had asked me, a couple of days earlier, to join the discussion group to ponder some issues with the Chairman's urogenital system. I was mortified to keep him and other leaders waiting.

"My motorbike was taken away from me, to be melted at our local backyard steel furnace and the buses are so overcrowded I could not get on one for over an hour. This morning I had three operations scheduled at two different hospitals and then cycled sixteen kilometres to get here. I'm very sorry, Comrade Wang, and apologize to all you comrades."

"I thought you were able to carpool with the other doctors in your Unit."

"Today there were ten doctors and only one car. A few of us waited at the bus stop for the driver to return, but when he did not, I took the bus. I am deeply embarrassed to keep you waiting."

We were informed that Chairman Mao was resting in the Chrysanthemum Fragrance Study next door. I was aware from earlier examinations that the Chairman had not bathed since arriving at Zhongnanhai. He swam in the sea and China's rivers a few times a year and found it invigorating. "Taking a bath is a waste of time," he used to say, and preferred his attendants, male or female, to rub him down with a hot towel as he read. I suggested that the Chairman might have a simple infection that could be treated with hot water and salt. But his physician, Dr. Li, responded, "His white blood cell count continues to rise, despite several days on antibiotics."

"May we see the patient?"

Several hours later, Dr. Li said I alone might accompany him to see Chairman Mao. He was sitting in a corner of his massive bed with books and newspapers littering the quilt. He was dressed in a cotton robe.

Opening my medical bag, I covered the Chairman's body in a clean white towel and proceeded with my examination.

"Dr. Li," I said, "have you been able to examine Chairman's urine and semen?" He had not.

Then, Dr. Li obtained the necessary excretions and I produced receptacles and slides and prepared samples for the laboratory. I was aware that there were those around the Chairman who recommended ancient treatments. I had been consulted by his medical team before. No matter how professional and dispassionate one is, how does one look the leader of China in the eye while conducting such a personal examination?

The Chairman broke the ice, laughing gruffly, "I don't have a problem becoming aroused, it's just painful achieving a full teapot, if you know what I mean."

"We will get to the bottom of the problem, rest assured and while we await the results of the tests, may I suggest immersing your body in a hot bath, Japanese style?'

We had to report back to the other members of the team that the Chairman was unwilling to take this advice, and one of the leaders present suggested, "One hundred virgins maintained the vigour of our Emperors for two thousand years. We must at least make some available to our Chairman." Another suggested, "Crushed rhino horn brewed with tree mushrooms and herbs were also used and have been sent by the Party leaders of Anhui province."

"I think we should await the results of the doctor's lab tests,' said Premier Zhou Enlai as we trudged out, exhausted, in the darkened early evening.

Wang Dongxing had arranged a car to take some of us to PUMC, where the tests could be conducted and where we would be able to use the doctor's dorm to get some rest. I felt weak from hunger and exhaustion.

I heard that the Chairman had been recommended Taoist and Tantric Buddhist exercises. The gossip among his medical experts was that in his bid for immortality he was attempting to practise Yin Yang exercises. I personally knew little about these matters, but thought I'd better become more informed. I read that the male should become aroused and not reach climax, but maintain the aroused state, regardless of his partner's level of arousal. It seemed an exhausting and pointless exercise, to me.

When Chairman Mao asked for my expert opinion, it was both an honour and a cause of anxiety. I was soon again consulted about sexual dysfunction on his behalf, and wondered why Mao was so preoccupied with this when we all knew that his wife, Jiang Qing lived at Diaoyutai, a compound of numerous mansions, several kilometres from her husband. But then I had also seen the beauties from the railroad carriages and nurses who massaged him. He was often surrounded by a bevy of personal assistants, most of whom were pretty young women.

* * *

The Great Leap Forward was a psychological, economic and human disaster wrought by one man's ignorance. Of course, Mao blamed the disaster on natural causes and on the anti-revolutionaries. He accused everyone and required the highest leaders to supply self-criticism. Even Premier Zhou Enlai was ordered to write a self-criticism; he almost had a nervous breakdown from the critics attacking him and undermining the causes he championed, calling them 'elitist' or 'capitalist'.

I noticed a surprising change in Jiang Qing, Mao's wife, around this time. Gone was the lethargic frailty, she was suddenly a lady with a mission. Mao had problems and she swept into office as his defender against all her old enemies – Zhou Enlai and his wife, Deng Yingchao, and Vice-Premier Li Fuchun and his wife, Cai Chang. She was ably assisted in this by her mentor, Lin Biao, PLA Commander-in-Chief and a Vice Premier.

> On 2 August, 1959, at the Eighth Plenum of the Eighth Central Committee, Mao was on the attack: "Some people want to attack the general line, to destroy the [Chinese Communist] Party. Right opportunists are launching a furious attack on the Party, on the leadership of the Party..."
>
> The reports Mao himself had commissioned were blamed for blowing the hardships out of all proportion. He now saw the private report by Defence Minister, Peng Dehuai, (which he had personally commissioned) as part of a pre-planned conspiracy and believed the conspirators were plotting to demolish the Party.

The Party secretaries explained that they were just the emissaries and blamed the advisers who gave them the misleading information about record productivity. All were sworn to secrecy and ordered not to divulge, or even discuss among themselves, the extraordinary political happenings that they witnessed.

Mao wrote, "Peng Dehuai and his supporters do not have the ideological preparation necessary… for socialist revolution." Peng and Li Rui[36], one of Mao's latest political secretaries, were classified as belonging to the anti-party group. Even Zhou Enlai turned against both of them, saying, "You have no right to speak."

Jieping explained, "Sometimes Zhou used the tactic of agreeing with the accusers in order to classify those accusations as less important than the good the accused had done.

I accepted Jieping's justification for Zhou's behaviour, as not even *his* position was secure at the time. Peng was removed as Secretary of Defence and Lin Biao promoted to his position.

Mao's waning self-esteem was now publicly supported by his wife, Jiang Qing – Limpid Stream – and the de facto Head of the PLA, the new Minister of Defence, Lin Biao. Lin used a collection of quotes from Mao to strengthen his image with the PLA.

Within a short time, millions of soldiers had memorized the contents of what became known as Mao's Little Red Book. Lin's prestige was greatly enhanced when scientists, working in a crash programme under PLA supervision, successfully built and tested China's own atomic bomb on 16 October, 1964.

As Jieping recounted this moment decades later, this unsentimental man had tears in his eyes.

Dr. Wu:

We cried with joy at this sign of China's resurgence and, in spite of all the mistakes the government leaders were making, I felt we were back at high table.

---

[36] Li Rui was an early recruit to the CCP, and one of the youngest ministers in the government. Mao was so impressed with his talents that he asked him to become his secretary. But Li was a truth-teller who would not dissemble in a meeting about the Great Leap Forward. For this "suicidal defiance" he was purged and almost starved to death. Rehabilitated after the death of Mao, he continued to be the "conscience of the CCP."

Jiang Qing, barred from the political arena at the time of her marriage, had bided her time and waited until Lin asked her to lead the cultural assessment and policies of the PLA.

Jiang was a beautiful divorcee who tried her hand at a number of jobs before settling on an acting career. She eschewed traditional roles in favour of a career as a revolutionary model. In Yan'an she researched and taught revolutionary theatre and performance. She had performed the role of Nora in *A Doll's House* in Shandong and arrived in Yan'an in 1937, where she gave the performance of a lifetime and captivated Mao Zedong. By 1938, Mao was in love with her. He divorced his wife (who had given birth on The Long March) and married Limpid Stream.

Mao's colleagues and advisers had insisted that Mao have his new bride swear not to become involved in politics. She was regarded by the old guard, and their wives, as a kind of she-fox. "When friends called on her in Yan'an, she proudly produced their new baby daughter, Li Na and seemed a sweet natured young lady," I was told by persons who met her at the time.

In the intervening years, Jiang Qing outmanoeuvred her critics and now embarked on the defining role of her life. She wished to emulate the success of the Tang dynasty Empress Wu Ze Tian, who as concubine, supplanted the Emperor to rule in his place for over twenty years. The Tang dynasty was a time of great prosperity and cultural growth, but China's male historians represented the Empress Wu as a witch incarnate.

Dr. Wu:

By the end of 1959, it was that clear the Beijing Medical School would revert to the Ministry; but before that happened, the municipality wanted to start its own medical school. I initiated the opening of that school in March 1960. My mission was to have the school up and running by the autumn, with our own building, faculty and syllabus in place. It was done.

Both the original Beijing Medical School and Beijing Second Medical School were under the control of the municipality, rather than the Ministry of Health. Our architects had already given me blueprints for another building planned on that site – so we took that as the first building block. We took one wing of the original building, about 2,500 square metres.

It was incredibly difficult. I tried to gather directors of affiliated hospitals to discuss the curriculum we should follow. I had the impossible task of finding building materials; the economy was in ruins and the factories were not producing construction supplies. All the steel was poor quality, so we went searching around the old wall of the city, and along the canal. There was a bridge, but it was not strong enough to carry the twenty-five-ton machine hauling cement. I was desperate and suggested to the man operating the machine to lay down steel plates to spread the weight over the entire surface. Because production had gone from private to state ownership, we had to apply to different government departments for the building materials, only to find at times that glass or nails were no longer being manufactured in the Units where they'd been purchased before. The construction industry was totally chaotic. But we managed somehow.

1960 was a bad year for China, because the Soviet Union withdrew its remaining advisers and specialists and demanded payment in grain for its heavy steel plants. In certain areas, we had become dependent on their expertise.

That year, when famine was killing millions, our students all helped out, including overseas Chinese from Indonesia. The students had to work harder, but they were ready for the entrance exam. We worked on everything, including manual labour, and all ate together, albeit rather sparsely. I had to fight for more nutritious food, as the students only got two eggs a week as their protein intake.

We started with thirty faculty members and three professors whom I selected. I gathered some lecturers and assistant professors from my old college, PUMC. I decided to send those faculty members to the different teaching hospitals I hoped to affiliate with. I told them the usual way was to select teachers in the pre-clinical departments – to educate and graduate as medical doctors. I sent them to check the clinical laboratories in those hospitals, to find out precisely what was going on in those laboratories; their work had to be very connected with the work being done there.

> Jieping took it upon himself to manage the hospitals and establish their specialties. He did not realize that he was also helping to construct a refuge where China's troubled leaders could nurse their political wounds.

CHAPTER FIFTEEN
HEROES AND HISTORY

In an effort to calm down and encourage the academics and university elite, Zhou Enlai invited them to discuss socialist principles. Jieping was troubled by this talk and wondered what he could do to improve himself.

Dr. Wu:

I thought of the old members of the Party I had admired so much at the beginning of the New China era; their devotion and responsibility were an example apart and made people think twice. An old Chinese proverb troubled me: "A hero is formed by his times." "Do heroes create history?" I asked myself, "Or does history create heroes?"

Certainly, history allows some men to rise up. But in my case, my particular speciality did not seem to have that effect. I could see that others, like my patient Marshal Chen Yi (Foreign Minister), did effect change through their work; but I did not.

> I observed the conflict in Jieping years later, when he clearly wished he had fulfilled some of his heroic ambitions. He was not at all satisfied with his level of achievement, or perhaps it was a higher level of recognition he felt he should have earned.
>
> By 1960, Jieping had frequent contact with Zhou Enlai. Their meetings invariably took place in the late evenings around 11 p.m., or even at midnight.

Dr. Wu:

Zhou would have the Political Bureau Conference and then receive foreign delegates up to 11 p.m., and only then did he have time to tackle problems like the health of the leading Party members. He would ask the other doctors and myself to report late at night. He took meticulous care, receiving the written reports, checking them and providing pertinent comments. He was reputed to sleep just three or four hours at night, only to be awoken by his fears for China. We would try to help him relax, often taking a stroll to distract him from national affairs.

Zhou was underweight and I often advised him, "You need several more hours of regular sleep," but he would cut me off with, "It isn't necessary to eat or sleep regularly – regularity ossifies the mind."

On one of our evening walks, I mentioned the talk he had given in 1956 on intellectuals and society, and how encouraging I had found it. But I told him I still could not see how ideology would change with my specialty.

"Oh, is that right? What are you doing right now in your specialty?" I told him about my study of TB and family planning. Zhou laughed and told me, "You have got it [a way of effecting change] but are not conscious of it. Why do you study these two subjects?"

"Because TB is a common problem. Some patients are doomed to die, so I am seeing what I can do to help them. And the rapid increase in population is a serious problem in our country, so I'm trying to contribute to finding a solution with my research."

Zhou responded, "That means that you are taking the practical problems of the nation as the objective of your research, instead of doing something just to show that you are capable of carrying out the research." I felt enlightened by Zhou's interpretation.

> While we all like a pat on the back, and Jieping was more sensitive than most, I found it interesting that this mature and, by now, celebrated doctor needed to be comforted and reassured that he was on the right track towards becoming an ideal communist.
>
> Zhou consulted Jieping regularly, on a broad range of health-related subjects. On one occasion when a young woman had sustained first degree burns in a heroic effort to save a factory and her colleagues from an explosion, Zhou raised the subject of her

long-term treatment in a way that really impressed Jieping with his thoughtfulness and attention to detail. He recognized that the girl would be unable to perspire in the summer heat, such was the severity of her burns, and he wanted an air-conditioned chamber, with a back-up generator, devised, where the young woman could live when her hospitalization came to an end.

Jieping kept faith with the basic principles of Communism for seventeen years, despite the doubts gnawing at his soul.

When I mentioned to Jieping that his attitude seemed contrary to much of the teaching at that time curtailing individualism, he was genuinely perplexed and said, "You can only serve the masses by *collective* individual perfectionism."

Then it was my turn to be perplexed and he tried to explain: "You cannot impose on others and you cannot allow emotions to affect your decisions." He felt that among the leadership, only Zhou Enlai exemplified this. Zhou had told Jieping, "You should know your feelings before acting on them."

Years earlier, Zhou Enlai had handed the leadership to Mao partly because Mao was well read in guerrilla tactics, which he displayed time and again on the Long March. *The Art of War* was his bible throughout and because he lacked bombast and understood the common peasant with whom he could chat and joke, he convinced Zhou, and most of those surrounding him, of his superior leadership capabilities at that time.

Jieping gradually realized, "The problem was that Mao rarely travelled abroad. He thought he knew everything and unfortunately, he did not."

Many years later, I asked Jieping how Mao Zedong could have made such mistakes.

Dr. Wu:

After 1960, things went wrong because of his age – a little sclerosis here and there – and Mao had become too powerful. We used to say, "Mao Zedong is against Mao Zedong Thought." Class struggle became central to his thinking, his old bête noir, the struggle between bourgeois and intellectual, between peasant and knowledge-bearer. He took class struggle as the main ideology of Chinese priorities to be corrected.

By the early 1960's, China had completely withdrawn and isolated its population behind a 'bamboo curtain' and Jieping felt more isolated than most. He had patients who needed a kidney transplant if they were to survive, but he could not consult anyone, even though he knew that kidney transplants were being successfully conducted in Boston. He longed to contact his American colleagues. But communication with the outside world would be regarded as treason.

Dr. Wu:

So, I experimented on dogs and eventually performed two human transplants successfully, but the rejection process could not be well monitored. The problem was how to procure healthy donor kidneys. My team was aware that we needed the consent of the donor or their family, but sometimes a spouse would refuse, saying, "What if my family needs a lung and you give it away to a stranger?"

So, we tried recent cadavers; to that end it would have been best to use kidneys from patients who were brain dead. But in China, brain death was not a legally recognized concept. An article on brain death was written and discussed, but I convinced the Editors not to publish it[37]. The lack of transplant organs was partially compensated for by the many executions: however, families would distance themselves from the disgraced criminal and their story and so did not freely give consent to the use of their organs.

> It seems callous to Western ears, but one feature of Chinese justice is that traditionally, all the immediate family members would be punished for the misdeed or crime of the accused and in China, a family would be tainted by the execution of one of its members.

---

[37] While some Chinese still believe that the body must be buried with all organs intact, they are now obliged to cremate the last mortal remains because there is no room for cemeteries to hold coffins, thus facilitating an acceptance of brain death and organ donation.

Dr. Wu:

In one case, we procured two kidneys from men who were due to be executed. The organs were in the warm ischaemic period, but we did not have the necessary immune-suppressive drug – Imuran manufactured by the Wellcome Laboratories – to prevent rejection. The operative process went well, but we could not succeed without adequate supporting drugs.

> While Jieping grappled with the means to transplant organs successfully, some of his patients dwelt on the turmoil in the leadership, and, as a leading doctor, Jieping could not avoid being roped into political arguments.
>
> Differences between the leaders on a range of issues, from China's relationship with the Soviet Union to involvement in Vietnam and its relationship with the US, were labelled "revisionist thinking" by Mao. He felt there was, "a need to change the way the Chinese think," just as there was a need to come up with a Chinese brand of communism.
>
> What China needed was a total change of outlook, to be achieved by a conscious, disciplined effort of will. A "cultural revolution", it was felt, would rid China of its own feudal thinking and of pernicious Western influence in its literature and values. Mao idealistically hoped to achieve a co-operative commonwealth, devoid of self-interest. He was not leading by example as Gandhi (1869-1948) had done, but seemed to think he could dictate this unrealistic way of life and challenged his team to support his vision.
>
> Reminding them of the record of achievements during the Han, Song and Ming dynasties, Mao asked whether they could doubt his and their capacity to make their utopian dream a reality, now that they were one nation in control of China's destiny. Whenever he felt his audience was in doubt about a new proposal, he always reminded them that they were finally one, a united China for which he, Mao, took sole responsibility. He reminded them, "After chaos comes order."

CHAPTER SIXTEEN

"DON'T LET VICTORY INTOXICATE YOU"

At the Tenth Plenary Session in 1962, there were many remarks to the effect that a new order was needed. What Mao said in essence was, "What we are familiar with is now over, we need to learn new ways."

Class struggle was always touted by Mao as a priority. He had decided, from his observations on Russia's handling of the uprisings in Poland and Hungary, that constant revolution was the only way to control the intellectuals: namely setting the masses against the elite.

Jiang Qing had been diagnosed with cervical cancer and was sent to the USSR for treatment. Fortunately, she was dispatched to the leaders' hospital and did not suffer the indignity of the common Russian. But she berated the Russian doctors as much as the Chinese. When one junior doctor answered her bell in the middle of the night when she claimed she was having a heart attack, he took her pulse and placed his hand on her heart. She barked, "Are you trying to pull teeth from the dragon's mouth?"

When she returned to Beijing, her entourage grew to include a team of nurses, a dentist, psychiatrist, immunologist, dancing master and piano teacher. She found her husband at war with himself and with the Central Committee. He moved from Zhongnanhai into the Great Hall of the People and Jiang Qing learned that his extra-large bed was shared with several young women.

When Vice Chairman Liu Shaoqi took responsibility for the economic disasters, instead of being grateful Mao decided it was a subterfuge and claimed Liu "only takes responsibility for the disasters in order to reassert his position at the centre, not because he believes he has done anything wrong".

While Premier Zhou tried to bolster the flagging self-esteem of the intellectuals who were forced to attend so many political meetings that they had to work through the night to make up time, he called another meeting to discuss "The Question of Intellectuals". Jieping was greatly relieved that Zhou felt empowered enough to argue that "to destroy superstition does not mean to destroy science". But Mao continued to despise the intellectuals, remarking, "They work in offices, eat well, dress well; they don't walk much."

Mao now wanted the nation's administrators, students and faculty, everyone, to spend five months doing manual labour in the countryside or factories. Without consulting Chairman Mao, Liu Shaoqi issued decrees for rehabilitating those purged during the Peng Dehuai debacle. Mao accused him of setting up an "independent kingdom".

It was bad enough that Liu had successfully dragged the economy from the brink of disaster, but he now took the Chairman at his word and got on with the job, rarely consulting him. There were still queues to buy the limited amount of fresh produce on the market, but there was no famine at this time. With Liu and Deng Xiaoping virtually in charge of the economy, Mao was at liberty and travelled constantly. He made the leaders come to wherever he and his hundred-man Praetorian Guard decided to show up. In September 1962, he told the Tenth Plenum, "The battle between the proletariat and the bourgeoisie will be protracted and sometimes severe. The country is facing the threat of capitalist restoration that must be fought through relentless class struggle."

Jiang Qing was mollified that a photograph of her as Mao's wife had finally been published by the *People's Daily*. It indicated her importance. But her composure didn't last long when she saw the photo of Liu Shaoqi[38,] in his ceremonial position as

---

[38] For fifteen years, President Liu was the third most powerful man in China, behind only Chairman Mao Zedong and Premier Zhou Enlai. In the photograph, Wang Guangmei wore the traditional Chinese qipao, in white silk, with a white handbag, shoes and pearls. In the other photograph, Jiang Qing wore a baggy Mao suit.

President of the PRC and accompanied by his wife, the tall and striking Wang Guangmei, receiving Mrs. Sukarno, wife of the first President of Indonesia.

Jiang Qing now acted as virtual publicist for her husband and her appearance changed considerably. There was no sign of the old ailments; she walked with her head held high and her nurse said it seemed to be a total recovery from neurasthenia. Lin Biao needed her "expertise" regarding improving the "ideology of the armed forces supported by literature and art". She travelled to Shanghai, where she co-opted the services of well-regarded publishers and editors.

Mao joined Jiang Qing in Shanghai, where he agreed with his wife's findings that "Academic and educational circles are dominated by bourgeois intellectuals". They were finally singing from the same hymn book when they named the worst perpetrators: the historian and Vice Mayor of Beijing Wu Han, the writer Liao Mosha, Vice President of Peking University Jian Bozan and the journalist Deng Tuo. They were accused of being "Chinese Communist Party members in appearance, but KMT members in thought and deed." Mao proposed a "Cultural Revolution in literature, history, law and economics".

Mao had learned expert political tactics from the leader of the KMT, Chiang Kai-shek: When your leadership is in doubt, take to the hills. On 16 May, 1966 the Circular of the Central Committee of the CCP clarified that the Cultural Revolution was Chairman Mao's "vigorous attack on bourgeois elements". Shortly after its publication, Chairman Mao retreated once more. In time he attributed the failure of the Great Leap Forward to a combination of "natural disaster, economic pressure from the Soviet Union and wrong work style of provincial functionaries". These same functionaries advocated "eating bitterness meals in dark halls" to distract the population from disappointment and frustration.

Posters bearing four-inch high characters announced:

A CULTURAL REVOLUTION TO STRUGGLE AGAINST COUNTER-REVOLUTIONARY TENDENCIES AND TO END EXPLOITATION AND OPPRESSION, SO THAT SUPERSTITIONS AND DELUSIONS WOULD BE REMOVED

It was intimated that this revolution would be characterized by ink, whereas others were wrought by blood. The big-character posters indicated a respect for one of China's most revered traditions, its literary heritage. But despite this reference, additional posters soon indicated that those very leaders of China's institutions were "capitalist roaders" – representatives of the capitalist class within the Communist Party – and "counter-revolutionaries". The writer spoke with a forked tongue. The infighting started in earnest and Jieping ran to his lab for cover, but even there he was not immune. It seemed Mao had complete control of the media.

Jieping was certain that knives were being sharpened and could only see Mao's support of this.

Somehow, under the guidance of Liu Shaoqi and Deng Xiaoping, by 1965 production levels had almost returned to levels of 1957, before the Great Leap Forward campaign; and a feeling of general prosperity and tranquillity ensued in the cities.

Jieping had a car authorized for his use and Junkai was relatively content because she was growing herbs in pots on her balcony, where she and other women also managed to keep some chickens.

Dr. Wu:

One late summer evening in 1964, my wife and I accepted an invitation from Cheng Zhing Qing, the female director of Beijing's ballet school, to attend the first public post-war ballet performance, The Red Detachment of Women. We were seated in the same row as Madame Cheng and, just before the performance started, somebody came from behind and climbed over the back of a seat, not wanting to disturb the other attendees. It was Zhou Enlai. My wife looked over at him and whispered, "I think life is returning to normal."

Little did she know.

* * *

The first graduating students of the Second Medical School and I had a spiritual understanding. In 1966, as the Cultural Revolution started, they were about to graduate. A few years earlier, in 1962, I had gone to treat President Sukarno and was decorated by the Indonesian Government for my help. The students had seen pictures of this and felt I brought respect and honour to China. It was in the papers, prized by the Party and Congress. I brought back two big stuffed tiger specimens that were a personal gift to me and I presented them to the college.

I had been in Guangzhou for a consultation with an old Party leader in March and when I returned to Beijing, my family warned that the city was full of rumours about a special movement ahead. But before I could find out what it was all about, I was sent to Shanxi and in May, I returned to Beijing and the Medical School.

At a self-criticism meeting one evening, a Party member had said, "Our Chairman believes contradiction is a permanent state. Disequilibrium is what we must always aim for. China needs a total change of outlook."

I contented myself with Zhou Enlai's interpretation that the aim of revolution was to change man himself. I felt this spiritual exercise could be achieved, with guidance, through a conscious effort of will.

The first day of the Cultural Revolution was 1 June, 1966. "Work teams" comprised of Party members had been sent to the universities and academies to dig out "revisionists" among the senior personnel, and stir unrest. I was back in the Medical School when the students announced "something critical" was coming. But I felt that the students and I had complete solidarity, which was in fact really based on my family's teaching.

But by 9 June, I realized I was wrong; what was being promoted was exactly what should not be done at this time. In this Cultural Revolution, students were exhorted to find the shortcomings and mistakes of those working with them. We were at Beijing Second Medical School. Less than a year earlier in October, seven months after we started working on that piece of open land, the school had opened in our own building, with our own faculty and our own short syllabus.

> How could the students find fault with Jieping and his hand-selected staff? He had overseen the construction and, when they were not finished to his satisfaction, had even helped build some parts of the

college with these very students. He had fought for better food rations for them, arguing successfully that young students could not survive on a diet that included protein only twice a week.

Dr. Wu:

The students circled the higher administrators of the college. They challenged the Dean, the Director of the Teaching Bureau, the President, but not me. So, I went right into the group and told them, "This is my responsibility. Don't blame others." After they'd interrogated the higher administrators for two hours, I succeeded in dispersing them in fifteen minutes. I did this successfully for the first few days. Anywhere I saw a group, I'd walk into it and have all their criticisms directed at me, because I was responsible for the College – that's what I mean by "solidarity".

But then after a few days, posters appeared against me as well:

WU IS TRYING TO DESTROY THE SPIRIT OF THE CULTURAL REVOLUTION

I explained to Gau Rui, my third wife, 'They were right! But they didn't realize how I was trying to obstruct them.'

Actually, from that first night of the Cultural Revolution, I did something subversive. That evening, students with loudspeakers called a mass meeting of students and faculty. They announced that a demonstration had started in Peking University, in the west of the city, and had moved to Tsinghua also in the west. Our college was located in Fengtai, in the south-west of Beijing, 25-30 km away. Our students wanted to go to the universities in the west, so I told them, "I support you. But it is so far away I will organize buses for you." Why? Prior to 1 June we already knew students were being deliberately provoked and the responsibility of school leaders should have been to stop their participation in the street demonstrations. So, by arranging buses, there would be no demonstrations in the streets.

> Thirty years later, Jieping laughed at having outmanoeuvred his students. "You think that to follow tradition should be right, but it turned out to be wrong."
>
> Jieping was not aware of the wrangling going on behind the scenes, nor did he have the time or interest in finding out.

Now Mao's name was used by his supporters and his detractors to score points, always using flattering language to honour his name and confuse the issues; on one occasion a paper accused Peng Zhen[39], a leading Party member, of spreading rumours that 'Comrade Mao supported postponement of the Cultural Revolution for two months, opposing proletarian thought, a shield for the reactionary bourgeoisie against Mao Zedong Thought."

The infighting was exhausting for Jieping and his circle. They knew not what to expect from the barrage of posters that appeared daily:

EVERYONE IS EQUAL BEFORE THE TRUTH, NEGATING THE CLASS NATURE OF TRUTH.

THEY ARE A BUNCH OF COUNTER-REVOLUTIONARIES....

THEIR STRUGGLE AGAINST US IS ONE OF LIFE OR DEATH.

The intellectuals whom Zhou had once pulled to the heart of the Party were living in the most dangerous times. Those who had Western connections, or had been influenced by the West, or studied there, were especially at risk. This obviously included Jieping, his brothers and most of his colleagues and, more pointedly, Zhou Enlai and Deng Xiaoping.

At the start of the Cultural Revolution, Mao claimed, "A thousand people will die this time"; and while still in Shaoshan, he had written and warned his wife in Beijing, "Don't let victory intoxicate you." So pleased was Limpid Stream with this seal of legitimacy that she had it printed and distributed for other members of the Committee, warning them not to gloat. Her title was, First Director of the Cultural Revolution.

Following four months of self-enforced exile from the capital, Mao had his famous swim in the Yangtze before heroically sweeping back to Beijing. It soon became apparent that the chaos he had

---

[39] Having led guerrilla activities behind Japanese lines, Peng Zhen was made Mayor of Beijing. But during the Cultural Revolution, he was accused of plotting to discredit Mao by supporting his vice mayor, Wu Han (see footnote 28). Peng Zhen was purged for his defence of Wu Han. He was rehabilitated in 1978. He died in 1997.

unleashed was a guise to trap his enemies: the same ones who had rescued China from his earlier whims.

By 18 July, Mao was back in Beijing denouncing Liu Shaoqi's "work teams" and the "fifty days of hell" they had caused at the universities. He was aware that a sixteen-point programme for the Cultural Revolution was being negotiated and that a "black gang" was trying to subvert the programme.

Dr. Wu:

I was made aware that Zhou had fought to include language in the programme that would "wrap a mantle of safety around his scientists": those involved in atomic and biogenetic research. I was greatly relieved to learn, from my younger brother, of a clause written by Mao that said, "Struggle must be conducted by reason, not by force."

> On 1 August, Mao wrote to a student at Tsinghua University's Middle School encouraging him to start a rebel organization. Soon, Red Guard rebels could be found in every school. It was their responsibility to chastise their teachers, elders and administrators, to lambast those who taught or even mentioned the classics. They were also encouraged to correct their parents and report their misdeeds to the Red Guard leaders. It seemed unthinkable, but Jieping's grandchildren confirmed that they, too, had been co-opted into a rebel group and no longer attended classes.
>
> The Cultural Revolution started a war of words between supporters of the intelligentsia and the workers. There were posters reviling aspects that Jieping was unaware of. They were full of contradictions. He read in *Xinhua News*, "The authors of *The Outline for the Cultural Revolution* praise academic authority and try to boost their own prestige… They hate and repress the militant new-born forces of the proletariat in academic circles."
>
> Living and trying to make sense of the contradictory arguments, Jieping could only guide his grandchildren away from pursuing an academic education. "It's much safer to be an ordinary worker right now," he told them. At that time, he realized he had to think as an individual if he was to survive in a collective society.

The *Outline* under discussion amounted to "prohibiting the proletariat from making any revolution". It was said to "openly resist the policy explicitly put forward by Chairman Mao of protecting and supporting the left… and building up their ranks. They are filled with hatred of the proletariat and love of the bourgeoisie. Such is the bourgeois concept of brotherhood by the authors of the *Outline* with prudence, caution, approval of leading bodies. All this serves to place restrictions on the proletariat… in order to tie their hands…"

It was clear to many that Chairman Mao was using the Cultural Revolution to get rid of most of his supporters, who had made him Chairman, so that no glory could reflect on them. He wished to be identified as the sole saviour of the PRC. In the final creation of this image, he was willing to destroy the people who had supported him, as well as their records.

Lin Biao, the Vice Chairman of the Party, ably assisted by Jiang Qing, were Mao's willing henchmen and set about destroying the reputations of those entrusted with the task of developing the Chinese economy. It is testament to their success that both Liu Shaoqi and Deng Xiaoping were now dispensable as "capitalist roaders". They had twice been the architects of economic recovery from Mao's disastrous programmes.

"In order to protect us scientists, artists and writers," Jieping said, "Zhou had to sacrifice the Ministries of Culture, Propaganda and Education. "What are doctors now?' he asked himself, 'Members of the proletariat as Zhou Enlai has suggested, or of the bourgeoisie as our inferiors suggest? How can we escape? We are obvious targets." He shivered, recognizing their impending danger.

That summer, fifteen million Red Guards travelled to the capital free of charge and joined Chairman Mao in denouncing their teachers, parents and elders. Within weeks, the smouldering embers of resentment and jealousy exploded into violent tumult. Homes were ransacked, treasures smashed, books burned as the youth of China rampaged out of control. Whether this was a reaction against controlled communist ideology and secrecy, or blind obedience to Mao's objectives, the ignorant youth gleefully took it upon themselves to destroy the old.

Dr. Wu:

Zhou Enlai, my most vulnerable patient, tried to talk and reason with the young visitors. They shouted and harangued him for twenty-two hours, until he lost his voice and succumbed to a heart attack in November. By January 1967, more than forty million workers were on a rampage; the country was spiralling into chaos.

I was aware of the power struggles between Jiang Qing and Lin Biao on the one hand, and Zhou Enlai and Foreign Minister Chen Yi on the other. And I was also Chen Yi's physician.

Zhou Enlai confided that he had seen a poster outside Zhongnanhai that read,

BURY ZHOU ENLAI ALIVE!

I was at my wits' end to be a calm and reassuring presence in a climate of constant psychological torture. The power struggle became public when the Red Guards mounted a criticism campaign against Chen Yi. Unable to destroy Zhou directly, Jiang Qing attempted to destroy those closest to him.

The Red Guards set up loudspeakers outside the western gate of Zhongnanhai, where both Chen Yi and Zhou had their offices, and shouted, **"DRAG OUT CHEN YI!"**

It was a terrifying time, although I didn't have all the sufferings that others had. My suffering was of a different order, more of a psychological type. I was able to start many operations in those years. So, for me and some of my patients, the Cultural Revolution had its bright side.

In the earliest days of the Cultural Revolution, students criticized their professors; and among the fifty-plus directors of colleges in Beijing, I was the only one not forced by Red Guards to bow down before them and my students.

> Thirty years later, I naively asked, "Do you now understand what was happening then?" Jieping replied quietly, "It was a divisive time – a time to split everything. It was a horrible time." Jieping raised his voice uncharacteristically loudly: "It was ALL STARTED BY CHAIRMAN MAO! He was fed up with all the historical experiences and was very familiar with history from the Warring States period to later dynasties; he had lost faith

in his supporters who were too terrified to level with him and tell him the facts."

Among the patients referred to Jieping by Premier Zhou Enlai during the Cultural Revolution was Pu Yi, the last Emperor. Pu Yi was being treated by Jieping for renal carcinoma.

Dr. Wu:

I was very impressed by him; someone who didn't know how to tie his shoelaces, or do up his buttons, learned to become a normal citizen. I'm afraid he learned a considerable amount about "normality" from the Governor of his first prison after he was returned by the Russians. It is said that when he left the Forbidden City, aged eighteen, he was very responsible and made sure that the eunuchs had their little boxes that showed they qualified for the position.

> The eunuch's little boxes contained their scrotums and penises without which they could not be buried. It was believed that without their complete body parts, they would be condemned to wander as ghosts in the nether world.
>
> Pu Yi became a gardener in the botanical gardens in Beijing and married a nurse. His medical condition interested Jieping, for he had a rare case of bilateral carcinoma of the kidney. Having directed the removal of one kidney, Jieping used various innovations that he had developed in an attempt to prolong Pu Yi's life. "I succeeded in keeping him alive for many years," he told me, "but he finally succumbed to the disease."
>
> Zhou also assigned some of the most vulnerable targets of the Red Guards to Hospital 301, the military hospital, where the medical staff co-operated by finding medical conditions warranting an extended stay. It required some diligence on the part of the 'Group in Charge of the Cultural Revolution' to track them down.
>
> Zhou Enlai convinced Mao that the economy was in such dire straits that he would have to change tactics and appeal to the nation. Instead, Mao called in the Army to restore order. Zhou warned, "If the economy is allowed to deteriorate further, the very foundation for promoting revolution will be destroyed."

Dr. Wu:

When the initial frenzy of the Cultural Revolution had died down, I discussed with the military medical authorities what we needed for successful transplants. I started peritoneal dialysis and haemodialysis, but we didn't have the right tubes. We used American bio-plasma tubes, but clots formed in the peritoneal cavity. We needed heparin to reduce clots and freshly prepared fluids. But a pharmacy would need at least twenty-four hours to prepare this, time we could not afford; and in the case of peritoneal dialysis, the patient could die while the solution was being prepared.

> On one occasion, Jieping had successfully treated a "class enemy" with the result that he was criticized for a "bourgeois way of research". Giving organs to save a life was decried as elitist.
> Little did anyone know, or care, about the lengths that Jieping went to in order to prolong the life of a patient or devise a way of making him more comfortable.
> Jieping's findings in contralateral nephrosis saved thousands of lives in the PRC. His findings were published in Russia, but because China was closed to the West, they were not disseminated in the UK or the US.

Dr. Wu:

In the mid-1960s, I took on a technical assistant and taught him filing, and how to use index cards, and my female research assistant also helped train him. That was a time when you could be criticized by anyone and instead of mounting a defence, the person being criticized had to make a further self-criticism. When the Cultural Revolution started, he criticized me for "experimenting" on human beings.

I was already at the Second Medical College at the time, so he and a young doctor came there to criticize and report on me. When their case did not hold up, they took their revenge in another way – the medical records on the two pioneering transplants disappeared from the Records Room.

But the Red Guards were not against me. If I had not had such a special position at the Second Medical College, the Red Guards could have beaten me to death. Nobody was safe.

Nobody in China was immune to the vengeance unleashed during the Cultural Revolution. Zhou Enlai's wife, Deng Yingchao, had had two miscarriages in the early years of their marriage. Thereafter, the couple became the surrogate and adoptive parents of a large number of children who had been orphaned; some were the children of friends.

One such daughter was jailed, with her husband, for failing to criticize Foreign Minister Chen Yi, for whom she had worked as a Russian translator. Unable to find out where their adoptive daughter was incarcerated, Zhou was only informed of her fate after she died. When he asked for an inquest, he received a notification: "Dealt with as counter-revolutionary. Cremated. Ashes not kept." Her biological mother had been an actress in Shanghai with Jiang Qing in the 1930s. While Jieping did not accuse Jiang Qing directly, the implication was obvious.

Dr. Wu:

Many intellectuals – and some of my colleagues – took their own lives, which led to the launch of another big character poster campaign:

MEMBERS OF THE COMMUNIST PARTY

ARE NOT ALLOWED TO COMMIT SUICIDE

That would deny the committee in charge of the Great Proletarian Cultural Revolution the right to hound them to death. Mao wrote his own big character posters, one of which read:

BOMBARD THE HEADQUARTERS

DESTROY THE DICTATORSHIP OF THE BOURGEOISIE

You see, in order to survive, I tried to remember and practise my mother's words, "When you yourself are right, nobody and nothing can hurt you." That saved me during the Cultural Revolution. My family did not suffer the way many millions did. We can't prohibit people from making mistakes; we must permit them to correct their mistakes.

This explains why Jieping did not "lift a finger" to help his children or grandchildren, as his wife had accused him.

Jieping's father was criticized by one of his former employees and while he defended everything he ever did, he died following his interrogation in 1966 and left a parting message to his family: "Believing that the body after death is unconscious, I request that you honour my Will of eighteen years ago. Please send me to the crematorium within eight hours of my death. A sad atmosphere may last that day only. I have had joy and love in the life shared with you all."

Following that advice, every family member who subsequently died was cremated, no ashes retained.

Once again, Jieping did not attribute his father's death to the treatment he received during the Cultural Revolution:

Dr. Wu:

Everyone was at risk of reprisal during the Cultural Revolution, and Mao's old colleague, Foreign Minister Marshal Chen Yi, was attacked for challenging the Red Guards for their excessive abuses.

We were kept awake, night after night, by the blaring loudspeakers and chanting Red Guards outside the Foreign Ministry. They only desisted when the ailing Premier Zhou Enlai intervened at the entrance to the Foreign Ministry and shouted to the throng of rebels, "You will have to walk over my dead body to get Marshal Chen Yi!"

Millions were exiled to hard labour in distant provinces, or beaten to death, or starved, in jails closer to home. Many preferred to take their own lives rather than succumb to the humiliation of dying at the hands of the merciless Red Guards.

Mao's posters exhorted the nation:

WAGE CIVIL WAR!

and

OVERTHROW EVERYTHING!

CHAPTER SEVENTEEN
"WHO WILL SAVE THE CUBS?"

Dr. Wu:

In 1967, a special group of radicals was charged with responsibility for collecting evidence against Zhou Enlai. They were known as The May 16th Group. They reproduced a KMT fabrication that identified Zhou by his pseudonym and charged him with trying to replace the Chairman. Mao ignored that fabricated letter, warning them, "That has been dealt with before." But they were out to destroy him and produced large character posters with unmistakable criticisms:

WHAT CLASS DOES ZHOU REPRESENT?

BURN ZHOU'S RIGHT-WING OPPORTUNISM AT THE STAKE

As this was a "class struggle", Zhou had to answer. Nine classes had been identified as counter-revolutionary and Zhou could have qualified for at least three. But he and Deng Yingchao stuck to their position that it was not birth, but attitude and experience that counted. The ninth class referred to bourgeois intellectuals, which Jiang Qing, as eloquent as her husband, referred to as the "Stinking Ninth".

By mid-July 1967, several provincial factions were involved in armed skirmishes, often resulting in fatalities. The leaders now worried there could be a number of uprisings. One faction required the PLA to intervene and restore order. It was soon reported that, "After a failed attempt by

Zhou Enlai to resolve the crisis, it took a show of military force by other PLA units for Chen Zaidao to eventually surrender."

> Chen Zaidao, the Commander of the Wuhan military region, had attempted to control the worst excesses of the Red Guards. He was instructed by Mao to admit 'the mistakes of orientation and line.' This he refused to do. In July 1966, he was summoned to Beijing by Jiang Qing and Lin Biao, to answer charges of being a counter-revolutionary. He was alerted by the Garrison Commander, General Fu Chongbi and escaped the mob circling the building only by hiding in a lift suspended between two floors. He was accused of having staged a counter-revolutionary movement and was dismissed. Mao later referred to him as a 'comrade'.

Dr. Wu:

This reference to a failure by Zhou Enlai was a rare opportunity on the part of Jiang Qing and Lin Biao to undermine the authority and prestige of Zhou Enlai, while claiming credit for their own organization.

Radical Red Guards and radical intellectuals would never see eye-to-eye and undermined the re-establishment of order. The Red Guards correctly charged that the principles of the Cultural Revolution had been abandoned; the sense of betrayal they expressed echoed many of the ideals once espoused by radical intellectuals. An especially-audacious group in Mao's home province, Hunan, charged that "Although the Cultural Revolution had purged officials, the bureaucratic and military machine remain and will continue to perpetuate the privileged system that has always repressed the masses." They even hinted that the Cultural Revolution should attack the military establishment. Above all, they wished to protect and maintain their utopian, anti-bureaucratic vision. Apart from Zhou Enlai, they singled out Hua Guofeng[40] from Hunan for special criticism.

In the madness at that time, some of my patients began to disappear. I was asked by a colleague to see Liu Shaoqi, who had been tortured by his own bodyguards on the instructions of the Red Guards. But before I could reach him, he had been "transferred to a better hospital". I felt pretty

---

[40] In 1975, Mao chose Hua Guofeng as his successor.

sure he would not get better treatment elsewhere and only discovered years later how terribly he had suffered.

The Red Guards continued to break into people's homes and ransacked them, searching for evidence of capitalism, anti-revolutionary literature, or family souvenirs. They smashed anything that was decorative or beautiful, calling the use of such objects a sign of decadence. Frequently, if they found nothing incriminating, they shaved the heads of the homeowner into a Yin-Yang hairstyle. Harsh treatment towards capitalist-roaders could begin with that insulting punishment, whereby the very distinctive Yin-Yang hairstyle – curved crescents – established their position as clearly as striped prison clothes and a shorn head would point to a common prisoner with whom contact should be avoided.

Chairman Mao conducted his revolution from his seat of power or wherever he chose to travel to with his private army on his private train. One month he would be in Shanghai, where he stayed at the former Swire mansion set in its own gardens in the centre of the city. Or he could be in Hangzhou at one of the former homes of Chiang Kai-shek, or at the best palace or mansion his Security Detail thought appropriate. There were times when the Premier did not know where, or how, to reach the Leader of China.

Such was his concern for stability, and fear for the Chairman's life, that Zhou encouraged Chairman Mao to return to Beijing. But he travelled between his hometown in Hunan, Shanghai and Wuhan where he rode in an open-topped jeep (through massive crowds who chanted, "Long Live Chairman Mao!") to prove he was still loved. His elite Praetorian Guard were dressed in Sun Yat-sen suits, like Mao and everyone else.

At this point, Mao recognized that the Cultural Revolution had taken on a force that was almost unstoppable. He later admitted that he had no idea how chaotic China could become. But this did not stop him fomenting anarchy and disorder.

On a fateful Sunday in July 1969, I had a wake-up call from Premier Zhou. He said, "I told our comrade Jiang Qing you would call on her this evening as she cannot sleep and has no confidence in her medical team. You will take over her health care and live at 7 Fisherman's Terrace. The PLA guards have been instructed to let your car through."

I thought the worst was over, but now I was being called upon in such a way that I knew I would never again have peace. Leaving Junkai was difficult, but our elder daughter came over as I was leaving.

I arrived at the gates of Diaoyutai at 5 o'clock. Two members of the PLA, rifles poised, motioned the driver to enter when they recognized the number of my car. We drove in and were stopped by the PLA sentries in their boxes. There was one more gate to open before I entered the den. I looked around me at the exquisite landscaping, such a contrast to the rest of the city where the flowers and grass had either been dug out or simply dried out from neglect.

We drove over a white marble bridge reflected in the still water of the lake below and, for a moment, I was transported to *Dream of the Red Chamber*, the classic that I had consumed so avidly as a teenage boy. We continued at a leisurely pace, the driver as enchanted as his passenger. There were sentries on duty outside each mansion. I opened my window to feel the air and was rewarded by a perfume I had not smelled in a long time. I asked my driver to collect me at 7 a.m. He knew that I would be doing surgery at various hospitals each morning and would expect to return to my new base afterwards.

The sentries at number 7 asked who I was before stepping aside, and I entered a large open lobby with some banquette seating and a few armchairs with white crochet antimacassars decorating the heads and arms. I was surprised that this vestige of Victorian style was permitted to remain. Several doors opened and my new colleagues, members of the medical team, poured into the lobby. The outgoing team leader took my arm warmly and showed me the room I'd been assigned. It was smaller than I expected and not big enough for my wife to join me. But it was more than adequate for my personal needs. He then showed me the communal washroom, equipped with a bath and two showers, before leading me to the Sitting or Common Room where we could relax between calls from Madame Mao.

As my workload had not been reduced, Premier Zhou had offered me the services of an assistant of my choosing. I chose another Dr. Wu, unrelated to my family, who had been unjustly criticized and imprisoned some years earlier. The whole team consisted of six other medics, including Dr. Wu who was yet to arrive from the countryside, and four nurses. Tea was poured and my team members explained the secret nature of their dealings and presented me with sheets of shabby paper, on which they had kept notes of their treatments.

We doctors addressed one another as *Tongzhi*, Comrade, and they told me it was how they also addressed Madame Mao, Comrade Limpid Stream.

Before I had been completely briefed, the telephone rang and I was summoned to Madame's presence. A Dr. Wei accompanied me to the mansion, where he introduced me as the team leader to the sentries and porters. He then withdrew and I was led to a cavernous and gloomy space. Madame Mao was seated behind a large desk, with a young male secretary whom she dismissed when we appeared.

"Welcome, Comrade Dr. Wu, I am glad you have taken this opportunity to serve the motherland. Chairman Mao is gratified I will be in the best possible hands from now on."

"Alas, Comrade Madame Mao, I am a *man's* doctor and have limited experience treating ladies."

"Please don't stand on ceremony like that. You will call me Comrade Jiang Qing and I will call you Comrade Wu Jieping."

"I should like to examine you," I said. "So we can get started, please tell me how you are feeling now."

She started with her teeth, and that her hair was thinning, and she had a sore throat (little wonder, I thought, from all the screeching and shouting from Mao's *Little Red Book*.) She was very sensitive to the cold and looked underweight. I told her, "You need building up and I hope you will let me suggest some dietary supplements like honey and cheese."

"I have the best Royal Jelly before breakfast each morning Comrade Jieping, look." She opened a large cupboard displaying a hoard of boxes fit for an imperial medicine shop.

"Naturally, you are ahead of me. Why don't I discuss your diet with the head nurse and porters and see what we can add?"

"You will not discuss my affairs with anyone but me. Is that clear? I will call my head nurse since she instructs the porter on my behalf." In those early days, she called me Comrade Jieping and her tone was polite, but I was left in no doubt as to who was superior.

I recommended Qi Gong breathing exercises in the fresh air, but she snapped, "Have you forgotten my sensitivity to the weather? I practise Qi Gong with Master Pan, in this very space, which is temperature-controlled for that purpose."

I nodded, thinking, "It smells of mothballs, stale tobacco and a pharmacy; the air hasn't been fresh in this inner sanctum for years." But I persisted regarding the merits of fresh air and suggested, "Why, Comrade Jiang Qing, I'm sure you could dress appropriately and take a walk before or after meals and in no time you will see the benefits."

"Is that the kind of medicine you learned at your smart American university? Peasants walk because they have no choice. But neither the Chairman nor I have the time. You don't know how busy we are. There are days when I don't even get time to eat."

"My instructions from Premier Zhou are to guide the medical team to boost your strength in every limb and organ, body and mind."

"From now on I issue the instructions," she said, "and you are not allowed to discuss my problems with anyone beyond this room. If you need to consult others, it will be in my presence."

It soon became apparent that Madame Mao was fussy and particular about almost everything. For example, she required the temperature always to be set at 21.5°C, whichever room she was in and scolded her staff very rudely, accusing them of lying about the temperature if she thought it didn't feel right. I did not get involved in these exchanges and she would complain, "Comrade Wu Jieping does not support me." If she was cross, which was not infrequently, she addressed me as Comrade Dr. Wu. The combined hands of the medical team were tied behind our backs as this intransigent woman charted her own course, usually telling the doctors what she was going to do or take. She believed that the aura of legitimacy attached to treating the sovereign Chairman was attached to treating his sovereign wife as well.

I sometimes had to apply to Wang Dongxing, the administrator of Zhongnanhai at the Central Committee of the Communist Party office, for funds to purchase her requests. At the time, like almost everyone else I was paid in coupons for food allowances and had very little cash.

I could not ask in such a way as to indicate that the items were for Jiang Qing but would simply explain, "I was asked to buy this or that." He always replied, "*Ni banme*," Go ahead. Sometimes, by the time the articles arrived and having forgotten why she'd ordered me to buy them, she would donate the items to a school.

"Let me know if you need anything," Zhou Enlai had offered at the outset. When we met a couple of weeks later, he asked, "How are you getting along with your new patient?"

I replied, "She needs a gynaecologist. I am not equipped to look after her complaints. She should consult Dr. Yan Ren Ying."

"But you should feel honoured that she insists you lead her medical team. This way you are serving the country and the Chairman; and we all must do so to the best of our abilities."

This was, of course, a reminder of the sacrifices that Premier Zhou was making himself; so I shut up and determined to do my best.

"Great Chaos will lead to Great Order," Mao had written a year earlier, and his words emblazoned posters around the city:

**THE DEMONS AND MONSTERS
WILL COME OUT BY THEMSELVES**

Jieping explained that Mao wrote to Jiang Qing:
"In order to protect our own interests, I have instructed the Premier to warn all employees of Zhongnanhai not to participate in revolutionary, rebellious acts."

Dr. Wu:

I occasionally remembered to count my blessings as I practised what I preached in the mornings, filling my lungs with the wonderful fresh air so unlike Chicago or the other polluted American cities I'd visited. We lived in a bubble at Diaoyutai and I was the only member of the medical team to travel around the city on a daily basis and gain some idea of the bedlam Beijing had descended into.

Premier Zhou was at a loss to figure out a means of controlling the chaos. The Politburo wasn't working and neither was the State Council, which he ran. He formed a new, ad hoc committee comprising the Central Cultural Revolution Small Group that included Jiang Qing and her three closest lieutenants, Mao's nephew Mao Yuanxin, as well as Zhou Enlai, Wang Dongxing, Xie Fuzhi (Minister of Public Security) and Lin Biao's wife, Ye Qun.

> It was a master move on Zhou's part and when Jieping questioned him about taking on these additional responsibilities, he replied, "If I do not enter the lions' den, who will save the cubs?" It was a means of communicating regularly with that notorious woman and thereby having some idea of what she was up to.
>
> In 1971, China joined the United Nations and Huang Hua, Wu Jieping's student colleague, became Ambassador there.

Dr. Wu:

Relations with the outside world were now a little more relaxed and some American-made luxury goods could be obtained. One day, Jiang Qing said to me, "I need something to distract myself. Get me a good deck of playing cards from the United States and some movies and games. I feel so cut off here."

"I'll bring you a deck tomorrow," I replied.

"No! Don't get me a Chinese set. I want an *American* one, like we played with in Yan'an."

Ordinarily such things would have been easy, but in this situation, it was fraught with difficulties.

One option was to just write to Huang Hua, who after all knew me from way back, and knew the position I was now in. But I worried how I would respond if Huang Hua should ask who was going to pay. I could not pay, as I had no foreign currency. But if I told Huang Hua who the items were for, I could officially be *found to be leaking a secret*. Although the sort of distraction provided by playing cards was part of Jiang Qing's therapy, this matter was not really related to health and I became very frustrated and worried. I contacted Wang Dongxing and told him the whole story. Then I telephoned Huang Hua and explained that I had been asked to buy this and that, but did not say by whom. Huang said just three words, 'Will do it.'

I was relieved Huang Hua did not ask me to pay for the goods, but if he had done, at least now I could refer him back to Wang Dongxing, who knew the whole story.

A couple of weeks later, when the goods arrived, I showed up filled with a sense of accomplishment and presented my hoard like a prize trophy. Jiang Qing couldn't look less interested.

"These are the cards and movies you asked me for."

She replied, "What are they for? They belong in a barracks or dormitory. Do I look like a child? You may look down on me, but I run a country!" She had completely lost interest. It had just been one of her whims.

In those days during the Cultural Revolution, I knew that anything could happen. I was in an awkward position, and just had to bear it. My wife grumbled that I never went home to be with my family. By now she was partly crippled, so it was particularly cruel to be deprived of time with her. I was trapped in the ivory tower of Diaoyutai, and of course my wife and others were suspicious.

Among other medical necessities, Jiang Qing had her own cinema, for therapeutic purposes, of course. When she wanted some new films from the US, I had again to solicit the help of Ambassador Huang Hua who, given the restrictions on the movements of diplomats and the abysmally low salaries to government employees, would surely regard this as an unnecessary indulgence. It showed Jiang Qing's complete disregard for our time, treating one of China's most important ambassadors and one of its most important doctors as messengers. I was furious that she could waste our time on such nonsense. But she claimed, "I need to divert my concentration and distract my thoughts." I couldn't help thinking, "If these things distract her from interfering, the entire population will be grateful." So, it was in that spirit that I was able to tolerate her abuse.

Eventually the films arrived, and I was summoned one Sunday evening and asked to translate the Fred Astaire, Ginger Rogers dialogue.

The room was so dark, lit by just two candles, that I had to squint before I got my bearings. I made my translation as intelligible as I could, but Madame sometimes had to stop the projector to find out what was going on. It was difficult to explain the subtleties, but I did my best and she seemed satisfied as I crept out exhausted at almost 4 a.m. I had my patients' health care on my mind and was not distracted by the film.

Zhou's nosebleeds were disrupting his meetings and his blood pressure was increasingly erratic. I could hardly trouble him with my problems when I was supposed to be taking care of his. I was aware that there had been some communication between the American government and our leaders and I dreamed of communicating with those medical scientists with whom I had worked twenty years earlier. I knew the country was recovering when the dynamics of Zhou's meetings changed and he charged a group of my colleagues with restoring scientific studies and research. Realizing there were spies everywhere, he told us, "We need to catch up with other countries."

I was aware that our Chairman was touring in the south of China and hoped this would give Premier Zhou some kind of break – and possibly a day or two off for myself. But no sooner had I telephoned my family to say I might be coming home, than I was summoned. It was about one in the morning.

I arrived at Jiang Qing's room with my brown medical bag, still buttoning up my tunic and expecting a medical emergency. When I entered the room and adjusted my eyes to the dimness, I noticed more candles than on previous occasions, and expecting to see my patient prostrate on a bed or couch, I wondered where her nurses were. I found my patient transformed into my hostess, wearing a figure-hugging, dark green velvet cheongsam. She was standing by a table laden with food and drinks and said with a smile, "Welcome, Comrade Jieping."

She walked over to the piano, sat down demurely and played a lullaby before telling me in a husky voice, "I have lost my voice. Do you have some medication?" I went through the contents of my supplies and found some soothing lozenges that would alleviate some of the discomfort.

"It's not really sore," she confessed, "just overworked from making announcements at Congress all day."

"You need to rest your voice for two or three days before you take up the microphone again," I said.

"I will take your advice; but first we eat, then you can help me relax. We'll switch on the projector and watch one of your favourite American films, but you'll have to translate. Think of it as my way of thanking you for looking after me."

She waltzed back over to me smiling. Sensing a trap, I told her, "You have no need to go out of your way on my account. I do my duty responsibly and that is its own reward."

"But we all need distracting from the grimness of life, and this evening we can be distracted together, Comrade Jieping."

I was determined not to become one of her diversions. But when I had to be her companion, I did it because I had no choice.

Knowing I liked cheese (which we Chinese never ate in those days and had to be imported) she cajoled, "Look what I've got especially for you." "No, thank you, Comrade Jiang Qing. I had dinner hours ago and for me, it's the middle of the night," I explained. "Eating cheese at this time will disrupt my sleep after the movie ends."

I was not about to be compromised over a piece of cheese, despite my longing, and told her, "I'm not hungry now, but I'll take a piece for breakfast." That seemed to appease her. She cut some for herself, put it on a plate with a piece of apple and two slices of toast, took a glass of tea and switched on the projector.

During one scene when a waltz was playing, she jumped up and waltzed by herself around the room, smiling serenely. When her steps stopped in front of me, she held out her hands and said, "Come, I'll show you. It's as easy as 1, 2, 3." And she moved as she counted the three steps. "Let's practise, first like this. Take my hand here and place your other hand on my shoulder and try to follow the music: one, two, three, starting on the right foot, stop. Then one, two, three starting on the left foot, stop. And repeat. It's that simple."

We made these movements together a number of times, but I moved so woodenly she asked in disgust, "Surely you learned how to dance in America? I've seen you at Chairman's parties."

"No, Comrade Jiang Qing, there was actually no time for relaxation and if there was, I liked to see different places and simply talk to people, to try to understand the American mind."

"You are very insulting," came her retort. "I've tasted more salt than you've eaten rice! Believe me, I know when I'm being rejected."

"It's nothing of the kind. I'd stand on my head if it made you feel better. It's just that I'm no good at dancing. My wife always complained that I have two left feet."

"Then you can massage my shoulders and feet," she told me, kicking off her shoes.

When I next met Wang Dongxing and told him the story, he challenged me: "You've touched Jiang Qing's body all over, you know how soft her warm belly feels under your firm hands; you know her smell, and her voice when she is being demure. How could you deny her a little dance?"

"I did not deny her, I am just not a good dancer."

"Well neither is the Chairman. The Premier is okay, as are a few of the top leaders. Sometimes you have to make a little more effort. It would take some pressure off the Chairman's shoulders. Anyway, she's asked the Chairman to make sure you are invited to all his dances from now on, so you're likely to improve before long!"

"Thank you, Comrade Wang. I'll try and keep that in mind if I'm ever summoned again."

> On 11 August 1971, it was rumoured that when Mao was returning to Beijing, the train on which he was supposed to be travelling exploded, which would surely have killed the Chairman.

The leaders knew that this attempt on Mao's life could only have been decreed by Lin Biao. It was announced a few days later that Lin had fled to the Soviet Union with his family and was killed when his plane crash landed on a Mongolian plain.

Jieping heard the rumours, but had intimations and anxieties of his own.

When Jieping finally got a few hours off to go home to his family, he told his wife that Jiang Qing was so desperate to bring down the Premier, she might resort to wild accusations. "If anything happens, just wait," he said.

"But if nobody knows anything, what am I to do?" Junkai asked him.

To his wife's great irritation, Wu Jieping lived in a mansion at Madame Mao's bidding and was initially allowed to visit his family once a week. But when this started to displease Jiang Qing, Jieping would go home "only when time permitted." With such an arrangement in place, his family would not necessarily know if something untoward happened to him.

"That woman wants you for something else," Junkai warned. "Look what happened to Liu Shaoqi – and he was more important than you."

Dr. Wu:

With her fiery personality, I knew Junkai could raise hell, but that would only cause trouble; so I kept quiet and advised her to do the same. There had been incidences of people disappearing, and not coming back, for much less. I just told my wife,

"I know there have been incidents, but if anything suspicious happens, wait a few days; and the most you should do is tell my younger brother that I did not come home." I knew my brother could appease my wife, if anything happened.

Documents discovered in Lin Biao's desk attacked Mao as a living emperor in the style of the first Emperor of China, Qin Shi Huangdi.[41] The document read, "We can't deny Mao's historical function in uniting

---

[41] Qin Shi Huangdi 259 B.C. – 210 B.C.. First Emperor of a unified China, after the Qin had conquered all the other warring states in 221 B.C..

China and this is why we've given him his rightful place and the support he deserves. But now, he has abused the confidence and status given him by the Chinese people. He is not a true Marxist-Leninist, but the greatest feudal tyrant in Chinese history. He puts on the cloak of Marxism-Leninism and exercises the laws of Emperor Qin Shi Huangdi." Lin Biao, on the other hand, determined to follow the teachings of Confucius and "Die to Preserve Virtue".

"Was this a suicide note?" I asked my brother, Wu Ruiping.

But my brother just said, "I need some fresh air. Let's take a little walk together."

When we were out of earshot, Ruiping said, "Who knows whether they were the Vice Chairman's papers, or whether they were planted. What *is* known is that Wang Dongxing got to the office before Jiang Qing and has all of their correspondence."

"Interesting."

"Well, I hope it isn't too interesting. We don't need another crackdown."

But in the wake of Lin Biao's treachery and desertion, we were waiting for reprisals: and we didn't have to wait too long.

It was 1971, right after Lin Biao's catastrophe, when more documents attributed to him came to light. The following afternoon, Jiang Qing collapsed, saying she had been poisoned. She instructed the guards to seize me and Dr. Hsutao, another assistant. We were under house arrest, but I recognized that she was "killing the chickens to scare the monkeys". I remained calm because I knew she had not been poisoned, and that she was over-sensitive. Worrying would achieve nothing. The blaring loudspeakers denouncing "running dogs" and those who "deviated from the Party line" allowed me no peace.

A couple of days later, Jiang Qing asked some of the members of the Political Bureau of the Chinese Communist Party to come to her house at Diaoyutai. My assistant and the guards all became very worried that she'd "arrested" me, when she called that meeting. Jiang Qing had no power to do this – she was only a *member* of the Politburo, not the Chairman or Secretary – but that did not stop her. She called the meeting anyway and they all arrived. From about 9 o'clock, I watched them all enter. Political heavyweight Li Xiannian came first, then Premier Zhou Enlai and a number of others, including two of Jiang Qing's closest associates (who later became known as members of the Gang of Four), Zhang Chunqiao and Yao Wenyuan. Shortly after came Wang Shenyue, Gao Weiren, Shen Yan, Marshal Ye Jianying and a couple of others. The furniture had been rearranged again.

I sat there, regretting my inability to waltz and my churlishness over the cheese. If it hadn't been the middle of the night, or for the fact that Zhou Enlai would need me the following morning at 6 a.m., I might have relented. But I just sat, hoping my rationality would prevail. Even with all those people in attendance, the house looked half empty.

> Jieping was worried when he saw how gravely Zhou Enlai treated the matter. Zhou was certainly worried; he understood that if she had been poisoned, he, as Premier, would also be held responsible. Zhou and Jiang Qing sat on one side of the huge banqueting table so recently filled with delicious treats. Wu Jieping sat opposite them. When Zhou asked a question, it was less as an interrogator, more a simple enquiry: "Who is the physician responsible for Jiang Qing's health?" This was an important distinction, and Wu Jieping knew it. "I am," he told the group as his confidence returned. Zhou then simply asked, "*zenme hui shir?*" – "What happened?"
>
> Jieping was not given the opportunity to say much in his defence.

Dr. Wu:

"Firstly," I said, "I did not find evidence of poisoning." I had not examined her, but I knew she was just making it up. Jiang Qing did not respond to that comment. Then I addressed the issue of her consumption of sleeping pills. I explained to the group assembled that she was taking too many sleeping pills and I waited for a comment from Jiang Qing, but she kept silent. Then I said, "I have recommended a gradual reduction of sleeping pills."

Jiang Qing shouted, "No, you have not!"

I calmly repeated that I had done so. She said again, "You did not and you have not examined me since the poisoning; so you know nothing."

I said nothing more, because I felt I had made my point.

The Premier then turned to Dr. Hsutao and asked, "Have you examined Comrade Jiang Qing?"

"I attended her a few days ago, when the dentist recommended she have dental surgery."

Then Premier Zhou very tactfully steered the conversation to talk about Lin Biao's use of sleeping pills and insomnia. He then told an amusing story from the previous General Assembly of the Communist Party. It was about what Lin did, and it was actually *top secret*. The story lasted for about three-quarters of an hour and Jiang Qing became very interested in what Zhou was saying. Since Lin Biao had championed her to the position she now enjoyed, I wondered if this was Zhou's subtle reminder that giants fall.

After a while, the impromptu tribunal began to dissolve as members excused themselves to use bathrooms and everyone left.

Zhou turned to me and said, "Doctor Wu, why don't you go and rest?" I said: "Thank you," for I was very tired, and I left. The ordeal had ended, for that day.

Premier Zhou Enlai tried to pacify Jiang Qing. He sat up talking to her until 7 o'clock the next morning. I had to wait for him to attend his appointment and he'd had no sleep.

I shook my head when he admitted consoling her all night and he replied, "All for a good cause. Comrade Madame Mao has been very nervous since Lin Biao's attempt on the Chairman's life. I think you should order bed rest."

"I do not expect to be summoned by her again."

In conclusion, Jieping told me that Jiang Qing's accusation was an attempt to distract the Politburo's attention away from her association with Lin Biao.

CHAPTER EIGHTEEN

"CHINA NEEDS ZHOU ENLAI, HE IS THE HOUSEKEEPER"

Dr. Wu:

At the time of President Nixon's first visit to China in February 1972, Mao was diagnosed with congestive heart failure. But he refused all medication, relying on Traditional Chinese Medicine (TCM)[42], which was not making him any better. When we explained that he would be in no fit state to greet the US President, he finally agreed that he would be seen by a team of doctors, each a specialist in his field. By now, he had moved into a room next to the swimming pool and a pungent combination of the pool chemicals, urine from his urinal and body odour made this an uncomfortable visit for all of us. He never used a toothbrush, so his breath smelled and his rotting teeth almost certainly added to his heart condition. His body felt clammy, like his wife's.

With so many sycophants surrounding him, it was difficult to diagnose Mao's condition and diplomatically and truthfully advise him. He was an eighty-three-year-old smoker who took no exercise and, as a result, was suffering from bronchitis and emphysema.

But fortunately, Mao was desperate to meet the American President and it was solely for this reason that he finally agreed to the recommendations

---

[42] TCM is an independent holistic system of medical practice, developed over the last 2,500 years. It uses Yin Yang concepts and identifies the body's meridians, to apply acupuncture. It also uses herbal medicines and Qi Gong to co-ordinate posture with breathing, to achieve balance. With many other Western medicine doctors, Dr. Wu dismissed it until it was recommended by a colleague who got his MD from Yale and also practised TCM. Jieping was planning a hip operation, but following his colleague's TCM intervention, he no longer required surgery. Jieping was converted.

of the medical team. And from being bed-ridden for six months, within a month he was exercising a little and getting some fresh air.

At the time of the meeting, Mao was still rather bloated, but this was well concealed under a newly tailored Sun Yat-sen suit. He was stronger than he had been since Lin Biao's attempt to kill him; but he was almost constantly reliant on the American-made respirator that Henry Kissinger had sent in 1971 after his secret mission to China.

The Gang of Four was still trying to bring Premier Zhou Enlai down, spreading rumours about illegitimate children he had fathered. In 1972, the Gang stepped up their attempts to trap Zhou, insinuating that his connections with the KMT meant that he was a spy. Because I had a family member who was married to a former leader of the KMT, I was worried that this connection could trap both the Premier and myself.

The medical diagnoses of all the leaders were secret, but when the Premier passed blood in his urine, we had to tell the Chairman and members of the Standing Committee. I was the head of the medical teams of three of the Leaders and still had my teaching and surgical responsibilities.

Jiang Qing continued to insist I be at her beck and call, despite her accusations and asked me one day, "If someone passes blood in their faeces, does it mean they have cancer?"

I had to watch my comments and movements very carefully.

"Comrade Jiang Qing, if you have passed some blood, it may just mean you have an irritable bowel; but it could be something more sinister and we should send a specimen to the lab."

"It was only an idle enquiry," she replied. "My cancer was cured by the treatment I received in the Soviet Union."

> Not having been seen publicly for several months, Mao laid to rest rumours that he was on his deathbed by appearing dressed only in pyjamas with a topcoat thrown over his shoulders at the funeral of the jolly, outspoken footballer, Chen Yi. He told Chen Yi's widow, "Comrade Chen Yi was a good man, as is Deng Xiaoping." Mao recognized that there were only a few people he could trust completely and at the Tenth Central Committee in 1973, Zhou was elected First Vice Chairman, Mao's chosen successor.
>
> Jieping was on tenterhooks and could no longer sleep as soundly as he once had. His anxiety was stoked as another war

of words was unleashed by a dozen writing groups producing hundreds of contradictory articles and pamphlets. This latest campaign gutlessly chose victims from the dead.

In 1973, the fashionable label from the Gang's pens was Confucianism. "Tradition, Education, Conservation", the revered hallmarks of Confucian thought, became associated with "rightist" thinking and behaviour. "Rule by the upright and superior person" they associated with Lin Biao and tried to trap Premier Zhou, accordingly.

The anti-Confucius campaign continued throughout 1974. Its slogan, *"Pi Lin Pi Kong"* meaning "criticize Lin, criticize Confucius", was amended to *"Pi Zhou Kung"* – "criticize Lord Zhou". Posters were pasted up overnight and speeches against Confucius and his disciples dominated the airwaves of the entire city. Jiang Qing explained that the campaign intended to trap those who infiltrated the Party and those who return by the back door. It was evident to many that the "Lord Zhou" referred to in the posters was Zhou Enlai, though none of the Gang was willing to risk saying this publicly because Mao no longer supported them. However much Mao was secretly antagonized by the Premier, he always said, "China needs Zhou, he is the Housekeeper."

By now, Mao had become very suspicious of his wife. He warned, "Jiang Qing wants to become head of the Party. She wants to make Wang Hongwen Head of the National Assembly, Zhang Chunqiao, Premier and Yao Wenyuan, Party General Secretary." It was he who first labelled his wife as leader of the "Gang of Four". Mao heard that, without permission from the Central Committee, Jiang Qing had spent weeks giving her story to an American biographer. He had Ambassador Huang Hua instruct the biographer not to proceed. The instruction went unheeded.

Because of Mao's failing health, the Gang of Four was not intimidated by his criticism and persisted in their persecution of Zhou and others. Zhou had approved the making of a documentary in China by the Italian film director Michelangelo Antonioni. Jiang Qing regarded all the arts as her territory, as it had been in the Lin Biao days, and ranted against the bourgeois values evident in the choice of music and beautiful cinematography. Her campaign was so successful that Antonioni was criticized by the Chinese Government in the international press and warned never to visit China again.

Now Jiang Qing set about enhancing her own self-image again: she took the unpopular images of Empress Wu Ze Tian and Empress Lü and had her favourite "pens" write glowing accounts of their rule. Both Empresses had long been reviled by China's male historians.

That Jiang Qing imagined that Chinese appreciation of these villainesses could be affected by *her* treatment of their stories, after almost a thousand years of vilification, is an interesting reflection on her self-assurance – or self-delusion.

Throughout 1974, everywhere there were rumours of Zhou's failing health. In a celebration of National Day, 1st October, 1974, the frail Zhou Enlai got out of his sick bed to lead the many citizens who had returned from the countryside, from prison and from house arrest, in a quiet but triumphant display of survival. He received a standing ovation from the Politburo and guests.

For the next year, heads of state from Europe, Africa and Asia flocked to China to bid Zhou goodbye. On Henry Kissinger's last visit in November 1974, Zhou was so weak he could only see Kissinger for half an hour.

On National Day in 1975, Zhou was not in attendance, but the man he had groomed to replace him, Deng Xiaoping, was present instead: an infuriating insult to Jiang Qing and her clique.

Dr. Wu:

Forty-nine veteran Party members who had been in disgrace reappeared that night. It was extraordinarily moving; *the Party was back*. It had not been destroyed by the Cultural Revolution, after all.

> The problem was that Mao still supported class struggle and continuous revolution. The Gang of Four supported him with even more contradictory articles. One claimed, "Historical truth is secondary to the appropriation of China's glorious past for current political purposes." This was a very troubling attitude, giving legitimacy to the distortion of facts.

Mao was installed once more like an emperor at Zhongnanhai, attended by a bevy of "nurses" and young men who were there to massage him. Jiang Qing and her assistants lived less grandly in the mansions of Diaoyutai. Following one unannounced visit by the Chairman's wife, Mao issued instructions that neither she, nor any of the top leaders, would be permitted to enter without his express permission. Thereafter, Jiang Qing had to announce herself and ask Wang Dongxing to seek an appointment with her husband.

Dr. Wu:

We all lived in terror of being called to account for deeds we could not imagine. And I had to minister to some of the most vulnerable of the abused. We heard of the public humiliations and beatings and although we were hungry and exhausted, sleep was troubled or did not come until the furies had exhausted us all.

> Jieping's daughter Wu Bing remembered:
> "One day, Grandmother Deng (Deng Yingchao, Zhou Enlai's wife) called and said she would like to visit. She did not ask to be met downstairs. Mother had been paralyzed down one side of her body for over ten years, but she still made all our clothes just with her left hand. When Grandmother Deng arrived, she held my Mother's right hand and told her, with deep emotion, 'You are an excellent wife and mother. People don't know that Jieping is Premier Zhou's doctor, or that he is rarely able to come home to be with you. I am very sorry about that.'"

Such was the level of mistrust that of course it had not been revealed that Jieping had responsibility for other "leaders", in addition to his surgical commitments. Nobody could admit that their left hand didn't know what their right hand was doing.

> "Grandma Deng told us she knew our Mother made all the family clothes, even Father's overcoat. She had no access to new clothes and had brought an old blue sweater and asked my Mother if she could make it into a cardigan without buying any new wool, because she was that poor. Mother pulled apart that

old sweater, knitting a new pattern with some dark blue wool she'd taken from her own sweater.

'We were all gratified watching Grandmother Deng, looking elegant on TV, wearing this "new" cardigan to meet foreign guests.'

Dr. Wu:

Zhou felt he needed to stay alive as long as possible. But we were impeded in his treatment by having to apply for permission to the ailing Chairman for certain medications. Zhou left no stone unturned in his effort as "Housekeeper," to hand China "swept clean" to his successors.

We kept him alive with blood transfusions and, in the middle of one, he was forced to stop to take a telephone call from Jiang Qing.

> Jieping told me that Chairman Mao had said, "She wants to be Party Chairman ... Her heart is rotten with ambition." And she almost managed it. Other battles loomed, battles that Deng Xiaoping would have to fight alone when Premier Zhou died.
>
> By the end of 1975, Zhou had had one hundred blood transfusions and six surgical operations. At his seventh, Jieping did another intestinal bypass to buy him some more time.
>
> "Have you been able to get the other drugs you prescribed yet?" the Premier asked him.
>
> "We have not yet had approval from the Standing Committee," Jieping admitted.
>
> "Without the drugs, exactly how long do I have?"
>
> Nobody was willing to lie and Zhou told Wu Jieping, "You had better attend to your other patients, whom you can help."
>
> On 7 January, 1976, with Wu Jieping and about thirty doctors and nurses surrounding him, Zhou suddenly opened his eyes, looked at Jieping and said,
>
> "Dr. Wu, I don't need you here, many other people need you more. You'd better go."

Dr. Wu:

The Premier was thinking of Kang Sheng (whose earlier death from lung cancer Zhou was left unaware of) and Jiang Qing, whose health he still felt responsible for because of his loyalty to Mao. Mao did not even visit the man to whom he was most indebted; and, like others who had helped and guided him, he resented his superior talents.

> Zhou Enlai died on 8 January, 1976. In keeping with the way he led his life, he asked that no special arrangements be made for his funeral or memorial service and that his body be cremated and the ashes scattered over the mountains and rivers of his beloved land. The Chinese have a definition of immortality, which Jieping described – those who are more spoken of in death than in life. Jieping's voice shook, and he wiped his eyes, as he recounted how he kept silent vigil over the spirit of a man he loved.
>
> Deng Yingchao had to be persuaded to allow some of her husband's colleagues to say goodbye and a couple of days later, Zhou's body lay in state for a select group to pay their respects.
>
> No announcement was made but, as the body was taken in an unadorned van to the Crematorium, an unprecedented spontaneous demonstration of about two million people silently lined the route. This forced his widow to announce that there would be no funeral rites in accordance with the Premier's wishes, but that his last remains would rest at the Workers' Culture Palace.
>
> For three days, hundreds of thousands of school children, students and ordinary workers left their homes before dawn. There was stillness in the air and in the hearts of the mourners. The ranks swelled even further in the evenings when work was finished and people filed past the photograph and ashes of China's great Housekeeper for the last time.

Dr. Wu:

We were forbidden from wearing traditional black armbands or white flowers. But the Government couldn't stem the tide of grief that overwhelmed the people. To commemorate Zhou Enlai's birthday, 5 March, children arrived by the busload and placed wreaths at the monument to the heroes of the revolution. Attached was a banner reading, "Beloved Uncle Zhou, you live in our hearts forever."

Tiananmen Square was cleared of all flowers and tributes by dawn. Soldiers came by the truckload and workers filled the square in the evenings. The torrent continued until *Qing Ming*, Tomb Sweeping Day, 4 April, when young poets recited sonnets, artists painted banners and singers sang hymns of praise and love to the memory of Uncle Zhou.

The following day, police arrived and began to arrest the "counter-revolutionaries".

> Just three weeks after arriving at Diaoyutai in 1969, Jieping had lived in fear of his life. Now, in 1976, following the death of Zhou Enlai, he was questioned about his care of the Premier. In the end he was defended publicly by Zhou's widow, Deng Yingchao. Jieping had been under the impression that Mao needed to keep Zhou alive and that gave him some protection; but now that Zhou was dead, Jieping felt vulnerable once more.
>
> Gone was the "Housekeeper" who had held China together under an unproven political system, the Chinese Communist Party system that Zhou recognized needed to hear "unpleasant truths and accept criticism".
>
> The power struggle continued to take its toll on both Jiang Qing and her husband. But on 9 September, 1976 Chairman Mao Zedong died, with the blood of at least thirty million innocent Chinese on his hands. Such was the level of fear and insecurity among the leaders of China that no preparations had been made for the Chairman's lying-in-state, because this could have been misconstrued to suggest the frailty of, or a death wish for, New China's modern-day God.
>
> Jieping was given responsibility for preserving Mao Zedong's remains to be presented to the world. The order came from Hua Guofeng, Mao's chosen successor, but was directed by the Gang of Four.

Dr. Wu:

I was given probably the biggest single responsibility of my long and troubled career, and was completely in the dark. Nobody in the team knew how to preserve a corpse, and I had no personal experience. The only case study I could draw upon was that of Sun Yat-sen, who had been embalmed almost fifty years earlier. It wasn't a welcome task because if it wasn't executed to the satisfaction of all, the potential for criticism would be substantial.

The body was moved to an underground complex built to house the military high command. That was when I found out that there was a whole secret underground world linking Zhongnanhai, Tiananmen, and the PLA's 301 Hospital with the Military Headquarters in the western hills. It was part of a honeycomb-like network of nuclear shelters, designed by Lin Biao at a time when he felt China might be attacked by the Soviet Union.

Almost a year later, in August 1977, the Chairman's body was still underground. I was on duty one night when an earthquake struck. It was the second earthquake to occur in that area in a short time. The first had hit Tangshan in July 1976, devastating a vast area and killing more than two hundred thousand people.

Jiang Qing and the Gang of Four had not bothered to visit Tangshan. They were preoccupied in Beijing with trying to bring down Deng Xiaoping.

Wang Dongxing and I had a little chat. Wang looked at me and laughed. I asked him what he was laughing at.

"You are a spy, a 'te wu'."

"Why do you say that?" I asked.

"Jiang Qing is claiming you're a spy. If you're not a spy, how else could you have bought movies, playing cards and other toys from the States?"

> They laughed together. It seemed typical. Jieping had been called a spy by Jiang Qing for doing what she asked! Nevertheless, she wanted him to stay beside her home and lead her medical team.
>
> Wang Dongxing reminded Jieping before he left, "One of Chairman Mao's last injunctions to our people was, 'Rise against the Party if it degenerates.' And never forget that in the long reach of history, he will be seen as the leader of the Gang of Five."

Dr. Wu:

I served that notorious woman until the 24 September, 1977, a year after Chairman Mao died. Diaoyutai was rife with rumours: Jiang Qing and her Gang of Four would purge the entire administration of the late Chairman; or Deng Xiaoping would destroy three of the Gang of Four and make Madame Mao Vice Chairman. There were endless permutations.

As the days passed, I learned that three or four of Deng Xiaoping's supporters had asked Wang Dongxing on 6 October to alert the male members of the Gang of Four that an emergency meeting of the Politburo was to take place at the Great Hall of the People. They arrived in due course and were immediately arrested when they entered. Jiang Qing was waiting to be escorted to the meeting when Mao's Praetorian Guard, Unit 8341, arrived and placed her under arrest. Simultaneously, the Gang's advisers, publishers and propagandists were quietly rounded up and imprisoned.

> Today, the grand State Guest Houses at 17 Fisherman's Terrace that housed Jiang Qing and her gang are open to paying guests for banquets and residence. The exclusivity of the setting will not allow a taxi to enter; only cars with sirens or official registrations are permitted. At Jiang Qing's residence, the guards at the eastern and western gates protect the privacy of wealthy foreigners, in the same way they once protected the life of the spouse of China's ruler.

* * *

Passing a large, framed picture, a decade later, at the entrance to PUMC hospital, Jieping laughed as if at a private joke. When I asked him what he had found so amusing, he admitted:

In order to save the calligraphy of one of China's great poets, Guo Morou, during the Cultural Revolution, we hung a large painting of Chairman Mao over it. We had to keep our wits about us in such times.

CHAPTER NINETEEN
RETURN TO THE USA

Throughout the fluctuating political turmoil, when not seeing his patients, Jieping immersed himself in research as his home life offered little solace. Junkai's last stroke had partially paralyzed her and she could no longer speak. She died of a heart attack in November 1978.

Jieping's relationships with other women were not trouble free.

Dr. Wu:

I used to share a lot of my anxieties with my wife and with a female classmate at PUMC who reminded me, "You don't even know what a white lie is."

Junkai used to accuse me, "You had four women in love with you."

The first she was referring to was a distant relative. That girl's mother was a widow and my sister was married to her brother-in-law. So, I was technically an uncle. She was unbelievably capable; she could dance, sing, spoke excellent English and later, at Harvard, she knew the prominent China historian Professor Fairbank very well. I was impressed that she understood what I wrote in my essay, "Adolescent Loneliness".

Thirteen years after I married Junkai, she finally married an architect and became very successful in the US. I went to visit in 1948 and met her husband, who worked with Frank Lloyd Wright in Spring Green, Wisconsin. She had left for New York City that day, so I had just missed her. We tried to meet in Cleveland, when I was en route to New York and again in Buffalo, Niagara Falls. But when we finally did meet, we never talked about my early infatuation – it was kept locked away in my own heart.

She had, in fact, been in China with her husband and son in 1973 during the Cultural Revolution. I had heard she was in Beijing but decided not to meet her because, as I told her later on, I knew that anything could have happened if I had gone. Being responsible to Jiang Qing, I ran the risk of being branded a spy if she found out about our encounter, and could implicate her, too. Prudence protected me. Junkai said this was the only good decision I took in our marriage.

But I knew which hotel she was staying at and would walk up and down the street for hours, keeping an eye on her window. I even knew her flight plans and thought to bump into her at the airport, but forethought forbade me. You may not realize it now, but during the Cultural Revolution anything could go awry if you took one wrong step.

> Interested, but unable to pry, I sat quietly as he revealed this unrequited love that had tugged at his heart since his teen years.

Dr. Wu:

I met my second wife, Yang Yuhua, in 1978, a year after Junkai died, when I was 61 and she was 43. She was the Editor of a medical publishing house in Shanghai and a graduate, in high standing, from Shanghai Medical School. Her family had been very wealthy and owned many important properties. They could have had a very difficult time later, but by the time her father died in the 1950s they had lost it all, just as my own family had.

> Despite the secrecy and egalitarianism of the times, Jieping had gained much prestige. Among a dozen roles, he was Chairman of the Family Planning Association, President of the Chinese Academy of Medical Science (CAMS) and was regarded as the leading urologist in China. And since treating Zhou Enlai's cancer, he was regarded as one of the country's leading oncologists.
>
> Jieping was sitting in conference with a number of male colleagues and became intrigued by the single female, whose elegance and command of her subject was startling. His male colleagues

were uncomfortable, but Jieping encouraged her and when one conversation led to another, he was surprised to find she was unmarried. He invited her to dinner, which was unheard of at that time. Afterwards, they strolled in the garden and both were astonished to find such compatibility in one another's company.

"Because we were editing a medical encyclopaedia in Beijing, the publishing house had to give her permission to move to Beijing," Jieping said. "But her colleagues gave her a very hard time."

The Cultural Revolution had largely ended, but Yang Yuhua was required to attend meetings that smacked of the self-criticism sessions that had characterized institutions of the previous decade. Her colleagues were both jealous of, and reluctant to lose, her dedicated expertise. Yang Yuhua lived with her mother and had never married. Her boss in Shanghai tasked her with a huge amount of work in Beijing.

Jieping was quite unselfconscious as he revealed his love for this woman, when we first met in the middle of their courtship. Since Jieping was already a grandfather, it would not have been seemly in Chinese society to start another family; but he told me openly that she would not have been able to conceive, as she had undergone a hysterectomy.

Jieping went to the US with a delegation comprised mostly of members of the CAMS. I asked him why he had not brought Yang Yuhua. He told me that it would have been frowned upon by his colleagues and, as the group were guests of an American pharmaceutical company, their tickets had been pre-paid. I suggested that he could have paid for her ticket, but he admitted he could not afford it. That fact illustrates rather well what the salary was for doctors in China at that time.

Yang Yuhua and Jieping were married in a quiet ceremony in Beijing, attended only by her mother and Jieping's family. She stayed at Jieping's apartment, but was unable to get a complete transfer from Shanghai[43]. Jieping's elevated position enabled him

---

[43] In the early 1950's, a system of family registration, *hukou*, was established in order to control migration from the countryside to the city, as well as from city to city, or village to village. All members of the Chinese population are obliged to return to their place of registration, once they finish their education. Migrant workers might work in a city for ten years and never qualify for the Hukou of the city where they have toiled. This system dogs the applications of thousands of brilliant professionals, to this day.

to request Beijing residency for his wife, but the jealousy of her colleagues threw a spanner in the works. They would not support her application. One critic accused her of 'marrying up': using the marriage to move to Beijing. This led to tragedy.

Dr. Wu:

Such was the mistrust created by the Cultural Revolution that nobody in authority was willing to help Yang Yuhua. A few months after our marriage in 1981, she disappeared and died. That was my Pearl Harbor. When Yang Yuhua disappeared, I spent ten very difficult days in Shanghai.

> Tracing his wife proved enormously challenging. It transpired that in preparation for her disappearance and suicide, Yang Yuhua had dressed in an old Mao jacket and trousers. She removed all personal objects and had only some tissues and sleeping pills in her pocket. She paid for a ticket to watch a long film. At that time, people believed in saving electricity, so she knew that the cinema would not be cleaned until the following morning – when she would be discovered. Of course, she could not be identified as she had removed any identifying clues.
>
> There were many unexplained deaths and suicides in China at that time. Finally, it was deduced, after searching all the city morgues, that she may have gone outside her district.
>
> Jieping eventually identified Yang Yuhua's body after visiting all the morgues in the city, and some outside, in the ten days after she disappeared. It was remarkable to learn of the lengths to which Jieping went in his determined efforts to trace his wife. He viewed more than forty bodies before he finally found her.

Dr. Wu:

The body of Yang Yuhua was in a morgue in a different district, across the Suzhou River and her mother wanted the cremation to take place in the more important, home district. But municipal regulations prevented a dead body crossing the river from that district to her home district in the former French concession, in the heart of the old city. It would have caused her mother further unnecessary pain to learn of this rule.

She was already suffering the loss of Yang Yuhua as the breadwinner of her family. I had to try to bend the rules, but I didn't know many people in Shanghai.

> It is an interesting reflection on the times that Jieping was one of the most important doctors in China, personal physician to China's most beloved leader Zhou Enlai, President of the Shanghai Chapter of the Jiusan Society, President of the CAMS, President of the Asia chapter of Planned Parenthood, and Vice Chairman of the CCPCC; and yet felt unable to appeal for help to grant his mother-in-law's wish for her late daughter to be cremated at her local Crematorium.

Dr. Wu:

I consulted her employers at the Publishing House and they suggested getting an ambulance from their side, to collect her body for the autopsy. That worked and at her Memorial Service, I spoke from my heart, thanking her comrades – I avoided explaining why she took her own life.

Yang Yuhua had been a very popular factory doctor and I was warned, when we held her Memorial Service, that the factory workers would accuse me, saying that she died for family reasons, and I could be held responsible. I later learned that the workers had been reassured and knew that I was not at fault.

I tried to help the family financially after Yang Yuhua's death, until her mother died.

> By the 1980s, the chief architects of the Cultural Revolution were either dead or in jail, but their legacy of mistrust and betrayal continued. Confucian family values, once the bedrock of stability in Chinese society, had been replaced by the cult of Mao, the untouchable Peasant Emperor. In his absence, the seeds of mistrust flourished and a sense of "every man for himself" pervaded society.
>
> I had befriended Jieping before he married Yang Yuhua in 1981. He seemed very happy and proudly sent photographs of their wedding. He was very keen to have us meet, but he was extremely busy as President of the CAMS, among a host of other boards

and associations. He still practised at the three main hospitals and while Zhou, his most important patient, had died, he still retained responsibility for the health of the new leaders of China.

Now it was in his clinical research that Jieping sought and found solace. Heartbroken at the loss of a kindred spirit, a beautiful, cultivated woman from the same background as himself, he immersed himself in his old, unfinished research.

Dr. Wu:

In 1949 when I returned from the US, I had not had any special training in the anatomy of the adrenal gland, but I had some experience of treating patients with problems in this area, and surgery related to the adrenal gland became part of my field. The two adrenal glands are positioned next to the kidneys. At the time, China's hospitals did not have departments for endocrine surgery, and despite the proximity of the adrenal glands to the kidneys, adrenal gland disorders did not traditionally fall under the remit of the Urogenital Surgical Department.

> Over the years Jieping found that some diagnoses were inaccurate because the kidney failure was a result of a blockage rather than TB. In 1954, he reported in the journals a system of treatment to prevent the loss of life in these patients.
>
> The following year Jieping identified a new condition, adrenal medullary hyperplasia (AMH), an increase in a secretion of the adrenal cortex. A tumour, adrenal medullar cytoma, had already been identified, but no such disease existed in hyperplasia.

I was very interested in Cushing's Syndrome, the symptoms of which are a fatter, shorter neck, a hyper-metabolic state, thin skin, high blood pressure and an increase of facial hair in women. In the adrenal cortex, a tumour or hyperplasia can be caused by the pituitary. In the medulla, the central part, the only disease known to arise is a tumour called pheochromocytoma. Hyperplasia does not occur.

> Jieping diagnosed a case of pheochromocytoma in one of his patients. During surgery he found no tumour, but he observed that the medulla was enlarged; and the pathological exam showed very

bad hyperplasia, tumour-like or pheochromocytoma hyperplasia. Hyperplasia is not the same as a tumour – tumours multiply without limit. Jieping removed the hyperplasic medulla and the patient was cured.

The physiotherapist wife of another colleague had chronic hypertension, which the doctors thought might be due to a tumour. Jieping operated and found one adrenal gland enlarged and no tumour, so he looked at the other one. This was not enlarged, so he removed the enlarged one and biopsied the normal-looking one.

The pathologist's report said it was pheochromocytoma-like hyperplasia, an overgrowth like a tumour. The normal-looking one was microscopically worse than the enlarged one. Leaving the cortex intact, Jieping curated the medulla with formalin to get rid of the bad cells. He called the condition adrenal medullary hyperplasia, which until then did not exist in the medical books.

Jieping became curious and started looking for other cases. He found only four papers in the history of medicine relating to this condition. Autopsies even insisted there was "no such thing as hyperplasia of the adrenal medulla". It is extremely uncommon, but nonetheless it did appear to exist.

"When a clinician solves something, it is simple," Jieping said to me. "Before it is solved, everyone accepts that the traditional concept is correct, which, of course, it is not."

In challenging accepted theory, Jieping showed an individual responsibility likely to get him into trouble in a society governed by the will of the masses. In the case of adrenal medullary hyperplasia, because it is so rare the traditional concept is even more difficult to challenge, as the opportunity to study the condition so seldom arises.

Jieping wrote up his findings in Chinese in 1977 and in English in 1979. His article was published in the *Yearbook of Urology* in the US. Editorial comments suggested that it was a new discovery needing the confirmation of other scientists.

Jieping's work began to get the recognition it deserved. Instead of dying of hypertensive crisis, patients now recovered. At the International Surgical Congress, one doctor commented: "Hyperfunction in the adrenal cortex can be caused by tumours or by hyperplasia. It's only logical to find that hyperfunction of the medulla can be caused by tumours and also by hyperplasia." Cushing's[44] contribution encouraged Jieping to question accepted findings and to trust his own judgement.

Jieping went back to review seventeen other cases. None of the patients showed any other endocrine symptoms. Jieping's studies, therefore, showed two distinct kinds of adrenal medullary hyperplasia. The first involved simply the adrenal medullary gland, and the other came to be known as Multiple Endocrine Neoplasia (MEN). This distinction was Jieping's contribution.

After hearing of Jieping's pioneering work, I could understand his disappointment that the condition was not ultimately recognized as "Wu's syndrome".

For many years, Jieping had discussed family planning policy with Zhou Enlai. From his efforts on sex education, his colleagues were not surprised that he was nominated to lead the recently-established China Family Planning Association (CFPA).

By the late 1970's, the population of China was approaching one billion and the new leadership, headed by Deng Xiaoping, considered curbing the growth rate. A voluntary programme in 1978 encouraged families to have no more than two children. In 1979, pressure grew for the limit to be no more than one child; but this was not universally required throughout the provinces. To standardise the policy nationally, the Central Committee of the Chinese Communist Party published a letter calling on everyone to adhere to the one child policy, for which 25 September 1980 was the official start date.

When it became evident that the voluntary system of reducing family size was not working, tougher action had to be implemented. As part of the one child policy, couples would need a permit from their Unit to have a child. This was monitored by (at one point forty-eight million) volunteers; and while every imaginable form of birth control was provided by the State, if a second pregnancy occurred, families were obliged to pay a fine or else there were forced abortions.

---

[44] Harvey Cushing (1869-1939) questioned accepted wisdom and pioneered neurosurgery, teaching at Harvard, Yale and Johns Hopkins universities.

To help alleviate the anxiety of men, Jieping contributed by devising a reversible form of vasectomy.

On my visits to China, Wu Jieping often invited me to join him on hospital rounds. On one occasion when we were in Changsha, he invited me to join him at the Obstetrics, Gynaecology and Paediatric wards. He explained, as he introduced me as Dr. Cox, that the three young women in the ward had all volunteered to terminate. It was very clear that at least one of them had been coerced and she cried when I spoke to her. The others explained that the Government issued birth control pills, but they had not worked.

In the face of low birth rates, a diminishing workforce and an aging population, Chinese officials announced the end of the policy in 2015. As recently as 2021, the Chinese government continued to legislate for the number of children (then three) that a married couple could have.

CHAPTER TWENTY
"REVOLUTION IS NOT A DINNER PARTY"

At the end of the 1970s, observers questioned how the leaders of China were going to handle the abuses and the history of the past twenty years of Mao's reign. Expose them or bury them? What actually happened is almost beyond the understanding of people in the West.

Jieping often used to quote a saying: "If you tell a lie a thousand times, it becomes the truth." Denial, and a will to forget, now seemed to be China's chosen path.

To preserve peace and order, Deng Xiaoping, the economic pragmatist who was Zhou Enlai's chosen replacement as Chairman, mapped the least disruptive plan for China's economic reform.

Dr. Wu:

Deng Xiaoping did a lot of things right, at the right time. Following his death, Mao was still regarded as a God by most of the population, and people believed his doctrine had to be pursued. Deng needed to somehow rectify this. He proclaimed, "You must follow the truth of reality, but you don't need to go into the details of what actually happened during the Cultural Revolution. You just need to have a general understanding. The former will cause conflict, especially between the old and young."

Deng strove to remove responsibility from the shoulders of the young, to avert a general national depression and claimed, "The young were misled: there have been instances when a father was rehabilitated and his children could not accept it. But when the young understood that they were in the wrong, there were many suicides."

If the Red Guards had denounced their fathers, they could only hope something good would come out of the next generation.

> This seems unimaginable today in the West, but given that China had suffered the disasters of the Opium Wars, the Boxer Rebellion and its punitive resolution, the betrayal by the Allies after World War 1, the Revolution of 1911 that terminated the Qing dynasty, their World War 2 lasting eleven years (from the strafing of Shanghai in 1937 to the defeat of Chiang Kai-shek in 1948), the Mao era and the Cultural Revolution, no price was deemed too high if it allowed for peaceful coexistence and development. The Chinese had learned, during those appalling times, how to bite their tongues and "eat bitterness".
>
> Jieping explained how Mao persuaded the masses to follow his lead.

Dr. Wu:

Mao started making landlords, teachers and successful businessmen wear white dunces' caps to mobilize the spirit of the peasants who, for generations, had been obedient to them. He said, "Revolution is not a dinner party, it is constant revolution," but during the Cultural Revolution, it was used too harshly with intellectuals.

> Jieping rationalized, "It's easy to be misled by people who are eloquent and powerful." The Cultural Revolution decade of madness was only possible because it was calculated. The grudges of Mao, The Great Helmsman, were nurtured silently, only to be repaid later.
>
> Jieping tried looking at these excesses from the point of view of the young and thus excused them, at least partially.

Dr. Wu:

My third wife, Gao Rui is very different from my second wife, Yang Yuhua, and in many ways Gao Rui thinks that my first wife, Zhao Junkai, was too harsh. Gao Rui is very emotional and explosive but her outbursts are usually over in two or three minutes – that's her asset. Her first husband died in 1980 and we met in 1983. He was an old revolutionary leader who dealt very nicely with the intellectuals. I knew him by name when he was a director of the Academia Sinica Institute. He was not a scientist, but formerly a director of the Institute of Mathematics and was older than Gao Rui, but not as old as me.

> Jieping chuckled happily. At 66, he was in excellent shape to woo and charm a simple woman who was the same age as his eldest child. The couple had been introduced at the suggestion of Gao Rui's daughter, Xiao Meng, later known to me as Marina. Having met Jieping's sister-in-law, she proposed they host a dinner and seated the widow beside the handsome widower. The rest, as they say, is history. Jieping was at that time living with his son who didn't get on with Gao Rui so he moved out.
>
> During his second marriage, and for a while during his third marriage, Wu Jieping's mother lived with Jieping, his son and daughter-in-law and their child. This ideal Chinese home of four generations under one roof continued until Jieping's mother died. But then trouble started between Jieping's son and Gao Rui. Although their house at the time was spacious – five bedrooms, which is rare for China – space was not as plentiful as it might have been. The main reason for this was Jieping's extensive library, which took up much of what could have been used as living space.
>
> Jieping told me that his family discriminated against his new wife because she was uneducated. She described herself as an "ordinary worker," so I asked, "What do you share with Gao Rui?"

Dr. Wu:

We take care of each other. She was born in 1932 and is fifteen years younger than me, but she has some physical weaknesses. My family sees this marriage as difficult. I try to educate and influence Gao Rui, although she thinks I'm a very weak person. But I challenge her, "How could a weak person reach this level of success?"

> I wondered if perhaps the death of his second wife made him determined to make a success of his third marriage. Jieping accepted his wife's criticism and tried to explain himself, but he never took it to heart. He was brought up with such expressions as, "Hold your sides tightly, don't wag your tail", meaning, "Be humble". Gao Rui thought he was often overly so; but wondered whether it was a family trait, as his brothers were also like that.
>
> Jieping took great delight in showing his wife the world, rather like a proud father educating his children. And as he travelled the world with her, showing her great cities, different cultures, introducing her to eminent people everywhere he went, it is tempting to wonder how often he reflected on the drive that earned him the position he achieved. Did the passion and energy that saw him single-mindedly stick to his goal through the Japanese pillaging, the tuberculosis, the crude conditions in Korea and the rampage of the Cultural Revolution, come from the efforts of another woman, his mother? Jieping never lost respect for her.
>
> About ten years later, he told me:

I came back from Australia three weeks ago. Foreign Minister Huang Hua was ill and I should have attended to him, but I had chest pains and Gao Rui insisted that I go to hospital myself. The medical consensus was that I was suffering from lung cancer. There were many letters from my colleagues urging me to have an operation. But I wanted to wait for a certain doctor to make the diagnosis. There were lesions on one of my lungs and I couldn't be sure whether they were the old ones from the TB, or new ones.

> Fortunately, he did wait and the diagnosis of lung cancer turned out to be wrong.

Gao Rui worked in a medical library and modestly described herself as an "ordinary worker". She was always warm-hearted and kind towards me and incredibly solicitous of her husband.

Aware of the family rift, of his son no longer speaking to him and the pressure and pain it was causing him, I had asked Jieping one day, "When your family is so different from Gao Rui, why did you marry her?"

Jieping did not hesitate in replying, "I need somebody to look after me and look out for me when I get old and Gao Rui is willing to be that person. In return, she will travel with me and have a lifestyle that would not otherwise be open to her. So, we will enjoy a complementary exchange."

I recall teasing him a little, "And as she is also a lot younger, you are bound to have a lot more fun…." Unable to maintain a serious expression, Jieping smiled, in spite of himself.

Perhaps the apparently great difference between the generations is that Jieping's children in today's China do not seem to have achieved a similar level of success in their own careers. While they clearly wanted to attend university and have professions, their education coincided with the dawn of New China when everyone was deemed equal. In that egalitarian society, Junkai and Jieping would have been severely criticized for pushing their children, or giving them any advantage.

That Wu Xing (the daughter who had volunteered for Korea and lost six years of education) managed to finally get the education that permitted her to lecture at one of China's great language centres is testament to her drive and hard work. Jieping's other daughter, Wu Bing, and his son, Wu Desheng, both rose to senior levels in their professions.

So accustomed had Jieping's family become to his taking no action on their account that they were only mildly critical that "he did not lift a finger to help his grandchildren". Communist Party leaders' children, or well-connected youth who had been sent "up to the mountains, down to the countryside" *(shang shan xia xiang)* by Mao's directive on 28 December, 1968, returned to their families or cities via the back door; but the less fortunate were stuck, including some of Jieping's grandchildren.

He had witnessed the abuse of the intellectual class, and been so subjected to the egalitarian propaganda of the 1950s and '60s that these combined to outweigh his father's teaching and his personal experience growing up. He clearly sought to believe that if he was able to strive with ill health to become the best in his field, others were equally capable of developing themselves.

Jieping's eldest granddaughter, Mingjia, lived up to his expectations, graduating as a medical doctor from the first medical school he had founded.

His second granddaughter, Lilian, had begun to assist her grandfather when his wife died and she helped him with some secretarial work, but she was displaced following his third marriage. Sadly for Lilian, she found that she was now 'surplus to requirements.' She asked for his help to study for her MA in the US, but he refused. It was against his principles, and her mother, Wu Xing, did not have her own mother's grit. Jieping's three children were among the most successful of that lost generation. And part of that success was due to their low profiles. They succeeded in not dying.

In some exasperation, Jieping said to me one day,

What we went through in the '60s was not a Cultural Revolution; it was cultural extermination and genocide of the educated elite.

> In 1987, a riding accident caused me to lose much of my memory and the book I was writing had to be postponed. I did not travel to China at that time, but fortunately I was able to meet Jieping on his travels to the US.
>
> When I visited Beijing in 1990, I was surprised at the way in which he had changed again. Apparently, during the student demonstrations of a year earlier, which culminated in the Tiananmen Square massacre, Jieping appealed to the student protesters in a TV broadcast in which he was reported to have cried. When he told me about this, Jieping's eyes filled with tears again and he explained:

I should have gone in person to talk to the students. I might have prevented the disaster of the massacre, because I understood the underlying frustration and resentment leading from the Democracy Wall Movement of 1978 right up to the Tiananmen Square 'incident' of 1989.

Throughout the 1990s, I would visit Jieping and Gao Rui on my annual visits to China, and on their visits to Europe and the US they would stay at my home. In 1994, we had started our chats about his life and memories, in order for me to write his biography.

On one of my visits in 1996, we were driven onto the station platform to board a private carriage to Chengde, where Jieping was going on a medical inspection tour. We joined Gao Rui, her daughter Xiao Meng and her eight-year-old son, as well as Jieping's secretary and a bodyguard. When ordinary travellers gaped at us I felt uncomfortable and, unable to stand their scrutiny, I retreated into the cabin.

Jieping was clearly pleased to be recognized by the masses, who called out his name and he waved in appreciation of their adulation. He seemed pleased to be able to expose me to a different way of life.

The Court (Astor) Hotel next to Jieping's family home.

Dr. Wu Jieping and Dr. Yang Yuhua following their marriage, 1981

Four generations of the Wu family following the wedding

The Chinese Medical Delegation visiting the Squibb Corporation in the United States of America, in 1979

Train to Chengde for the medical inspection tour
Security convoy alongside the train with a private carriage, awaiting the arrival of Dr. Wu

L – R : Bodyguard; Gao Rui; Olivia Cox-Fill; the Secretary to Dr. Wu; and Dr. Wu Jieping

The Government Official Guest House, Chengde,
Hebei Province: street scene with Security Detail

The Government Official Guest House:
Gao Rui on the terrace

Gao Rui and Dr. Wu Jieping on their visit to Chengde

"REVOLUTION IS NOT A DINNER PARTY"

L – R : Dennis Fill; Dr. Wu Jieping; Huang Dongsheng; Olivia Cox-Fill; and Haematologist Dr. Teng. Circa 1981.

L – R: (back row) Dr. Teng; Dr. Wu Jieping; (front row) Distinguished Obstetrician and Gynaecologist Ran Yen Ying; and Olivia Cox-Fill.

The Chinese Academy of Medical Sciences (old building)

The Friends of Peking Union Medical College

**The Friends of
Peking Union Medical College**

The Friends of the Peking Union Medical College will be administered by a Committee of sixteen chaired by: Deng Jia-dong (Teng Chia-tung), Chairman, Class of 1933, Professor of Medicine, Former Vice President of Peking Union Medical College; and Wu Jie-ping (Wu Chieh-ping), Vice Chairman, Class of 1942, Honorary President of College, Professor of Urology.

An incorporation under the title of "The Friends of Peking Union Medical College, Inc." was established in the United States for fund-raising to support the Foundation in Beijing. To coordinate the work of the Foundation in Beijing and the Incorporation in the United States, two PUMC alumni sit on both Committees.

*Executive Committee
in the United States*
Charles A. Sanders, M.D.
Co-Chairman
Wu Jie-ping, M.D.
Co-Chairman
Members
Robert H. Ebert, M.D.
Dennis C. Fill
Olivia C. Fill
Nancy Huang, M.D.
Richard S. Ross, M.D.
Sheldon J. Segal, Ph.D.
Gene C. Szutu, M.D.
Daniel C. Tosteson, M.D.

Address:
The Friends of
Peking Union Medical College
P.O. Box CN5207
Princeton, New Jersey 08543

The Friends of Peking Union Medical College, narrative

Although Chengde is only about 180 kilometres from Beijing, it took two or three hours and a good lunch with wine, a siesta, afternoon tea and snacks to get us there. I continued interviewing him until we arrived in Chengde. A Mercedes limousine drove onto the platform here, too, and we were swept along to the allocated destination. Soon, we were being ushered into the Government Guest House with its enormous library, where I interviewed Jieping alone, away from the family, before another rest and a banquet.

Next morning, bright and early, I accompanied Jieping and a couple of officials to two hospitals, where I witnessed him examining a woman with a swollen abdomen. The way in which he quietly instructed the nurses and doctors, as he rearranged the clothing around the patient, after first touching her arm and introducing himself, spoke volumes.

Jieping told her, "I'm Dr. Wu from Beijing and I'd like to help my colleagues to diagnose your illness." He respected this lady's dignity and inspired her confidence, before touching her.

Jieping's instruction to the other medical staff had been along the lines of, "We must protect the dignity and privacy of our patients, because we don't know whether we will be able to help their medical condition or not."

He had a way of not infringing on the space or dignity of his patients, which the medical staff had overlooked in their excitement to have the famous Dr. Wu give his opinion.

Jieping pressed the woman's abdomen in different places, asking her questions about the levels of discomfort, having already been debriefed by her doctors. He suggested additional diagnostic procedures, as well as a couple of possible diagnoses. Then he squeezed her arm gently, before covering her abdomen with the sheet and telling her she was in good hands. From the expression in her eyes as we left, it was evident that Jieping had given this lady hope and a sense of self-assurance that would sustain her. It reminded me of the biblical healing miracles, and I laughed inwardly, as Jieping and I were both atheists. It was his display of humanism that touched everyone around him. His special signature was a unique quality of care that had been honed by his teachers and mentors along the way.

Jieping's next patient was a boy of about fifteen. Here again, he was noticeably solicitous about the boy's privacy and introduced me as an English doctor so the boy would not be embarrassed. As it concerned a urogenital issue, this diagnosis was right up Jieping's street and he recommended a simple procedure to encourage the boy's second testicle to drop into the scrotum. Failing that, he recommended other simple procedures, while encouraging the boy to play sports and study hard at school. He asked what his favourite stories were and otherwise deflected the boy's attention from his examination.

After two days of chaperoned hospital visits, we had a morning off and he decided we should go to a local museum. I was astonished at the pushing and shoving we experienced as we tried to enter. After all, this was a man of over eighty and the youths had no regard for his frailty. I suddenly understood the justification for the body-guards, chauffeurs and private train carriage.

On another occasion, we were invited to see a new statue erected to memorialize Chairman Mao. Such is the propaganda machine created by the Communist Party to preserve the reputation of the leader of communist China, that whole swathes of the population still nurture respect for the one and only Chairman Mao.

* * *

Jieping and I were in constant communication about the content of our talks until I gave him the printed version, after the handover of Hong Kong in 1997. When he handed it back, he said,

"Did I really tell you all of that? Of course; you couldn't have got it from anyone else. But if you publish that now, you will probably never see me again."

I was incredulous and asked why.

"Because I shared with you a number of what would be regarded now as 'state secrets', for which I will be punished."

"But you are one of the leaders and above all that. After all, you are Vice-Chair of the CCPCC, Chairman of this, that and the other…"; but he was certain he did not want it to be published then.

"I must be seen as an example to the young members of all the organizations where I have a position. Please wait until I die."

I understood his instruction to hold off the publication of my book, but was disheartened. I was obliged to honour his wish and wait until Jieping's death, which occurred in March 2011.

CHAPTER TWENTY-ONE
FRIENDS REUNITED

The following year, 1998, while staying at the Grand Hotel in Beijing with my son Jason, I received word that Jieping was ill in hospital, following a stroke, but wished to see me. As both he and Gao Rui were very fond of Jason, I took him along.

Jieping's appearance shocked me at first – he no longer had the trademark jet black hair like most members of the Consultative Conference committee of which he was Vice Chairman. Now, his grey hair made him look more distinguished and he seemed a little frail.

We talked in English about the book I had been writing, as he had introduced me to a few of the important women who were portrayed in it. After a while he lapsed into Chinese and I gently requested that he speak more slowly, because I had lost the memory of most of my Chinese and could not really understand him. Obviously, his stroke had not affected him too adversely as, a few minutes later, he was teasing my son in English, admonishing him to study hard at university.

Jieping and I remained in frequent touch by telephone and we met on my regular visits to China. I moved to Beijing in 2006. When I finally got a response from his phone, I was, surprised to learn from his stepdaughter Marina (Yang Xiaomeng), that he was in hospital in the suburbs. I had sent a number of faxes, letters and left phone messages and I had also met his secretary many times, but received no replies.

Jieping had previously taken me to visit the offices of the Wu Jieping Medical Foundation in 2001, in the central block of the Beijing Hotel. He also proudly showed me the museum shelves dedicated to him at the Urology Hospital.

Marina called one day in early 2007, in response to calls and faxes I had sent to Jieping at the Foundation. She asked if I had time to visit Jieping in the afternoon. I told her I was occupied until 4.00 p.m. and she said, "I'll send my Dad's driver to collect you then."

Jieping always arrived early for our meetings or dinners, so I expected the chauffeur to arrive promptly. Telephoning from his mobile phone to announce his arrival outside, he had parked several buildings away, as there was no parking in the hutong outside my courtyard house. When I walked out, he flashed his lights to indicate his presence. I noted the shaded glass windows typical of the 'A' registration plate indicating a VIP, and knew it would be Jieping's driver. The chauffeur got out and I recognized the man who had driven us onto the platform alongside Jieping's private railway carriage ten years earlier, on our memorable outing to Chengde. My neighbours in the *hutong* also noticed and registered the event for their usual report to the local Security Bureau.

We picked up three young men about five minutes from my neighbourhood, who were presumably joining the meeting with Jieping. They didn't speak English and I worked out, from my scanty Chinese, that they all worked for the Wu Jieping Medical Foundation under Marina. I was decidedly perplexed as to our destination as we sped out of the city along the Badaling Expressway, miles past anything I recognized. We drove past the departure airfield famously used for Lin Biao's fatal last flight, and I wondered if I was being whisked to some sort of Shangri-La. Past the Air Force Museum, past some villages and miles of cultivated fields later, we turned into a guarded complex with a fine hotel outside, describing itself as a sanatorium. I guessed we had arrived.

My friend the driver and the three other occupants led me inside. Marina appeared, very attractively dressed in a knitted St. John suit, and said, "My Dad will be ready soon. When did you arrive?"

I told her I'd been back six days and she said, "What a shame you weren't in touch earlier; we had a big birthday party at the National People's Congress on the Twentieth. But this is his family party so really, you are here for the most important one. He was only able to stay at the Congress for twenty minutes."

Of course – Jieping was ninety years old. We would be celebrating our friendship of twenty-seven years.

Marina and I made small talk about our sons, our Christmas plans and so on, when she suddenly said, "Let's go." We walked to the end of a corridor where I was ushered through to a large room. There sat Jieping, blanketed in a wheelchair, with a woolly hat covering his head, surrounded by seven or eight people. His beautiful eyes watered slightly when he saw me and I wondered, as he spoke to me in Chinese, just how much he remembered. I sat next to him, holding his trembling hands until they were quiet, and wondered if it was a sign of Parkinson's disease. Tea was brought and an older, grey-haired, slimmer Gao Rui appeared to greet me warmly. I was slightly surprised that both of them had given up dyeing their hair. By this time, my Chinese had recovered somewhat and I told him, "Dennis sends his warmest greetings and would like to come to China to see you."

I was surprised by his response, "I don't know a Dennis." My ex-husband Dennis was President of the Squibb Corporation when we first met Jieping in 1979. When we started the Capital Medical Foundation to improve hospital care in the capital, Jieping headed the Delegation to the US: a trip that also marked his first time back in the States since he finished his post-doctorate training in 1949. That delegation was sponsored by Squibb Corp.[45]

I decided to leave it at that as we chatted in and out of English. His hands in mine gradually became still, so Jieping's grasp improved and the sadness that filled his eyes seemed to plead for my understanding. He was surrounded by people and yet, seemed so alone.

---

[45] See Chapter 20 photograph, *Chinese Medical Delegation visiting the Squibb Corporation in the USA, 1979*

(L-R) Gao Rui and Wu Jieping with Olivia Cox-Fill at their favourite Beijing Restaurant, c. 1995

Marina came and sat with us as I asked after his family. She told me that two of his brothers had died in the last year (one of whom I had known about) and we finally got around to his younger brother, the now more famous President of Beijing Hospital. We chatted about the state of health of our mutual friend, Huang Hua and the fact that he, too, had lost a lot of weight and depended on an oxygen tank for several hours each day.

Jieping said, "Well, the oxygen hasn't made any difference to me!" and I thought he was pretty focused, when the subject interested him.

He closed his eyes and Marina asked if he wanted to rest, which he acknowledged by an imperceptible nod. Again, as I disengaged my hand, Jieping opened his eyes and that same, haunting expression returned – a little like my mother's, the last time I saw her. I was overcome with sympathy at the helpless position he found himself in, totally dependent on others for everything.

Outside in the corridor I said to Marina, "Oh, I forgot to take his photograph, I'd love to do that." I was grateful when she replied, unexpectedly, "We're going to have dinner in his honour and see him later for his birthday cake."

We went back to the strangely utilitarian reception area where I had first been waiting. There I was introduced to two or three different doctors, some of whom spoke a smattering of English, and to Dr. Frank Fang, the Secretary General of the Wu Jieping Medical Foundation, who, Marina told me, came from close to the North Korean border where she had been in late December. Several nurses were introduced before she announced it was time for the family birthday party.

We entered a large, lavishly decorated room where two tables were laid for ten, with red velvet chairs trimmed with gold sashes and bows. A side table offered refreshments. I sat between Marina and Dr. Fang. Marina whispered, "He's great fun after a few drinks" and she proceeded to fill his glass and challenge him to *gan bei!* (the Chinese for "bottoms up") with the other doctors and nurses. He was more than willing to oblige with a variety of drinks, red wine, beer, cider and a light, sweetened red wine like fermented Ribena. Many of the good red wines imported into China were "altered" at that time to suit the Chinese palate, with the addition of wolfberry juice.

The guests all seemed to advise or be employed by the Wu Jieping Medical Foundation, which is run under the auspices of the Ministry of Health. Well into his cups, Dr. Fang elaborated to me on the mission of the Foundation. When I asked about the funding, he told me, "We are well supported by Bristol-Myers Squibb (formerly the Squibb Corporation) and the Pfizer Corporation whose public relations is run by the granddaughter of the famous North West warlord, Feng."

The Wu Jieping Medical Foundation was established on 28 February, 2002 in Beijing by the Ministry of Health. The Foundation's objective is to unite all medical professionals, in and outside China, who share an interest in the development of medicine and health through financing various academic activities to promote the medical profession and health education in China.

Soon, Jieping returned to the party and the birthday cake arrived. We all got our cameras out and my friend was allowed to remove his woolly cap for the photographs. After elaborate preparations, Gao Rui and Marina helped him cut his birthday cake, and he indicated that I should come closer to him. I felt decidedly embarrassed as I supplanted Gao Rui, who luckily was distracted by the arrival of another lady doctor bearing an album she had made of some of Jieping's most memorable moments. As he was shown this, Jieping mentioned many of his patients by name, Marshal Ye, Chen Yi, Deng Xiaoping, Zhou Enlai and others; but interestingly, no mention of The Great Helmsman, or Madame Mao.

When the party broke up, Jieping's bodyguard came to take him back to his room. I was relieved when Marina told me that her driver would be taking me back to the city, as I had noted how many times Jieping's driver had challenged Dr. Fang to *gan bei* and didn't fancy my chances.

Marina was very merry, although we'd each had only two tiny glasses of red wine. We dropped the Ministry doctor off at what, I presume, was the visitors' hotel for the sanatorium, then proceeded onto a highway where workers were already preparing to welcome the Year of the Pig. Lots of police cars had stopped trucks that would not be allowed to enter the city until later.

I was home by 9.45 p.m., after what seemed like several hours in Wonderland.

* * *

I was regularly surprised by how much China was changing in the free market society,

I texted Marina about Jieping's biography and whether she could check with him if I could revisit that subject. I had mentioned it in passing to him as one of the highlights of traveling with him and Gao Rui, saying that Dennis was urging me to publish it, to which he responded, "Good." But whether he really took it on board or not I couldn't be sure, until we were one-on-one again.

Once, when Marina and I were having dinner, she revealed, "When my mum married Wu Jieping, she went to live in his apartment behind the Beijing Hotel. I was then living with three girlfriends, all of whom had boyfriends and I had just broken up with mine. I have no brothers or sisters; my Mum was spending all her time with someone who was very kind to her and all my friends had their boyfriends and I was very lonely. Every time I saw my Mum, she told me of the kindness of Dr. Wu and I realized how much she loved and admired him. I suppose I felt sort of excluded. Everyone wanted me to meet someone. My father's secretary introduced me to a cousin of his and I married him."

I was surprised that she confided this to me. This was before private ownership was permitted in China and private apartment buildings were not yet being constructed. In any case, Marina would not have had the means to buy an apartment on her own.

"I still had to live in housing allocated by my work unit, as nobody had any savings and there were few rental apartments. Dr. Wu shared everything he knew and experienced with my Mum and when I was with them, there was no difference; he shared with me also and never treated me any differently. There are no romantic men like my father Jieping in China now."

Having watched Jieping in action with Gao Rui on various travels – ever the born teacher – he would point out aspects of life to her that I would find distinctly annoying, (perhaps because I knew them already, or because it would show the inferiority of my own education), but which she took with a fervent and childlike grace that always surprised me.

The more I see of Marina, the more I like and admire her spirit. She is quietly spoken, not aggressive and tells me she goes out to the sanatorium every day, either for lunch or for dinner, with her parents. She says, at seventy-five, her mother expects her support, but never listens to her advice and when she says, "Baba can answer for himself or feed himself," she gets brushed off by her mother.

Later that month Marina suggested we meet at 6.00 p.m. for an early dinner; she mentioned a restaurant called Beijing Gong, where I had dined with her parents and Michael ten years earlier.

When the "concierge" had made sure that I was expected, I was invited into another formal reception room where Marina greeted me and introduced me to the owner and several other friends of hers.

Everyone seemed to know who I was because of a photo taken on the occasion when we had visited with Jieping, He Liliang and Huang Hua, on Michael's first trip to China in 1997.

Marina had just been driven back from seeing her parents and said they were both in terrific form.

"My father goes out twice a day to enjoy the fresh air and sunshine, and even manages to walk a little."

She was very encouraged by both his physical and mental condition. She said that his being well made her mother feel better. When I suggested she take the leftover desserts for them, she reminded me that neither of them could eat sugar because of blood sugar problems.

I was very touched by her assessment of Jiang Qing, Madame Mao:

"What chance did she have, married to someone like that? She was forced, as all girls were and some still are, to marry someone her mother thought suitable, who was taking her as a third wife or worse. She ran away, changed names and remarried a handsome student who could not feed her or keep up with her, but probably kick-started her acting career. By the time she arrived in Yan'an, she had nothing and nobody, so of course her head must have been turned by the attentions of this charismatic leader. Would she have preferred a little romance or some personal attention? Of course she would. But Mao was surrounded by people who did not trust her; so I think that warped her."

Seemingly in the know, she continued quietly:

"Later on, she became a pawn and was used terribly by 'The Great Helmsman'. And in this egalitarian society," Marina laughed ironically, "Mao's son lives far above the normal standard and his two daughters, one from his second wife and the other from Jiang Qing, do as well. They're pretty old by now."

Marina is very well connected, through Wu Jieping, to the academic world. She has invited university presidents onto the board of the Wu Jieping Medical Foundation. As Jieping was both President of the Jiu San Society and Vice Chair of the National People's Congress, Marina was smart enough to put them also on the Board of the Foundation; she now has their support and has progressed from General Secretary to President and now to Chairman.

She told me that all present that night did not give a fig for the education they might have had, or missed. They are all self-made entrepreneurs who worked hard and, with total determination, forged ahead mostly in the business world. She said that one or two are not above asking for government introductions.

Life continued for the next couple of years with me spending seven to eight months a year in my courtyard house in Beijing[46]. During this time, I took Mandarin classes for a few hours each day, visited friends, walked and jogged in the former Imperial Parks, hiked and generally enjoyed life as a resident tourist. I started a charity with my good friend, Mme. He Liliang, to help impoverished girls of the Hui minority in Ningxia Autonomous Region. I travelled there a couple of times each year, accompanied by Ms. Wei Xie who ran the charity under the auspices of The Soong Ching Ling Foundation. I also helped other friends with their charity work for children and animals.

Marina would call me from time to time, to suggest a visit to Dr. Wu or just simply a get-together for the two of us. I usually left Beijing in June and returned in September, dividing my time between our family home in Princeton, New Jersey and trips to the UK and Ireland.

After my return home in 2009, I failed to get any response from efforts to contact Marina, or Jieping's Secretary. I could not understand why Marina had become incommunicado.

After eighteen months of silence, I called Marina from Princeton, when I got news of Jieping's death on 2 March, 2011. I was shocked to learn that he had spent the last several months as a patient at PUMCH, which was close to my home and where I had spent quite a lot of time with him.

I arrived back at my courtyard house in Dongcheng District at 2 p.m. on 8 March; but I could not reach Marina until the next morning, when she told me, "We are at Babaoshan (the National Cemetery)[47] waiting for Hu Jintao and Wen Jiabao." Moments later, she rang back suggesting, "You can watch it on CCTV (China's state television broadcaster)." I was so surprised and hurt that I could not bear to turn on my computer and search for the coverage. I had expected to be invited to pay my respects at the funeral.

---

[46] See Epilogue, Author's Reflections

[47] Babaoshan is the Arlington National Cemetery, or Westminster Abbey, of China, where the most distinguished have their last rites. Hu Jintao and Wen Jiabao were the two most senior leaders of China immediately preceding Xi Jinping.

I was stunned when our mutual friends told me that they had been invited to attend and they had assumed I was out of the country.

I debated changing quickly and jumping into a taxi to Babaoshan (where I had earlier attended the funeral rites for Huang Hua with these same leaders). But after a few moments thinking about the character of a man I had come to love, I decided to take myself to Beihai Park, where I had occasionally walked with Jieping en route to the famous imperial restaurant, a favourite of his and of Empress Cixi. I sat in the restaurant and contemplated the memories of our charming times and why I had admired him so much.

When I returned home, I was mollified enough to find the proceedings live on my laptop. Watching the funeral service, I was interested to see that his widow Gao Rui, who had been married to him for twenty-five years, was in tears much of the time and looked very shaken, and his younger brother, the last of the four eminent Dr. Wu brothers, looked ancient. Jieping's children, who were about the same age as his widow or younger, looked so much more composed. I later learned that the Premier and President had been informed of Jieping's death before his brother was told. It was only through a loyal connection that his daughters and son discovered he had died.

There now also exists in Beijing a Wu Jieping Urology Centre and the Wu Jieping Medical Centre, with two hundred and nine beds.

According to Jieping's belief that "science should be imparted to the public", the Urology Centre has dutifully carried out several exhibitions concerning sexual health.

Na Yanqun, President of Peking University Shougang Hospital, said that the Centre would embody Jieping's advanced skills and endeavour to become one of the most advanced urology medical centres in the world.

On 22 March, 2013, the Founder Group and the Wu Jieping Medical Foundation signed a co-operative agreement on jointly promoting the development of urology and other medical fields in China. The report of the signing identifies the participants and his stepdaughter's elevation: "Academician Wu Jieping's wife Gao Rui, Director-General of the Wu Jieping Medical Foundation Xiao Meng, NPC Standing Committee member and academician of the Chinese Academy of Engineering Liu Depei, Director of Peking

University's Wu Jieping Urology Centre Na Yanqun, and several other academicians attended the signing ceremony."

Neither Jieping's brother nor his children were invited.

The term "princeling" is commonly used to describe the younger generation of Chinese who succeeded as a result of their name or connection to a famous member of the Communist Party. When Marina is described as such in commentaries about her, the irony is not lost on Jieping's children. As her chauffeur-driven Mercedes swept past their bicycles, they did not reveal their thoughts, for fear of denigrating their father's memory.

China's Man of La Mancha is gone. My hope is that his idealism and innocence were passed on to some of his students. Certainly, his children don't seem to recognise these characteristics in themselves. They remain concerned that Jieping's reputation may be damaged since it has been hijacked by others.

(L-R): Jason Fill; Olivia Cox-Fill; Dr. Wu Jieping; Gao Rui; and Dennis Fill

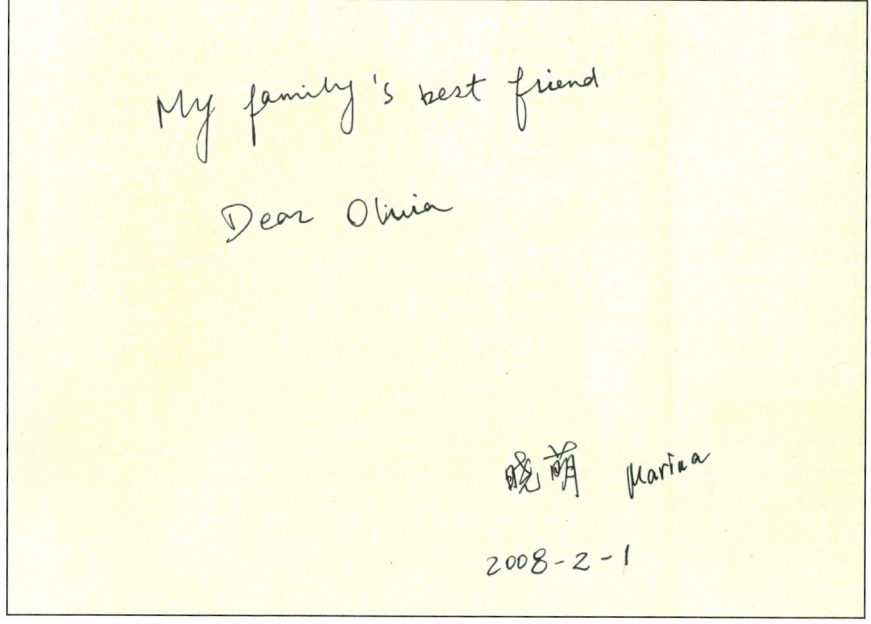

Dedication to Olivia Cox-Fill by Dr. Wu's stepdaughter Marina, Yang Xiaomeng

Wu Jieping Speaks at the Opening of the Chinese Academy of Medical Sciences and Peking Union Medical College, 6 June 2001

'An Extraordinary Journey and a Colourful Life: the Album of Wu Jieping'
ISBN No. 9 787 1170809-4-1

He Liliang and Olivia Cox-Fill

Olivia Cox-Fill visiting Huang Hua at home

The Forbidden City
By kind permission of Dennis Fill

The Forbidden City: golden roof tiles
By kind permission of Dennis Fill

MAP 1

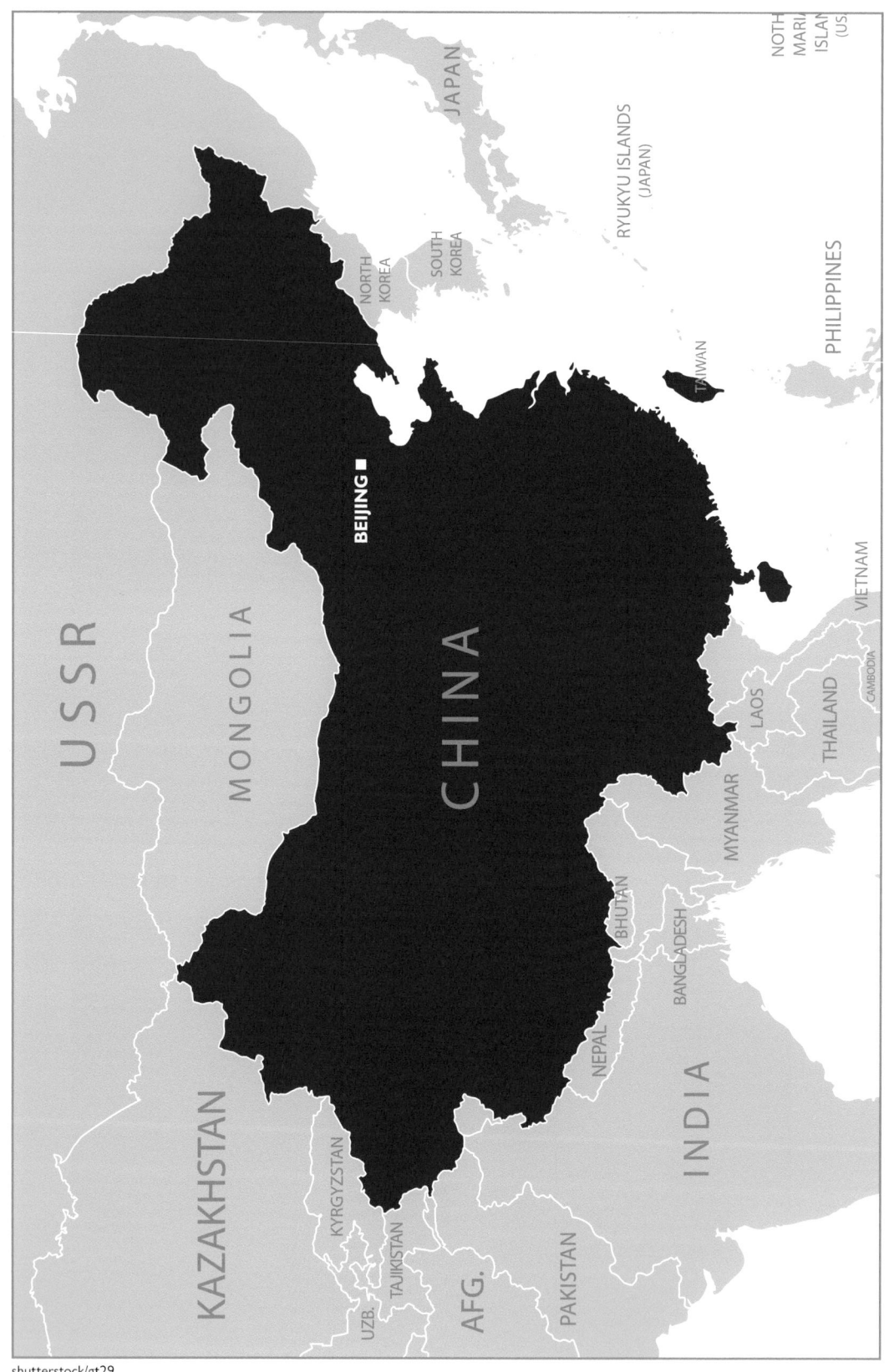

MAP 2

MAP 3

MAP 4

EPILOGUE

Zhou Enlai recognized that Jieping, like himself, was incorruptible; but since their deaths, China has changed and the Chinese people deserve to see examples of the noble sacrifices that both of these men endured on behalf of the Chinese people.

When Jieping and his brother read the big character posters and heard the Gang of Four's followers baying, "DOWN WITH LORD ZHOU!" they worried that their friend and patient would not be able to stand up to another attack; but Zhou had the willpower to endure. Like the Furies of Greek mythology, the din continued morning, noon and night. The Furies were baying for blood and Jieping was at his wits' end. His patient was dying and suffering from severe headaches, almost sleepwalking through a quagmire of meetings and responsibilities that could not be discharged by others. He wanted to have China back on track before he left.

Early in the Cultural Revolution, when associates had cautioned him to be careful, Zhou had responded, "If I do not enter the lions' den, who will save the cubs?" Jieping reflected that he had asked himself whether Zhou had ever guessed at the living hell to which he would be subjected.

As fearlessly as the dying Zhou fought those Furies, Jieping and his team guarded his back. Jieping could be credited with preventing Jiang Qing from tripping him up and thereby protecting the Premier on one specific occasion when she accused him publicly. But there is no record of the number of times she tried to get Zhou Enlai ousted.

The last time I visited Jieping at the sanatorium, with his wife Gao Rui by his side, his eyes appealed for my understanding. I squeezed his trembling hand and reassured him, "Never forget that in protecting Zhou Enlai for such a long time, you helped save China from that 'notorious woman'."

A rare look of contentment was followed quickly by a gentle nod, as his hands stilled and his rapid eye movements increased, telling me he was asleep.

I believe Jieping felt he had entrusted his life story to a pair of safe hands.

Author's Reflections

When I submitted this book to my Chinese publishers they sat on it for a long time; their stalling tactics made me realise that they had no intention of publishing it. I was living in a more open and liberal Beijing and assumed, naively, that the facts recorded on what Dr. Wu Jieping experienced in the 1960's would be regarded as a valuable lesson on the mistakes made by earlier revered leaders.

Some Chinese friends warned me that history repeats itself, that controls and restrictions of the 1950's and '60's could be re-imposed; but my retort was, 'You can't put the Genie back in the bottle'.

At that time, the path to openness led from the top. Jiang Zemin (1926-2022), paramount leader of China, 1989-2002, was open to modernisation. He presided over more than a decade of dramatic economic growth following the 1989 crackdown on pro-democracy protestors in Tiananmen Square. Under his leadership, China opened fearlessly to international expansion. He was followed by Hu Jintao, (1942-) under whom development continued, 2002 – 2012, and progressed towards greater openness.

With the selection of Xi Jinping in 2012, the anti-Imperialism jingo of earlier years initially became China's defence for 'protecting' the adjacent, disputed islands. But gradually, restrictions on expression coincided with interventions into private corporations, placing Government watch-dogs into the senior management. This Government intrusion grew out of all proportion with the onset of the Covid Pandemic; leading to the ejection of former leader Hu Jintao, who, readers may recall, was forcibly frog-marched out of the Great Hall of the People in October 2022, during the National People's Congress.

China's technological progression stole up on the rest of the developed world. The US wanted to believe the Chinese claim that it was a Third World country, with a massive peasant population living in poverty. China managed to hide its development *under a bushel*. Today, China is very advanced in outer-space exploration and possible space colonisation.

These technological advances have allowed massive numbers of peasants to move from their subsistence farming to labour in city factories, where they work, on average, twelve-hour days, six days a week. The White-Collar workers live in the factory compounds and, on their days off, can take the factory transport to the city. I ask whether the sacrifice of personal freedom for the security of a regular salary is adequate compensation? This is not a question that workers in China ask themselves, because of the lack of social safety nets. The vast population means that competition for these jobs is fierce.

There is minimal infrastructure of state education, or medical care, for the vast majority. The provision of welfare-for-all is not a Chinese construct. The Government wants to lift the maximum number out of poverty so that they can provide for themselves. The disabled and orphans are cared for, but help must be provided by the family and the community.

The concept of a Welfare State finds little favour in the meritocracy that is China. Neither Russia nor China lives up to the original ideals of Communism, equal sharing of a nation's resources. Far removed, in fact, from these communist virtues, both nations have become oligarchies. The concept of political freedom has never existed for either society. Both countries had been subjected by imperial might for millennia, while their present leaders now govern as dictators. Like most peoples, Chinese workers do not have time to think about political freedom; they mostly wish to work and be compensated.

It is perplexing that the educated intelligentsia appear to be neither willing to learn, nor care, about the repressions in China today. Those who 'make it' do not want to rock the boat. My questions in this regard were countered with a mild rebuff by Chinese friends: that the leaders knew what was best for the Chinese people. I recognise that the massive population needs to be controlled using its own value system. I ask why it is deemed necessary to suppress debate. I understand that fear has been so instilled that people cannot risk inviting the horrors of the Cultural Revolution upon themselves again. Why does repression of the masses succeed? The so-called 'Reform Schools' in Xinjiang are reported to be necessary re-education centres for unskilled workers. Can nothing be learned from differing cultures, or from those with opinions which differ from our own?

Against the many oppressive sacrifices that Chairman Mao inflicted on his people, he encouraged education and equality among China's minorities. Today, those minority languages, arts and ways of living are deliberately withdrawn from curricula and teachers are punished if they teach them.

The freedom to think and to criticise is being crushed, once again. What is the perceived, innate threat from the survival of the differences?

Once lost, a vital link to China's cultural development will be swamped by the dominant Han culture. The artist, revolutionary and polymath, Ai Wei Wei refers to "the withering of spiritual life" that marked the 1950's.

I invite readers to consider the premise that all Absolute Monarchies, followed by all Absolute Dictatorships, use fear of the outsider as a control mechanism.

Now, it seems that history is about to repeat itself; that government advisers, worldwide, are afraid to convey to their leaders anything that might indicate weakness in the present administration. This was a fact of leadership under American President Trump and Russian President Putin: and it continues under China's leader, Xi Jinping. Xi Jinping has imprisoned his critics and competitors. Nobody has the courage to challenge him. People must shelter, or hide within the regime, rather than challenge oppression. The personal cost of exposure is too great. They were not raised with an expectation of freedom of expression. It comes down to 'Food, not politics' – and the Chinese are a very pragmatic people. Xi Jinping does not have a Zhou Enlai equivalent to balance the equation.

The present 'Special Military Operation' in Ukraine was reported to be necessary because of the threat NATO poses on Russia's border. Putin will not stop until he has access to the ports that he requires. He will destroy everything, in his determination to recreate the Russian Empire. Yet China considers this to be "an internal matter" and will not criticise him unless the trouble reaches their own border.

I recall the secrecy insisted upon by Zhou Enlai at the establishment of the Communist Party in France and which permeated its establishment in China. And the fact that members were encouraged to use aliases. Regrettably, this secretiveness has become part of the character of the modern Chinese. How can society thrive when a lack of trust has become part of its DNA?

Should China's administrators not acknowledge and learn from the mistakes of the past, these are bound to be repeated in future. The Chinese people crave peace and development. Having been subjected by the British, Europeans and their allies for over one hundred years, and the Japanese more recently, small wonder that they did not trust the West and Democracy. Now, despite its growing economic power, China still cannot trust the West; and Western countries reciprocate by not trusting China.

It is also understandable that China should seek trade with Africa: but hopefully without bankrupting many African countries in the process. Is China now transposing the behaviour to which it was subjected onto another Continent?

Since China has been able to 'ride the tiger' for the past thirty years, it does not need to be repressive at home and should refuse to be goaded into defensive action. Sadly, I believe that people's faith in the propaganda of the Chinese Communist Party will see them marching towards a future that neither matches their potential nor fulfils their personal ambitions.

Having had a taste of alternative cultures, experienced through education and lives lived outside China, will Chinese students be content to return to live with the apparent trappings of the West, without the freedoms of expression? 'Make yourself richer, but don't rock the boat?'

None of the publications in China today take note of the brain drain that has occurred over the past decade. The majority of hard-working, brilliant, successful tycoons have left, forced to abandon their culture by the interference of government agents. Like Ai Wei Wei, they have lost "a sense of belonging" and must try to recreate a substitute in a foreign culture. And, as he so knowingly puts it, China "rejects memory and refuses to honestly address the task of building a healthy society… Its moral decay simply spreads anxiety and uncertainty in the world."

It could be argued that because of its latent myopia, China is engendering mistrust of its intentions worldwide, forcing the major powers to arm themselves for what might lie ahead.

The Future

The Chinese people are afraid to speak against repression by 'the strong man'. Despite claims of growth, the economy has been in freefall, since Covid paralysed it. Basic foodstuffs are unavailable and inflation means that people can no longer afford the basics they ate yesteryear.

The leading members of the Government and armed services are dominated by fear of their leader. Like earlier opponents, contenders for power could easily be purged and nobody would dare to question it. Likewise, members of the press and the intellectuals.

> *"….. when a fierce silence falls, we should be on our guard…."*
> Lu Xun, 1881-1936

The Chinese are a superstitious people, more so than people in the West:

"….When we see something like a poisonous snake gliding among the corpses, or an avenging spirit rushing through the darkness, we should be even more on our guard: for this is a sign that 'genuine fury' is coming."

Lu Xun was an ardent revolutionary who waged war with his pen and supported those rebelling against Imperialism, and bureaucrat-capitalism. The "fierce silence" he wrote about in the 1920's is all the more worrying, since today it follows the so-called "Opening Up" of the 1980's to 2015.

It is to be hoped that the present intellectual population will continue to find ways to express their dissatisfaction. History shows us that the oppressed will always find methods to challenge, if not overcome, suffocation by the powerful. I cannot write here what I have learned about the methods or language they use to disguise what they are writing about, lest the army of Internet spies and editors spot these; but it is some consolation that the people are not all committed to repression by silence.

My hope for my friends in China is that the march towards a more liberal society resumes; that people be allowed to maintain their traditions, be they religious or cultural; and that the diversity of the minorities be respected and protected. If we remain silent, we are complicit in the erosion of freedom and the exploitation of the Chinese people by those entrusted to guide and protect them.

In what now seems like the good old days, Wu Jieping was so worried about reprisals as an old man, that he asked me to wait until he died before publishing his life story. The leaders cannot get to him now and I believe he would want, more than ever, for the Chinese people to know what he had witnessed.

APPENDICES

Chronology of Chinese History 1911 – 1976

1911 Sun Yat-sen's armed insurrections cause the collapse of the Qing dynasty and signify the end of Imperial rule.

Sun Yat-sen forms the Kuomintang Nationalist Party (KMT).

Sun is President, but is side-lined by the coalition of warlords in Beijing.

World War I **(1914-18)** and the Versailles Peace Treaty of **1919** lead to the May 4th Movement, an anti-imperialist and anti-foreigner student political movement which grew out of protests in Beijing's two main universities and spread throughout the country.

1920 The Chinese Communist Party (CCP) is formed (by two visiting Comintern officials sent by Moscow), in Shanghai in August.

1921 Mao Zedong is invited to its first Chinese Communist Party Congress.

1924 Alliance between communists and nationalists.

1924 Huangpu Military Academy formed, with Zhou Enlai as Director of the Military Department.

Mao and Zhou are members of both the CCP and the KMT.

1925 Sun Yat-sen dies, in March.

Zhou Enlai leads Huangpu cadets against warlord Chen, defeats him at Shantou. His reputation soars, but he is discredited inside the leadership of the Communist Party.

1927 Chiang Kai-shek assumes leadership of the KMT.

Russian advisers offer contradictory advice to continue the alliance between the CCP and the KMT, and prepare a workers' up-rising.

1928 Japan annexes Manchuria.

1930-1934 Chiang Kai-shek leads the Kuomintang (KMT, or Chinese Nationalist Party) in launching a series of five military encirclement campaigns to annihilate the Chinese Communists (the fore-runner of the People's Liberation Army) in their base of the Jiangxi Soviet, on the border between Jiangxi and Fujian in south-eastern China. The first four of these are unsuccessful, resisted using tactics of guerilla warfare adopted by Mao.

1932 Japan bombs Shanghai.

1934 The fifth KMT military encirclement campaign involves seven hundred thousand, better-armed, troops and uses cement blockhouses to surround the Communists. By now, the Chinese Communist Central Committee has ousted Mao Zedong and returned to regular warfare tactics. Those tactics result in heavy losses.

1934-1936 The Long March: in fact, a series of marches which start from the border base in October 1934; led by Zhu De, a soldier with no political ambitions. Beginning in Jiangxi province, heading west and then north, the 6,000 mile trek crosses eighteen mountain ranges and twenty-four rivers. Zhou Enlai is the political commissar. During this military retreat by the remaining eighty-six thousand troops and some administrators, "Chairman" Mao emerges in January **1935**. About ninety percent of those who leave Jiangxi do not complete the March: lost in warfare, to disease or to starvation.

Ultimately, the Long March results in the relocation of the Communist base from south-western to north-eastern China. The reported heroism inspires many young Chinese to join the Chinese Communist Party during the late 1930's and early 1940's.

1937 Japan invades China.

1939-1945 World War II.

1945-1949 Civil War in China.

Mao and the CCP are victors.

1949 New China: the establishment of the People's Republic of China (PRC).

1950 The Korean War.

1958 The Great Leap Forward.

1966-76 The Cultural Revolution.

1969 The existence of the Gang of Four is acknowledged with contempt by Mao.

1971 Vice Chairman Lin Biao plans to bomb Mao's train, but dies during his attempted escape.

1973 Rehabilitation of Deng Xiaoping.

1976 Zhou Enlai dies in January.

Mao Zedong dies in September.

October **1976** Arrest of the Gang of Four,.

Key Dates in the Life and Times of Dr. Wu Jieping 1917 – 2011

1917   Born in Jiangsu province, about 180 km from Shanghai and 1,000 km south of Beijing.

1922   The Wu family move to Tianjin. Tianjin is 1,130km north of Shanghai and 114km south of Beijing.

1931   Introduced to Zhao Junkai.

1933   Enrols to study at Yenching University, a stepping stone to Peking Union Medical College (PUMC).

Stepping stone to Peking Union Medical College (PUMC).

1933   Marriage to Zhao Junkai.

1935   Political Awakening.
Birth of children: Daughters **1935** and **1936**; Son **1939**.
Graduation: B.Sc. **1937**; M.D. **1942**.
Beijing Medical College. Several career progressions.

1945   Re-joins PUMC.

1947   To the USA for post-doctorate research, sponsored by the American Board for Medical Aid to China (ABMAC).

1948   December, returns to China.

1950   Korean War.
Joins the Voluntary Medical Corps, March **1951** as Captain and Chief Surgeon.

1952   Applies to join the Communist Party, but is directed instead to the Jiusan Democratic Society.

1957   Performs the first surgical operation on Premier Zhou Enlai.

1958 – 1973   Beijing Medical College.

1969   Appointed personal physician to Jiang Qing.

1977   Death of Zhao Junkai (his first wife).

1978   Meets Yang Yuhua, who becomes his second wife in 1981.

1979   First meets the author, Olivia Cox-Fill.

1981   Marries Dr. Yang Yuhua in May. She dies later that year.

1983   Marries Gao Rui, his third wife.

1993 – 2003   Vice Chair of the Standing Committee to the National People's Congress.

2011   Dies, aged 94.

Key Achievements in the Life and Times of Dr. Wu Jieping

Wu Jieping regarded as a huge project the mission to remedy the backward status of China's healthcare services. During more than sixty years of medical study and administering care, he was tirelessly dedicated to medical education in China. During the three-year, 'difficult period', with no financial support available, in an old temple Dr. Wu established Beijing Second Medical College (which became known as Capital Medical University) and he held the first Presidency. Another eminent physician, Han Qide (Vice Chairman of the Standing Committee of the National People's Congress), described this as a hard time for teachers and students as they pulled together, through thick and thin, to begin their careers.

Dr. Wu was appointed president of the Chinese Academy of Medical Sciences and Peking Union Medical College. He held the chairmanship of the Medical School of Tsinghua University and was the honorary president of many other well-known domestic medical institutions.

Dr. Wu published 150 articles and edited 21 books, 13 as Editor in Chief.

He was the recipient of seven national scientific and technological awards. Dr. Wu received also the 1st All-China Scientific Award on Population; the 1st Award of Distinguished Professor of Beijing Medical University; the Science and Progress Award of the Ho Leung Ho Lee Fund; the Ruby Award of Paris; the Grand Medal of Paris; and the Suzuki Urological Medicine Award of Japan.

Dr. Wu received international acclaim and recognition for his contributions. He was elected to the membership of the Third World Academy of Sciences; honorary membership with the American Urological Surgery Society; he received an Honorary Fellowship from the Royal College of Surgeons of Edinburgh, UK; Honorary Membership with the International Association of Surgery; and fellowship of the College of Surgeons of Hong Kong.

Distinguished colleague, now a former Vice-Chairman of the National People's Congress, Han Qide noted that Dr. Wu was active in political affairs. 'In the 1960s, under the direct arrangements of Chairman Mao Zedong and Premier Zhou Enlai, Wu led a medical team to Indonesia for the treatment of President Sukarno, finally overcoming substantial difficulties to successfully accomplish what was also an important political mission. During the Cultural Revolution (1966-1976), a time of chaos, Wu continued his healthcare work for the central authorities, with dedication. Myriad complications and tough challenges did not affect his perseverance based on correct political principles; instead, he acted skilfully and resolved many complicated issues'.

Later, Dr. Wu was elected chairman of the Jiusan Society (the September 3 Society), vice-chairman of the standing committee of the 8th and 9th NPC.

Han Qide observed that at that time:

> 'Wu is a living symbol close to the heart of national intellectuals. The exemplary life he has led and his remarkable career represents the advancement of generations of Chinese intellectuals, the prominent traditions of whom have to a great extent centred on his personal character. Following the lead of his banner, Chinese intellectuals will be encouraged to strive forward to realise a renaissance in China.'

Key Places Mentioned in the Text

Beidaihe

Roughly 150 miles north of Beijing, on the Bohai Sea coast, this is the closest seaside resort to the capital. English railway engineers were the first Europeans to discover the fishing village in the 1890s and it was not long before wealthy Chinese, along with foreign diplomats from Beijing and Tianjin, made the village a popular destination. The beach of approximately six miles is covered with fine, yellow sand stretching one hundred metres to the sea. With an area of twenty-seven square miles and coastline of twenty-four miles, it is also known as a birding haven. The water is shallow.

The resort was further developed by European diplomats and businesses in the 1900s. After the Civil War, Beidaihe became well known as the summer retreat of the Chinese Communist Party (CCP). After Mao Zedong led the CCP to power in 1949, Mao had a summer resort here and the new rulers developed a taste for the seaside atmosphere. The leaders built underground shelters adjacent to their mansions, in case of a nuclear attack. The airport was reserved for Government officials.

Sanatoria sprang up to reward the efforts of model workers in every industry. A very large Friendship Guesthouse was constructed in 1954, one of dozens across China, to receive the Soviet 'elder brothers' who – before tensions emerged between the Soviet and Chinese leaderships – came to assist Chinese development.

Beidaihe became the location of many important official conferences. The most infamous event here involved Lin Biao, Mao Zedong's anointed successor who, after being accused of plotting a coup, fled on 13 September 1971 with his wife and a son to his villa here. They boarded a plane at the airport, heading to the Soviet Union; but the plane crashed in Mongolia, killing everyone on board.

In the summer of 1995, access to Beidiahe was achieved via badly-maintained roads. There was an official State Guesthouse, which was only then beginning to welcome Chinese tourists. Lush vegetation, caves, decorated pavilions, secluded paths and winding bridges made it attractive to visitors from throughout China.

The CCP conferences were abandoned by order of Hu Jintao in 2004, because they 'did not convey the frugal image the Party wished to convey to the masses'. Hu's leadership sought to work through formal party and state mechanisms, rather than informal gatherings. However, the Beidaihe meetings resumed in July 2007.

Changsha

Situated on the Xiang River, thirty miles south of Dongting Lake, providing excellent access to south and south-western Hunan. As provincial capital of the northern province of Hunan, Changsha was the ancient seat of many schools and academies.

From 1664, Changsha prospered as one of China's principal markets for rice. Opening to foreign trade in 1904, Changsha also became a centre for Western schools including a missionary medical college. It is the site of the Hunan Medical University (1914). In 1918 the opening of the railway, to Hankou in Hubei province, generated further development. Although a commercial city, before 1937 the city had little industry other than small cotton-textile, glass, non-ferrous metal plants and handicrafts enterprises. During the Sino-Japanese War (1937–1945) Changsha was the site of three major battles. Destroyed by fire in 1938-39, Changsha was captured by the Japanese in 1944. In 1949 the city was rebuilt.

Changsha was the city nearest the countryside where Mao Zedong (1893 – 1976) grew up.

Changzhou

Since 600 BC Changzhou, an historical walled city of Jiangsu province on the central east coast of China, has been a major trading city. Changzhou borders Zhejiang to the west and Wuxi to the east and is almost in the middle of two major metropolises, Nanjing and Shanghai.

Nicknamed the Dragon Town, it is situated on the southern bank of the Yangtze River. Criss-crossed by rivers, lakes and canals, Changzhou was one of the earliest-developed national and provincial industrial centres. After the construction of the Grand Canal, linking it with Shanghai, Nanjing and Suzhou, Changzhou became a canal port and a trans-shipment point. In the 1920s, Changzhou started to attract mill owners for the cotton industry and that industry finally made Changzhou a national centre for textiles. At the time of the 'unequal treaties', the Germans favoured Jiangsu province and added industrial manufacturing to the already-established textile and food commodities that had attracted them. The Changzhou Benniu Airport was established in 1963, approximately eighteen miles from the city. Changzhou continues to be regarded as of national importance and the fifth city for productivity.

Changzhou is the birthplace of Dr. Wu. His family tablets, or 'soul tablets', have been there for several generations. Although the family home was burned down, when the author visited with Dr. Wu in 1995 the external walls remained: protecting the ghosts of yesteryear. Zhou Enlai also was born and grew up in Jiangsu. He and Dr. Wu spoke the local dialect. This would have entitled them to regard one another as elder and younger brother.

Chengde

A city in Northern Hebei province, approximately 180 kilometres north east of Beijing and 69 kilometres north of the Great Wall of China, Chengde lies in the mountains separating the North China Plain from the plateaus of Inner Mongolia. Rich in cultural and historical treasures, Chengde is now one of China's major destinations for tourists.

From the beginning of the Qing dynasty, the Manchu leaders made Chengde their summer palace and imperial hunting ground. In the early 18th century the Qing Emperor built a summer residence, Bishu Shanzhuang, to escape the heat of Beijing. It became known as the Secondary capital where the imperial family and officials encouraged diplomatic visits by other 'minorities'. A replica of the Potala palace was built to make the Tibetans feel at home. Official residences of many minorities, in their individual architectural styles, followed suit. The Mongols, Tibetans, Uyghurs, Koreans and Hui were all part of the inter-provincial summer enclave which sometimes lasted for several months. It supported the Emperor's claim of uniting all people as one family, *neiwai yijia*.

Guiseppe Castiglione (1688-1766), the Jesuit priest and artist from Milan, served as imperial artist to four Emperors and painted hunting scenes here.

It was to Chengde that the first British diplomatic mission was finally invited, known as *The McCartney Embassy* in 1793. Sent by H.M. King George III, the mission was intended to secure more favourable diplomatic and trading conditions for the United Kingdom and the party of several hundred was received by representatives of Emperor Qianlong (1735-96).

Chengde grew into a flourishing city, given administrative status. In 1911, Chengde became a regular county and the surrounding area became a special administrative district. In 1928, the Nationalist government established the new province of Jehol, with its capital at Chengde. The Zhenggui Army was quartered there as a defence against the Japanese expansion from Manchuria (North East China).

Following the conquest of northern China by the Japanese in 1937, a railway line was built linking Chengde directly to Beijing. After the establishment of the People's Republic in 1949, Chengde grew steadily and from the late 1950s, developed as a centre of heavy industry. In 1956, Jehol province was abolished and Chengde again became part of Hebei province.

The official residences continued to be very well maintained. Knowing the author's love of hunting, Wu Jieping was especially pleased to invite her on a semi-official trip to reside at the Official residence. She accompanied Wu Jieping on a medical inspection tour to Chengde in 1996, with his family, by private railway carriage.

Diaoyutai (meaning, Angling platform)

A large retreat built in Haidian District, about a mile from the Forbidden City, at the start of the New China era, on the instructions of Zhou Enlai.

The State Guesthouse was a diplomatic complex, erected to house guests securely in the early 1950s. The walled fortress was guarded at each entrance by armed PLA soldiers. To host foreign dignitaries, the State Guesthouse included twenty mansions with gardens. The Guesthouse also accommodated visiting provincial government officials. During the Cultural Revolution, the State Guesthouse was used as the office of the Central Cultural Revolution Group and residences the size of manor houses were allocated to Zhou Enlai as Foreign Minister, to Chen Boda, Kang Sheng and Jiang Qing (Madam Mao).

The complex was used also as a sanctuary for Chinese leaders during the Cultural Revolution, when Jiang Qing occupied 17 Fisherman's Terrace. The other members of the Gang of Four also lived there, as did Dr. Wu Jieping. Due to Jiang Qing's demands, Dr. Wu rarely managed to go home to see his family.

Since the 1990s, the State Guesthouse has been open to paying customers and the author has stayed there occasionally.

The Chinese President and Communist Party General Secretary, Xi Jinping, invited British Prime Minister Theresa May to tea there in 2018. In the same year, the President of North Korea, Kim Jong-Un, stayed at the Guesthouse's Number 18 villa during his trip to China.

The Forbidden City

Located in the centre of Beijing, the Forbidden City is the supreme model in the development of ancient Chinese palaces, providing insight into the social development of late Dynastic China, especially the ritual and court culture. It lies within the confines of the former Imperial City in which Zhongnanhai and the former Imperial parks, Beihai and Jingshan, are situated. The hutong in which the author resided for five years was also within the Imperial City.

The layout and spatial arrangement of the Forbidden City reflects and embodies the traditional characteristics of urban planning and palace construction in ancient China. It features a central axis, symmetrical design and layout of outer court at the front and inner court at the rear, with the inclusion of additional landscaped courtyards deriving from the Yuan city layout. (Yuan dynasty; ruling, eventually, all of China from the early 12th century to 1368.)

As the exemplar of ancient architectural hierarchy, construction techniques and architectural art, the Forbidden City influenced official buildings of the subsequent Qing Dynasty, over a span of three hundred years. The religious buildings, particularly a series of royal Buddhist chambers within the Palace absorbing abundant features of ethnic cultures, are a testimony to the integration and exchange in architecture among the Manchu, Han, Mongolian and Tibetan cultures, since the fourteenth century.

Meanwhile, more than a million precious Royal Collections, articles used by the Royal family and a large number of archival materials on ancient engineering techniques including written records, drawings and models, are evidence of the Court culture and law and regulations of the Ming (1368-1644) and Qing (1644–1911) dynasties.

Unlike during the first few centuries, when the Imperial Rulers were in residence, the Forbidden City has been opened to the masses for over forty years. Now known as the Palace Museum, it is visited by thousands, daily. Visitors and their possessions are scrutinised carefully and anything controversial is removed from them before they are allowed entry.

In the middle of the old city, situated conveniently close to the Forbidden City and Zhongnanhai, stands a large teaching hospital. The building was formerly the palace of a Manchu prince. Peking Union Medical College Hospital (PUMCH), also known as Beijing Xiehe Hospital, was funded in 1921 by the Rockefeller Foundation. It is affiliated to both the Peking Union Medical College and the Chinese Academy of Medical Science (CAMS).

Sun Yat-sen, the Founder of the Kuomintang and the Republic of China, died at the PUMCH on 12 March, 1925. Dr. Wu treated the last Emperor of the Qing dynasty, Prince Pu Yi, there. He died at the hospital on 17 October, 1967. During the Cultural Revolution, it was renamed 'The Anti-Imperialist Hospital'. It continues to be regarded as the best teaching hospital for medicine in China.

Dr. Wu studied medicine at PUMC. In 2001, he addressed the Opening Ceremony of the new Library building at Chinese Academy of Medical Sciences and Peking Union Medical College. His wife received treatment at the hospital and two of his children were born there. Dr. Wu received end-of-life care at this, his favourite hospital.

Tianjin (meaning, Heavenly Ford)

The largest coastal city and the leading port in North China; the major seaport for Beijing, bordered by the Bohai Gulf which is a shallow inlet of the Yellow Sea. Located to the east of Hebei province, at the north-eastern extremity of the North China Plain, central Tianjin lies about seventy-five miles east of central Beijing and about thirty-five miles inland from Bo Hai (Gulf of Chihli). After Shanghai and Beijing, it is the third largest municipality of China. Tianjin is also the most important manufacturing centre of North China.

Tianjin has been an important transport and trading centre since the Mongol\Yuan dynasty (1206–1368). The development of modern Tianjin began during the Ming dynasty (1368–1644), when the national capital moved from Nanjing to Beijing. Formerly known as Tientsin, Tianjin was developed as a walled city in the 15th Century. By the beginning of the Qing dynasty (1644-1911\12), it had become the leading economic centre because of its location at the northern terminus of the Grand Canal. Following the Second Opium War (1856–1860), Tianjin became a Treaty Port, giving access initially to the British and additionally to seven other countries, who carved up the city, dividing it into various foreign concessions where the Chinese were allowed to enter only as servants. The incoming traders built European-style homes and churches.

At the time of the Boxer Rebellion in 1900 it was from Tianjin that the combined Expeditionary Forces from the eight countries marched to "relieve" Beijing from the Society of Righteous Fists, also known as the Boxers. At that time, numerous European-style buildings and mansions were constructed in the concessions, many of which are well preserved today.

The maritime orientation of Tianjin and its role as the commercial gateway to Beijing fostered the growth of an ethnically-varied and commercially-innovative population. The city was noted for its woven carpets, handicraft products, terracotta figurines, hand-painted wood block prints and extensive seafood cuisine.

The municipality of Tianjin extends to an area of 4,540 square miles, with a population of in excess of fifteen million. Tianjin now has excellent academic credentials. The municipality is highly industrialised and is an electronics and IT hub, with development parks akin to the status of Silicon Valley in the United States of America.

When the author visited with Dr. Wu in 1986, the car journey from Beijing took almost six hours. Now, Tianjin is accessible to Beijing in thirty-five minutes by high-speed rail. Dr. Wu proudly demonstrated the location of his first home in the city, on the banks of the Hai River.

Zhongnanhai

Adjacent to the Forbidden City, Zhongnanhai is a former Imperial garden with two artificial lakes which gave it its name. It is a compound housing the offices of, and serving as a residence for, the leadership of the Chinese Communist Party (CCP), the central government. The term *Zhongnanhai* denotes the power of the central government and its leadership at large. Surrounded by twenty-foot high vermilion walls, it is an impregnable fortress guarded by PLA soldiers at each entrance.

The current, basic, outline of Zhongnanhai emerged during the Ming dynasty (1368–1644), when the southern-most of the two lakes was created in 1421. By the late Qing dynasty (1644–1911\12) Zhongnanhai was used as the *de facto* centre of government, with the Empress Dowager Cixi (1835–1908) and later, the Prince Regent Chun (1883–1951), building residences there instead of within the Forbidden City.

After the creation of the first Republic of China (1912–1949) the new President, Yuan Shikai (1859–1916) remodelled Zhongnanhai to become the formal centre of government. In 1949, after the establishment of the People's Republic of China, Chairman Mao Zedong moved from the western hills into the Beijing complex. He received many important foreign leaders in Zhongnanhai, including Nikita Khruschev, First Secretary of the Communist Party of the Soviet Union; Che Guevara; US President Richard Nixon, French President Georges Pompidou; Prime Minister of Japan, Kakuei Tanaka and Prime Minister of Pakistan, Zulfikar Ali Bhutto.

Mao's favourite places in Zhongnanhai were the Library of the Chrysanthemum Fragrance (his personal residence, filled with bookshelves) and the Pool House, where he would spend much of the day swimming, or reading books and reports by the pool. As Dr. Wu discovered while preserving Chairman Mao's body, Zhongnanhai is connected by underground subways to other very important locations in and around Beijing.

During Jiang Zemin's tenure as leader of China (President 1993–2003), an underground passage connected the new Concert Hall directly to Zhongnanhai. Jiang Zemin was a great music-lover, very happy singing karaoke with family and friends.

Key Personalities: Short Biographies

Chen Boda (1904-1989)   Originally from Fujian, he joined the CCP aged twenty. Chen attended university in the Soviet Union. When he returned to China, he followed Mao to Yan'an, where he was made a member of the Central Committee. He became Mao's Personal Secretary and wrote many well-received articles on Chinese communism. He was allied to Lin Biao and jailed for supporting the Gang of Four.

Chen Yi (1901-1972)   A top communist military commander during the Chinese Civil War and later, Foreign Minister of China for ten years. He met Zhou Enlai and Deng Xiaoping in Paris, where he had been part of the work-study group of students. In France, he worked as a dishwasher and barge loader, and also worked for Michelin and took art courses. He could recite classical poetry and was an enthusiastic and gregarious footballer.

He Liliang (1926-)   The widow of Huang Hua. Her father, He Sijing, was credited with writing the Chinese Constitution and was honoured in his lifetime by Mao Zedong, but beaten to death by the Red Guards. His colleagues believed that Mao felt threatened by the help "Pioneer He Sijing" had given him in translating *The Theory of War* by Carl von Clausewitz. This led to Mao's famous book *On Protracted War*, which owed much to He Sijing's interpretation.

He Liliang had her own independent career at the UN and was part of the team that negotiated the Law of the Sea.

Huang Hua (1914-2010)   Foreign Minister from 1976 to 1982 and, concurrently, Vice Premier from 1980 to 1982. He was educated at Yenching University where he also joined the CCP. In 1936, he accompanied the American journalist Edgar Snow to Yan'an, acting as interpreter between Snow and the communist leaders, including Mao Zedong. He was involved in the truce talks following the Korean War in 1953 and was part of the Delegation to the Bandung Conference with Zhou Enlai in 1955. Huang spent much of the 1960s abroad, serving as ambassador to several African countries. When he returned to China during the height of the Cultural Revolution, he was exiled to the countryside but was soon rehabilitated and appointed the PRC's first Ambassador to the United Nations in 1971.

Jiang Qing (1914-1991) The fourth wife of Mao Zedong, Jiang Qing had two marriages behind her before she met and married Mao in 1938. She attended drama school in Jinan before moving to Shanghai to start out as a professional actress. She is said to have attracted the attention of Mao following her performance as Nora in Henrik Ibsen's *A Doll's House*. Having joined the CCP in 1933, Jiang was arrested and jailed by the KMT in 1934, but was released after three months.

Following her marriage to Mao, she was forbidden from engaging in public politics. However, in 1962 she was selected as an arbiter of the artistic merits of film, opera and theatre for the Party, and eventually held significant influence in affairs of state, particularly in the realm of culture and the arts. At the height of the Cultural Revolution, she formed a close political alliance with three other CCP officials, which would become known as the 'Gang of Four'.

Jiang Qing led campaigns against Zhou Enlai and Deng Xiaoping, and by the mid-1970s, Mao had denounced her as "too ambitious" and they reportedly separated. However, this news was not widely known; so Jiang continued to exploit her position as Madame Mao, a ruse that she kept up even after Mao's death in September 1976. Her notoriety as an overly ambitious, self-appointed leader caused her to fall out of favour with the Central Committee and the public; and she was arrested, together with the other members of the Gang of Four, in October 1976.

Jiang Qing took her own life in 1991, after being released from prison on medical grounds.

Lin Biao (1907-1971) Having been admitted to Huangpu Military Academy in 1925, Lin Biao joined the Nanchang uprising under the command of Chen Yi. In retreat, he escaped to the remote communist bases where he met Mao Zedong and Zhu De. He joined the Long March to Yan'an, where he gained much influence and rose to power. Lin Biao was ranked third of the ten Marshals of the Revolution in 1955. He eventually became head of the PLA and was named as Mao's successor following the downfall of Liu Shaoqi. During the Cultural Revolution Lin Biao became so powerful that Mao felt threatened. Following his aborted attempt to bomb the train on which Chairman Mao was travelling, Lin Biao commandeered a jet and was flying with his wife and son towards Russia. It was reported that the plane crash landed on a plain in Mongolia. There were no survivors.

Liu Shaoqi (1898-1969) Hunanese by birth, Liu Shaoqi joined Mao's New People's Study Society in 1918. He joined the Communist Party in 1921; that same year he went to Moscow to study. When he returned to China in 1922, he set up underground workers' movements and agitated on their behalf. In 1925, he became Vice-Chairman of the All-China Federation of Labour. He was very well connected to intellectuals through the universities of North China. A Party theoretician and remarkable organizer, he made speeches and wrote key documents on discipline during the early to mid-1940s. Having *rescued* the Chinese economy from some of Mao's disastrous policies, Liu Shaoqi was seen as a challenge to Mao's supreme control; yet he carried on his leadership policies steering the country away from one Mao-inspired disaster after another. He eventually incurred the wrath of Mao, who encouraged his political oblivion and physical torture during the Cultural Revolution.

Mao Zedong (1893–1976) (also 'Mao Tse-tung'). Leader of the Communist Party from 1935 until his death in 1976. Chairman (Head of State) of the People's Republic of China, 1949–1959.

Born and raised at Shaoshan, in the countryside near the city of Changsha, in the southern province of Hunan. The son of a former peasant who had become affluent as a farmer and grain-dealer, Mao left home at the age of thirteen to pursue his education, rather than work full time on the family farm.

While attending secondary school in the provincial capital of Changsha, he became aware of new political ideas from the West formulated by political and cultural reformers Liang Qichao and the Nationalist Revolutionary, Sun Yat-sen. In October 1911 fighting against the Qing Dynasty broke out. Mao enlisted in a unit of the Revolutionary Army in Hunan. The new Chinese Republic emerged in the Spring of 1912 and his military service ended.

From there, Mao's education continued and he eventually graduated in 1918 from a school in Changsha which offered a higher standard of education, embracing Chinese history, literature and philosophy as well as Western ideas. He also gained his first experience of political activity by helping to establish student organisations.

Mao secured a position and worked for some months as an assistant in the Library of Peking University in Beijing, China's leading intellectual centre of education, but was not admitted to study. This led to his life-long resentment of not only Peking University, but all university graduates. While working there, he was influenced by two key figures in the foundation of the CCP: Li Dazhao and Chen Duxiu.

In 1919, Mao observed the emergence of the May Fourth Movement: student demonstrations protesting against decisions made at the Paris Peace Conference to hand over German concessions in Shandong to Japan, instead of returning them to China. Those activities acted as a trigger for many of the changes that were to take place in the following fifty years. The May Fourth Movement evoked a period of rapid change, including in 1915 the abandonment of Western liberalism in favour of Marxism and Leninism as the solution to China's problems and, in 1921, the creation of the Chinese Communist Party.

It was during the notorious Long March that Mao emerged as Leader of the Chinese Communist Party. Map 5 illustrates the route taken.

In 1966 Mao launched the Great Proletarian Cultural Revolution, which lasted until his death in 1976. The four aims were to replace the designated leaders with people more in tune with his thinking on Communism; to rectify the Chinese Communist Party; to provide the youth of China with a revolutionary experience; and to achieve policy changes which would make the education, healthcare and cultural systems less elitist.

Qin Shi Huangdi (259 B.C.–210 B.C.) First Emperor of a unified China in 221 B.C. Born Zhao Zheng, his Father was King of the Qin state in North West China. He ascended the throne at the age of 13 and took the name 'Emperor' on completion of the conquering of the warring states in 221 B.C. His political and economic reform ambitions were to standardise practices of the earlier states. His work included unifying the walls of all the diverse states into the Great Wall of China and a new, national road system. He developed a strong bureaucratic government and military organisation, as the basis for a totalitarian state philosophy. He was buried in a gigantic funerary compound, known now as the 'Qin Tomb'. Excavations began in 1974 and this led to the discovery of the Terracotta Army in Xian. The ground became a UNESCO World Heritage site in 1987.

Zhou Enlai (1898-1976) The first-born child to a family of scholar officials in Huai'an, Jiangsu province, an island port on the Grand Canal of which his grandfather had been made prefect. To uphold Confucian family values, Zhou's mother was obliged to give her first-born son up for adoption to her sister-in-law, Lady Chen, to redeem the life of her husband dying childless of TB, because without the adoption the dead man would be erased from the family's lineage. Zhou's childhood was spent most happily in family libraries, until his mother and adoptive mother died and money ran out.

When he was left destitute aged twelve, his childless uncle living in Manchuria offered to educate him. He was the first generation to follow a curriculum of "new learning", studying European languages, science and maths following the termination of the Imperial Examination System.

Revolution was in the air and Sun Yat-sen finally managed to overthrow the Qing dynasty, and proclaim China a republic, when Zhou was just thirteen years old. Failing to pass the entrance exam for Tsinghua University, he enrolled at Nankai College in Tianjin. His uncle and his concubine moved to Tianjin to keep the young man company for his first year at college. Zhou graduated from Nankai in 1917 and, with funding from friends, travelled to Tokyo with the intention of studying to become a teacher. He enrolled at the University of Kyoto, but did not become a full-time student as he was short of funds. He returned to Tianjin in time to take part in the May 4th Movement, which saw students protesting against the conditions of the Versailles Peace Treaty.

The coalition of warlords of North China had sent three hundred thousand labourers during WW1 to support the allied war effort in the factories. In recognition of this support, the allies would consider and hopefully rescind the unequal treaties imposed on China. But France and Great Britain had secretly promised Germany's 'sphere of influence' to Japan. When this became known, protestors prevented China signing the Treaty and students all over China participated in the May 4th Movement.

Zhou Enlai edited the Tianjin student newspaper, organized marches and agitated for workers' rights. He later joined youth organizations, was imprisoned and went on hunger strike. In jail he read Economics, English, History of Law and Marxism. Through the Awareness Society he met Deng Yingchao, a lively young girl who was a socialist organizer. After a couple years, Zhou was selected to go abroad to study. He was disappointed not to be sent to Russia and left for Paris, with one hundred and ninety-five other students, in late 1920. His personal mission was to learn how China could restore its dignity. He returned in September 1924, competent and self-assured. By that time, he was recognized as the prime organizer of communist cells in France, Germany and Belgium. His absolute secrecy protected his alias, John Knight, from the continental security establishments.

In France, the students would be admitted to universities funded by the Boxer Indemnity Fund, administered by the Sino-French Committee; but they would also work part-time in factories.

Dissatisfied with his unfair reception as a foreign student, Zhou moved to the UK, where he studied the coalminers' tactics for improving their work and living conditions, the formation of the Labour Party and the work in the docklands. He read the English newspapers avidly, dictionary in hand, and was accepted at the University of Edinburgh. However, he could not afford the cost of living there, so returned to France where he was inducted into the Communist Party with several friends who had been part of Mao's New People's Study Society. He wanted to find a means of changing China and decided to give Marxism a go.

One of Zhou's first run-ins was with the Chinese government, represented by the northern warlords, who had arranged a loan for flood relief of 300 million francs. Zhou discovered that one-third would be paid as commission to the warlords and French arms companies, and the remainder would be used to purchase weapons from these same arms dealers. As collateral, they would receive concessions on the railroads and on local taxes. Zhou was incensed and wrote articles that were published in the Tianjin newspaper, *Yi Shibao*, denouncing the loan. His revelations caused such an outcry that the loan was cancelled.

Zhou Enlai became joint political leader with Mao Zedong leading the Red Army, the People's Liberation Army (PLA), on The Long March. Zhou stepped down and handed the pre-eminent position to Mao. Thereafter he was regarded as number two to Chairman Mao, until he became Foreign Minister in 1945. He retained this position until his death in 1975.

Zhu De (1886-1976) Also an alumnus from France, Zhu De was a most unlikely candidate for the CCP. He was a warlord with several concubines and an opium habit. But as a result of the May Fourth Movement, he decided to put China's salvation before his own. He paid his way to France, tracked down Zhou, who was living in Germany at the time; and after six days, Zhou sponsored him to become a member of the Communist Party, requiring total secrecy. They had in common a love of classical music.

Zhu became one of China's greatest military leaders as Commander of the Red Army during the Long March. In 1945, following the Japanese surrender and resumption of the Civil War, Zhu commanded the renamed People's Liberation Army which defeated the Nationalists and drove them to Taiwan. It was his guerilla tactics in the countryside that were key to crushing the Nationalist Army which was concentrating war on the cities.

Zhu was later First Secretary of the Central Commission for Discipline Inspection. He served as Chairman of the National People's Congress (NPC), of which Dr. Wu became a Vice Chairman.

BIBLIOGRAPHY

A MORTAL FLOWER by Han Suyin

CHINA 1945 by Richard Bernstein

CHINA HANDS by James Lilley/Jeffrey Lilley

CHINA SHAKES THE WORLD by James Kynge

DELIVERANCE IN SHANGHAI by Jerome Agel / Eugene Boe

ELDEST SON by Han Suyin

HISTORY OF MODERN CHINA by Jonathan Fenby

HUNGRY GHOSTS by Jasper Becker

INSIDE THE CULTURAL REVOLUTION by Jack Chen

JOURNEY TO THE WEST by Wu Cheng'en

MAO by Jung Chang / Jon Halliday

MAO by Philip Short

MAO'S GREAT FAMINE by Frank Dikotter

MAO'S LAST REVOLUTION by Mac Farquhar / Schoenhals

NO DOGS AND NOT MANY CHINESE by Frances Wood

PRISONER OF THE STATE by Zhao Ziyang

RED STAR OVER CHINA by Edgar Snow

SPARROWS, BEDBUGS AND MORNING SHADOWS by Sheldon Lou

TAO TE CHING by Laozi

THE PENGUIN HISTORY OF MODERN CHINA by Jonathan Fenby.

THE SEARCH FOR MODERN CHINA by Jonathan D. Spence

TEN YEARS OF TURBULENCE by Barbara Barnouin and Yu Changen

THE CHINA FANTASY by James Mann

THE MORNING DELUGE by Han Suyin

THE POLITICAL THOUGHT OF XI JINPING by Steve Tsang and Olivia Cheung

CHINA'S WORLD VIEW: DEMYSTIFYING CHINA TO PREVENT GLOBAL CONFLICT by David Daokui Li

INDEX

A

A Doll's House, Henrik Ibsen 133
American Board for Medical Aid to China (ABMAC) 79, 82, 86
Academia Sinica Institute 190
adrenal medullary hyperplasia (AMH) 184
Ai Wei Wei 231
American Red Cross 83
Anti-Rightist Campaign 123
Antonioni, Michelangelo 171 – 172
atomic bomb, China builds and tests 132

B

Babaoshan, National Cemetery 215
Bacon, Francis, scientist, teaching philosophy 85
Bandung Conference 118, 119, 245
Bao'an 56, 63
Baochen Spinners, factory 11, 17, 39
Bauer, Max, German arms broker 43
Beida (Beijing University) 52, 88
Beidaihe, government coastal resort 2, 40, 238
Beijing 32, 64
Beijing Gong, restaurant 213
Beijing Medical College 77, 79, 95, 111, 133, 235
Beijing Municipal Bureau of Engineering and Architecture 106
Beijing Paediatric Hospital 98
Beijing University (Beida) 52, 88
Beiyang University 9
Bethune, Norman, Canadian doctor who worked in China 2
Bishu Shanzhuang 240
Blueshirts 78
Bolshoi Ballet 102
Boring, Alice, professor 59
Boxer Indemnity 52
Brand, Dr. William 69
British Broadcasting Corporation (BBC) 65
British concession, Tianjin 26, 29, 37
Brothers of the Robe, secret society 55
Burton, Arthur, son of American engineer 25, 28, 50, 73, 85
Butto, Zulfikar Ali 244

C

Cai Chang 131
Capital Medical University 236
Castiglione, Giuseppe, Jesuit priest 240
Central Hospital 77, 79
Changimen, western gate of Peking (Beijing) 65
Changsha 66, 187, 247
Changzhou (formerly Yanling and Wujin) 9, 11, 36, 64, 66

Chen Boda, Secretary to Mao Zedong 5, 241
Chen Duxiu, key figure in foundation of the CCP, 247
Chen I-wan, friend "Chenny", 20
Chen Yi, Marshal and Foreign Minister 135, 149, 152; challenges Red Guards 153; 212
Chen Yun, Vice Chair of the Eighth Standing Committee, 115
Chen Zaidao, Commander of the Wuhan Military Region, 155
Chen Eugene, Minister of Foreign Affairs in Sun's government, 29
Cheng Zhing Qing Director of Beijing's ballet school, 143
Chengde 194, 204
Chiang Kai-shek: appointment as Military Commander, 16; and the progressives 22; appointed by Sun-Yatsen as overall Commander, KMT, 57; after death of Sun-Yatsen 1925: emergence of military rule, 23; Commander-In-Chief, campaign for reunification of China 1926, 26; leadership of the KMT 1927, 29 – 33; march on Shanghai with KMT army, 29; military advisers, tactics 43 – 44; Tangku Truce with Japanese 49; use of German strategists, 54; Red bandits in death throes 56; Japanese suppression of communism in China, 57, 59, 62, 73, 77 – 79; kidnapping, 62; "disciplinary" measure, 1941, 73; Peace charade, tactics in 1945, 77 – 79; in Taiwan, 86
Chicago, University of 82
China Family Planning Association (CFPA) 186
Chinese Academy of Medical Science (CAMS) 180 – 181; 202 (photograph); 236
Chinese Communist Party (CCP) 103, 106, 231, 233, 238, 248
Chinese Medical Association 119
Chinese Medical Board, New York 74
Chinese Society of Biochemistry 84
Chongqing, Sichuan, KMT seat of government 73
Chronology of Chinese History, 1911-1976 233
Chun, prince regent 244
Cixi, empress dowager 40, 244
Class struggle 140
Clausewitz, Carl von, *The Theory of War* 245
Coalition government, transition to, 1945-46 80
Comintern, (Communist International) 44
Concessions, Shanghai 29
Concubine 19
Confucius 97, 166
Confucian ideas 8, 26, 35, 105, 183, 248
Confucianism, attacked by Gang of Four 171
Court Hotel, Tianjin 37; 194 (photograph)
Covid pandemic 228
Cult of Individualism xxv, 117

Cultural Revolution 1, 4, 20; definition and self-criticism, 143 – 151; prohibition of suicide, 152; the Red Guards, 155 – 160; Cultural Revolution Small Group, 160; ending of, 181-3; Deng Xiaoping thinking, 188 and Mao 189; effects on culture and the educated elite, 193
Cushing, Harvey 186
Cushing's Syndrome 184

D

Dadu River 56
Daimler-Benz 44
Deng Jinxian, Dr., 95, 105
Deng Tuo, journalist 142
Deng Xiaoping: 115, 141, 143, 146, 148, 168, 170, 172, 177, 186, 188, 212, 234
Deng Yingchao, wife of Zhou Enlai 4, 131, 152, 154, 173, 175, 249; defends Wu Jieping, 176
Dewey, Thomas, US Presidential Candidate 1948, 85
Diaoyutai, government compound 5, 131, 157, 160, 162, 166, 173, 176, 178
Donald, W. H., journalist; negotiator, 63
Drama at Sea, opera 21
Dream of the Red Chamber, novel by Cao Xueqin 39, 157
Du Yuesheng, 'Benevolent Gangster' 29, 31

E

Education in China 38, 42, 46
Educational Workers Union 93
Epsteins, aspiring family in Shanghai, late 1930s 16
eunuchs 150
executions in China 138
extraterritoriality 47, 60, 78

F

Fairbank, Professor John K., historian 179
Falkenhausen, Alexander von 54
famine of 1959-60 115
Fang, Dr. Frank, Secretary General of the Wu Jieping Medical Foundation, 211
Ferguson, Dr., PUMC registrar 75
Fill, Dennis 209, 212; 218 (photograph); 221 (photograph)
Fill, Jason 207; 218 (photograph)
Fleming, Alexander 70
Forbidden City Beijing 87, 88, 150, 221 (photograph)
French concession, Tianjin 27
Fu Chongbi, General, Garrison Commander 155
Fujian, province 44

G

Gang of Four 5, 166, 170 – 172, 176 – 177; arrested 178, 227, 234, 246
Gao Rui, third wife of Wu Jieping 145, 190 – 192, 194; 198 (photograph); 207, 209, 210, 212 – 213, 216, 227, 235

Gelao minority 55
Geneva Conference, 1954 104
Georgia, USSR 118
German concession, Tianjin 27
German industrial strength, contribution to China's industrial development, 44
Gong Peng, diplomat, interpreter to Zhou Enlai 58, 60
Gong Pusheng, diplomat, Ambassador to Ireland 58, 60
Gordon Hall, Tianjin 40
Gordon Park, Tianjin 40
Great Hall of the People 115, 140, 228
Great Leap Forward, The 111 – 112, 114, 131, 142, 234
Great Wall of China 31, 56, 240, 248
Green Gang 16, 31
Guangzhou 26, 119, 144
Guardian newspaper 65
Guevara, Che 244
Guizhou province 55
Guo Morou, poet 122, 178

H

Hakka minority 6
Halsted, Dr. William, eminent doctor, 69
Han culture 230
Han dynasty 139
Han Qide, former Vice-Chairman of the National People's Congress, 236 – 237
Han Suyin, writer 50
Hangzhou 156
Hardoon, aspiring family in Shanghai, late 1930s 16
Harvard Medical School 7
Harvard University 51
He Liliang, wife of Huang Hua 213, 215
He Sijing, accredited author of the Chinese Constitution, 245
Heavenly Maiden Scattering Flowers, opera 21
Heilonjiang province 23
Henan province 47
Hiroshima, atom bomb 77
Ho Yingching, General, pro-Japanese Defence Minister, 58
Hodgkin, Dorothy, Nobel Prize winner, 70
Hsutao, Dr., assistant, 166 – 167
Hu Hanmin, leader of right-wing faction in coalition KMT government, 23
Hu Jintao, President of China 2003-13, 215, 228, 238
Hua Guofeng, successor chosen by Mao, 155, 176
Huang Ching-yung 29
Huang Dongsheng 201 (photograph)
Huang Hua, Ambassador to UN, Foreign Minister, 50, 58, 60, 80, 160 – 162, 216
Huangpu Military Academy 16, 26, 246
Huangpu River 12
Hubei province 9, 55, 239
Huggins, Dr. Charles, (1901-1997) University of Chicago 1947, 83 – 84, 110
Hui minority, Ningxia Autonomous Region, 215

Hukou, 1950s system of family registration 181
Huang Guo'an, fellow outstanding student PUMC, 70, 72; later meeting, 75
Hunan province 155
Hunan Medical University 239
Hunan Report, The published by Mao Zedong 1927, 108
Hundred Flowers movement 122 – 123
Hurley, Patrick, United States Ambassador 80

I

Imperial Bank of China 9
Imperial examinations 8 – 9
Imperial University, Beijing 52
Imuran, immune-suppressive drug 139
Industrialisation, 1930s 33

J

James, Edmund, President of University of Illinois, scholarships for Chinese students, 53
Japanese aggression 11, 30, 33, 49, 64, 72, 234; and Chiang Kai-Shek, 16; Japanese suppression of communism in China, 57; Second Sino-Japanese War, 239; Japan and Chinese Medical Association 119; Japan and Twenty-one Conditions, 61
Japanese concession, Tianjin 27, 40
Japanese Emporium 40
Jews, in Shanghai 16
Jian Bozan, Vice President of Peking University, 142
Jiang Qing, wife of Mao Zedong admitted to Politburo, 4; appearance in Henrik Ibsen's A Doll's House, 246; appointment of Wu Jieping, 1 – 2; arrest, 178; assistance to Lin Biao, 142; power struggles, 148 – 149; early career, 133; role in supporting Mao, 131 – 132, 142; leading the cultural assessment and policies of the PLA, 133; First Director of the Cultural Revolution, 146; class struggle 1967 and evidence against Zhou Enlai, 154; temperament and conduct, 160 – 164; reprisals following Lin Biao's treachery, 166; Gang of Four, 170 – 175, 246; death of Zhou Enlai 175 – 178; and the Cultural Revolution, 142, 178, 227; health, 140, 170; support for Traditional Chinese Medicine, 98; treatment by Wu Jieping, 6, 7 and Qi Gong, breathing exercises, 158; self-image and the Empresses Wu Ze Tian and Lu, 172; marriage to Mao Zedong, 4, 72; revolutionary operas, 5; death, 246
Jiang Zemin, leader of China, 228, 244
Jiangsu province, Wu's family origin 2
Jiangxi province 44, 54
Jilin, northern province, 33
Jinggang mountains 44, 54
Jiusan Society 103, 237
Johnson, Lyndon B., U.S. President xvii
Junkers, armaments 44

K

Kadoorie, aspiring family in Shanghai, late 1930s 16
Kang Sheng 175, 241
Katsuki, General, Japanese commander-in-chief 66
Ke Ling, Dr. 119
Kennedy, John Fitzgerald, U.S. President xvii
Khrushchev, Nikita 109, 244
Kim Jong-Un 241
Kissinger, Henry, U.S. Secretary of State, 170, 172
Korean War 100, 234-5, 245
Krupp, armaments 44
Kung, H. H., Minister of Finance, 103
Kuomintang (KMT) Army: 26, 31, 50; and Central Executive Committee, 31; and December Ninethers, 58; and executions, 28; First Congress, 17; and government, 22; and Overall Commander Chiang Kai-shek, 57 and movement against the Japanese 63, 65; and massacre of Chinese communist garrison, 7 January 1941, 73; and US recognition of, and renouncing right to extraterritoriality, 37; and Wu Jieping's attitude in 1946 towards 79; 234; 244

L

Land Reform 108
Langfang 65 – 66
Langrunyuan 54
Leaf, Earl 4
Let a hundred flowers bloom, Guo Moruo 122
Li Dazhao, father of Chinese communism 30, 64, 247
Li Feng, husband of Wu Xing 102
Li Fuchun 131
Li Keqiang, premier of China 30
Li Na, daughter of Jiang Qing 98, 137
Li Rui 132
Li Xiannian 166
Li, Dr., Mao's physician 130
Liang Qichao 274
Liao Mosha, writer, condemned by Jiang Qing as bourgeois intellectual, 142
Liao Zhongkai, leader of left-wing faction in coalition KMT government, 23
Liaoning province 33
Lilian, Wu Jieping's granddaughter 193
Limpid Stream, see Jiang Qing
Lin Biao, Chinese Military leader, a Field Commander of the Red Army: 246; and Beidaihe 2; association \ relationship with Jiang Qing 4, 168; design of nuclear shelters 177; PLA Commander-in-Chief and a Vice-Premier 131, Secretary of Defence 132; plot against Mao 4; treachery 166; undermining the authority of Zhou Enlai 155; Vice Chairman of the CCP and power struggles 148 – 149; death in crash 5, 165 – 166
Literary Gazette, The, publication of Mao's rationale, 123
Little Red Book, Mao's, 132, 158
Liu Bosen, friend of Old Wu, 11, 30
Liu Depei, Director of Peking University's Wu Jieping Urology Centre 216

INDEX

Liu family, Wu Jieping's mother sold to this wealthy family 17 – 19
Liu, mother of Wu Jieping 17 – 18
Liu Shaoqi, Chairman of the People's Republic of China, 1959-68: decentralisation policy, 109; and New China, hardship and famine, 1959-1960: role in engineering economic recovery, 115, 140, 143, 147, 155, 165
Lloyd, Harold, actor, 46
Long March, The 3, 55, 57, 72, 133, 137, 234, 246, 248, 250
Longevity Hall 94
Lu Cui, China's "Joan of Arc" 60
Lu Xun, 232
Lü, Empress 172
Lugouqiao, Marco Polo Bridge Incident, 64, and the Chinese 37th Division, 66

M

Manchu leaders 240
Manuel, Dr., surgical assistant to Dr. Charles Huggins, 83
Mao Anying, son of Mao Zedong, death of 101
Mao, Madam, see Jiang Qing
Mao Yuanxin, Mao's nephew 160
Mao Zedong: philosophy to serve the people, 1; philosophy on education and equality of minorities, 229; effect of economic policies, 4; base in Jinggang Mountains, 44; sweeping to power, 52; leading Red Army, 54-55; guerilla tactics and The Art of War, 56; progression to Chairman of the Politburo, 57; marriage, 72; tactics for dealing with nationalist forces, 77; emergence of Red Peasant dynasty, 87-88; address at end of the civil war, 90; On Practice and On Contradiction, 93; The Importance of Peasants in Hunan, 108; residence, Chrysanthemum Fragrance Study, 94, 129, 173; conflict between communist values and his behaviour, 110; and food tasting, 97; swims Yangtze, 146; behaviour, and The Great Leap Forward, 109 – 114; New China, hardship and famine 1959-1960, 115; self-criticism, 115, 121; discredited, 116; failure of The Great Leap Forward, and his demands of others, 131; emergence of the Little Red Book, 132; political tactics, 137, 141-2; class struggle, and relationship with Liu Shaoqi, 140-141; the Hundred Flowers Movement, barrage of criticism, 146; Mao Zedong Thought, 146; The Cultural Revolution, 146-148, 154-156; Cultural Revolution an almost unstoppable force, 156; itinerant lifestyle 156; Revisionist thinking, 139; abuse of power, described by Lin Biao as feudal tyrant, 165-166; suspicious of Jiang Qing, 171; 'Revolution is not a dinner party' 189; Cult of Mao replacing Confucian family values, 183; health, 118, 129-130; congestive heart failure diagnosis, Traditional Chinese Medicine, 169; death, 1976, 176; statue, 205; regarded as a God,188; at Zhongnanhai, 244.

Marco Polo Bridge Incident, 1937 64
Marshall, George, US General, negotiator in talks for a coalition government, 80
Marx, Karl xviii
Marxist thinking, 89
May 16th Group, in Cultural Revolution 154
May, Theresa, British Prime Minister 241
McCarthy, Joseph, U.S. politician xvii, 85
McCartney Embassy 240
Mei Lanfang, opera artist 21
Meiji Restoration 60 and n
Methodist school 37
Ming dynasty 139, 242, 244
Minnesota, University of 50
Murphey, William Rhoads, geographer 12
Murphy, Dr. John B. eminent doctor, 69
Museum of Revolutionary History 115

N

Na Yanqun, Peking University's Wu Jieping Urology Centre, 216
Nagasaki, atom bomb 13, 77
Nanjing, Japanese atrocities 66
Nanjing, Nationalist capital 32
Nanjing, peace talks 77
Nankai school 27, 126
National Military Council 43
National People's Congress (NPC) 103
National Revolutionary Army 26
Nationalists, Wu Jieping's attitude to 79
Nehru, Jawaharlal 104
Ningxia Autonomous Region 215
Nixon, Richard, U.S. President, xvii, 169, 244
North-eastern Border Defence Army 33
nuclear shelters 177

O

Old Wu, father of Wu Jieping, 8, 24, 35, 57; hardship, 64; resilience, 72; perception of Mao, 97; 80th birthday party, and Rectification Campaign,123; violence suffered, 124; death of, 153
On Contradiction, by Mao Zedong 93
On Practice, by Mao Zedong 93
One Child policy 186-187
Opium, use in off-setting trading imbalance, 14
Opium Suppression Bureau, c. 1927 30
Opium Wars unequal treaty system,16; legacy fears, 109; 189; Second Opium War 1858, 24, 243
Outline for the Cultural Revolution 147

P

Panscheel Treaty, the Five Principles of Peaceful Co-existence, 104
Pasteur, Louis 70-71
Peace Conference, Paris 60, 248
Pearl Harbor, Japanese attack 73
Pearl Harbor, my: Wu Jieping's description of personal impact of disappearance and death of his second wife Dr. Yang Yuhua,182

Peking Union Medical College Hospital (PUMCH) Sun Yat-Sen death in 1925, 41; Wu Jieping as a patient, 215; 242
Peking Union Medical College (PUMC) 6, 23, 51, 59, 70, 74; temporary closure January 1942, 77; 94; 219 (photograph); 235
Peking Union Medical College (PUMC), Friends of, 202
Peking University Shougang Hospital 216
Peng Dehuai, Defence Minister 131-132, 141
Peng Zheng, Mayor of Beijing 146
People's Liberation Army, (PLA), see also Lin Biao, 80; attitudes within, 89; medical team of, 100; Jiang Qing, leading the cultural assessment and policies of, 133; provincial factions, 154; guards at Diaoyutai,157; emergence 1930-34, 234; headed by Lin Biao, 250
People's Republic of China, established 1949 90
Pfizer Corporation 211
Pheochromocytoma, case of, 184
pidgin English 25
Pompidou, Georges 242
Pu Yi, puppet governor emperor 40, 150, 242
Putin, Vladimir, Russian President 230

Q

Qianlong, Emperor, 1735-1796, 240
Qin Shi Huangdi, first emperor of a unified China 165-166, 248
Qing dynasty 8, 9, 52, 189, 242, 243, 244, 249
Qing-Mei, feeling of closeness, between US and China 100
Qing Ming, Tomb Sweeping Day 176

R

railroads 40, 44, 66, 239, 240, 250
Ramos and Ramos Amusement Company 39
Red Army (see also PLA) 54, 55, 65, 73, 250
Red Detachment of Women, The, ballet 143
Red Guards 20; 147; denouncing parents, elders and teachers, 148; criticism campaign against Chen Yi, 149 – 150; undermining the re-establishment of order, 153 – 154; beating to death of He Sijing, 245
reform schools, Xinjiang 229
Red Peasant dynasty 87
Rehe (Jehol) 33
Reunification of China campaign 26
Revolution of 1911 8, 189
Royal Enfield, Wu Jieping's motorbike 113
Rujin (Red Army station) 54
Russian concession, Tianjin 27

S

Salt tax 14
Sassoon, aspiring family in Shanghai, late 1930s 16
Seekt, Hans von, military adviser to Chiang Kai-shek 43, 54
self-criticism movement 123
sex education in China 21, 126

Shanghai, location at mouth of Huangpu River, 12; in 1930s, 16, 24; international city 1947, 87; bombed by Japanese, 63; the Shanghai Experimental School 1932, 39; Shanghai foreign concessions, 32; general strike and the Shanghai General Union, 29; Shanghai Medical School, 180
Shen Chang-huan, future Foreign Minister of Taiwan, 58
Shen Yan, present at inquisition led by Jiang Qing, 167
Sheng Xuanhuai, promoter of foreign technology, founder of Tianjin's Beiyang University, opened Imperial Bank of China, 9; introduced Old Wu to shipping tycoon Liu Bosen, 11
Shimonoseki, Treaty of, 41
Snapper, Professor Isadore, Clinician at PUMC 70
Snow, Edgar, journalist, 245
Song dynasty pagoda, 139
Soong Ai-ling 15, 30, 103
Soong Ching-ling 15, 31, 63; Soong Ching-Ling Foundation 215
Soong family influence, 73, 103
Soong Meiling, wife of Chian Kai-shek xvii, 30, 39, 63
Soong, Charlie 30
Soviet Union 109, 134; conflict among the leadership over involvement with, 139; 140, 142, 177
Squibb Corporation 196 (delegation photograph); 209; Bristol-Myers Squibb, formerly the Squibb Corporation, 211
Stalin, Josef 33, 44, 118
Stray Thoughts, by Lu Xun 228
Stuart, John Leighton, President of Yenching University, 51; becomes US Ambassador, 80
steel production 109, 112, 113
student strike of 1919 60
Sukarno, Mrs 142
Sukarno, President of Indonesia 116, 142; treatment by Wu Jieping, 1962, 144; 236
Sun Chuanfang, warlord 29
Sun Tzu, *The Art of War* 56
Sun Yat-sen, leader of Republic of China, 11, 13, 16, 32, 57, 177, 233, 242, 247, 249; death of 17, 23
Sun Yat-sen University (former Chung San University) 119
Swire Mansion, Shanghai 156

T

Taiwan, xvii, 24, 58, 63, 78, 86, 90
Tanaka, Kakuei 244
Tang dynasty 133
Tanggu Port 26
Tangku Truce, with Japanese 49
Tangshan earthquake, 1976 177
Tao 130
Tao Xingzhi, educator and reformer 38
TCM (Traditional Chinese Medicine) 98, 169
Teng, Doctor, haematologist 6; 201 (photograph)
Terracotta Army 248
The Importance of Peasants in Hunan, by Mao Zedong 108
The Long March, 3, 57, 72, 137, 234

The Meiji Restoration, 60
The Romance of the Three Kingdoms 74
The Will to Live, opera 21
Theory of War, The 245
Tiananmen Square, 88, 90, 115, 117, 176; massacre 193; crackdown on protestors, 228
Tianjin, 15, 17; port city, 23; description of, 24; *concessions*, special zones, 27; 31, 33, 36
Tianjin Steamship Company, 38, 43
Tianjin Volunteer Corps, 40
Tientsin, now Tianjin 243
Traditional Chinese Medicine (TCM) 98, 169
treaties 78
Treaty of Nanjing 28
Treaty of Shimonoseki 41
Treaty Ports 25
Truman – Dewey (candidates) U.S. Presidential Election, 1948 85
Truman, Harry S., U.S. President xvii, 80, 85
Trump, Donald, U.S. President 230
Tsinghua University the 'Harvard of China', 18; 1911 creation of, 52; Wu Junkai representations to, 106; demonstration 1966, 145; Mao's written encouragement to student to start a rebel organisation August 1966, 147
tungsten, in armaments 43
Twenty One Conditions, Japanese control in China 61

U

Unequal Treaties, between Great Britain and China 24, 239, 249
United Nations, China joins in 1971, 160
United States of America (USA) xvii, xviii; recognises KMT, 37; support in education 52; role in supporting KMT (Japanese suppression of communism in China) 57; migration to, 78; duplicitous tactics in the face of diplomatic negotiations 1945-46, 80; Wu Jieping experience of, 82; conflict among the leadership over involvement with the USA, 139; President Nixon visit 1972, 169; Tianjin comparison with Silicone Valley, 243
USA, the American Board for Medical Aid to China (ABMAC), withdrawal of support to mainland China for medical education, 86
University of Chicago, xxv, 82, 96

V

Versailles, Treaty of, (1919) 60, 233, 249
Vietnam, colonization of, 104; conflict among the leadership over involvement, 139
Vietnam War xvii
Voluntary Medical Corps 100

W

Wang Dongxing 1, 2, 94, 129, 130; administrator of Zhongnanhai 159; 160, 161, 164, 166, 173, 177, 178

Wang Guangmei 141n, 142
Wang Hongwen 171
Wang Jingwei, leader of third faction in coalition KMT government, 23
Wang Shenyue 167
Wanping, Japanese entry 65
Warlord Period 11
Warlords 14, 26, 29, 40, 50, 54, 233, 249
Wei Xie 215
Wellcome Laboratories 139
Wellesley College 50
Wen Jiabao, Premier (Prime Minister) of China 2003-2013, 215
Wenham scholars 7, 72, 74, 95
White Russians, immigrants to Shanghai 13, 40
Wolff, Otto, German industrialist, engineer 44
Wong, Dr., Zhou Enlai's surgeon 118, 119
Workers' Culture Palace, Zhou Enlai's final resting place, 175
World Health Organisation (WHO) xiv
Wright, Frank Lloyd 79
Wu Anran, Immunologist, brother of Wu Jieping 22
Wu Bing, daughter of Wu Jieping vii, 62, 76, 106, 173, 192
Wu Desheng, son of Wu Jieping 75, 107, 192
Wu, Dr., assistant to Wu Jieping 157 and formerly Chief of Medical Service, Beijing Hospital 3
Wu family (photograph) 195
Wu Han, historian and vice mayor, Beijing 105, 146; condemned by Jiang Qing as bourgeois intellectual, 142
Wu Jieping, early education, 21; pre-medical studies at Yenching university, 50, 58 – 60; receives B.Sc, M.D., 1942, 75; post-doctorate, University of Chicago 1947, 82; courtship and first marriage, Zhao Junkai, 49, 51; death of Zhao Junkai, 179; second marriage, Dr. Yang Yuhua and death, 181; third marriage, Gao Rui, 190; appointment as personal physician to Zhou Enlai, xxvi; and communism, 89, 110; and the Great Leap Forward, 112; role in sex education, 125; instruction by Zhou Enlai to take over the healthcare of Jiang Qing, Madame Mao, 156; first consultation with Jiang Qing, 159; her behaviour, 1, 159; accused of poisoning Jiang Qing, 166; and kidney transplants,138, 151; rare case of bilateral carcinoma of the kidney, 150; identifies adrenal medullary hyperplasia (AMH), 184; embalms Mao Zedong, 177; health: renal tuberculosis, 68; stroke, 207; death in 2011, 215
Wu Jieping Medical Centre 86, 226
Wu Jieping Medical Foundation 208, 210, 214
Wu Jieping Urology Centre and the Wu Jieping Medical Centre, 216
Wu Lili (Wu Guangwei), (photograph) 4
Wu River 55
Wu Ruiping, Paediatrician, brother of Wu Jieping 22, 48, 94, 105, 166; and children's hospital, 94, 105; anecdote of Mao's behaviour,110; anecdote, aftermath of death of Lin Boao, 166

Wu Weiran, surgical specialist, brother of Wu Jieping 22
Wu Xing, daughter of Wu Jieping vii; birth, 60, 62; 76, 83, 101, 107, 112, 192
Wu Ze Tian, empress 133, 172
Wuhan, the defence of, 73
Wuhan massacres 29

X

Xi Jinping, President of China current philosophy, xviii; consequences of selection 2012, 228; treatment of competitors and critics, 230
Xi'an, capital of Shaanxi, controlled by the KMT 57; under siege by the Young Marshall, and kidnap of Generalissimo Chiang, 62; under threat of bombardment 63
Xiang River, doomed expedition, start of the Long March, 1934 55
Xiao Meng, Gao Rui's daughter 190, 194, 216
Xie Fuzhi, Minister of Public Security 160
Xinhua News 147
Xinjiang 'Reform Schools' 229

Y

Yale in China programme 66
Yan Ren Ying, Dr. 159; 201 (photograph)
Yan'an 3; new communist base 62; Mao directing operations from, 73; new order emerging from, 87; 245
Yang Huchen, KMT General 57
Yang Xiaomeng, also known as *Marina*, step-daughter of Wu Jieping, 207- 215; 218
Yang Yuhua, second wife of Wu Jieping 180 – 183; 190; 195 (photograph); 235
Yangtze, famous river swim by Chairman Mao 146
Yao Wenyuan, writer recruited by Jiang Qing 5, 167, 171
Ye Jianying, head of the Office of Confidential Secretaries, Marshal 167
Ye Qun, wife of Lin Biao 160
Ye Zilong 97
Ye, Marshal, patient of Wu Jieping 212
Yearbook of Urology 185
Yenching 39; Yenching University 50 – 53; student movement 1935, 58 – 60; 79; 235, 245
Yi Shibao, newspaper 250
Yin Yang exercises 130
YMCA, Beijing 90
"Young Marshal", Zhang Xueliang 31, 33 – 34; 62 – 63
Yuan dynasty 28; 242 – 243
Yuan Shikai, general 15 – 16; 244

Z

Zhang Chunqiao, writer recruited by Jiang Qing 5, 166, 171
Zhang Xueliang, known as the "Young Marshall" 31, 33 – 34; 62 – 63
Zhang Zuolin, Marshall, Manchu warlord 29, 31

Zhao Junkai, first wife of Wu Jieping, 2; meeting 48; marriage 50; life with, 75, 93, 111, 143, 156; studying 89; deteriorating health 116 – 117; visited by Deng Yingchao, wife of Zhou Enlai, 173; 235
Zhenggui army at Chengde 240
Zhong Huilan, Dean of Central Hospital, 76
Zhonghe hospital 76
Zhongnanhai, northern section of Forbidden City 1, 88, 93; clinic 119; 129; Mao departure for the Great Hall of the people, 140; protests at 149; 159; Mao returned to, 173; underground complex 177; position in the former Imperial City, 241; 244
Zhongnanhai clinic 119
Zhou Enlai: 1, 2; residing at Diaoyutai 5; head of political department of CCP 16; Vice Chairman and Political Commissar of the army, 55; 'Housekeeper' 57; 'Inhuman is he who slays his brother to feed the wolf' 62; negotiations with Chiang Kai-shek 1937, 65; prediction of Japanese expansion into Asia, 73; coalition government peace talks 1945-46, 80; calling the intelligentsia to return 1940, 90; tasting of Mao's food 94, 97; guidance of and influence over Wu Jieping, 104, 122, 136; handling of border dispute with India 1954, 104; withholding Junkai's bad health news from Wu Jieping 117; health, 118, 162; failing health c. 1972, 172; the class struggle and suggesting a campaign for free discussion, 121; experiences criticism of the *Hundred Flowers Movement*, gives seven-hour talk, *Communist Party View on Intellectuals*, 122; aftermath 123; gives sex education lecture, 126; family planning policy discussions with Wu Jieping, 186; encouraging academics and the university elite to discuss socialist principles c. 1960, 135; growing relationship with Wu Jieping 136 – 137; *The Question of Intellectuals*, 141; concern for safety of scientists in the era of the Cultural Revolution 147; argues with Red Guards 149, 153; convinces Mao to change tactics in light of economic deterioration, 150; May 16th Group, class struggle 154 – 156; concern for stability, 156; measures to control chaos, 160; role in handling Jiang Qing accusations 166 – 168; Gang of Four attempts to entrap him 170; aspirations despite failing health, 227; death 175
Zhou Yichun, economist 62
Zhu De, Commander-in-Chief, 1935 4, (photograph); 55, 234, 250
Zhu Futang, Dr., Paediatric Department Director at PUMC 95, 105
Zhuang Zedong, table tennis champion 7
Zhuangzi, father of Taoism 41
Zunyi, location of key meetings 1935 55 – 56